MATRIX

OF THE GODS

Books by John Nelson

Transformations: The Next Step
Starborn
Matrix of the Gods

MATRIX
OF THE GODS

John Nelson

HAMPTON ROADS PUBLISHING COMPANY, INC.

This book is dedicated to those who cherish
and allow the free exchange of ideas.

For information write:

Hampton Roads Publishing Company, Inc.
891 Norfolk Square
Norfolk, VA 23502

Or call: (804)459-2453
FAX: (804)455-8907

If you are unable to order this book from your local
bookseller, you may order directly from the publisher.
Quantity discounts for organizations are available.
Call 1-800-766-8009, toll-free.

ISBN 1-878901-97-4

Printed on acid-free paper in the United States of America

Acknowledgements

The writing of this novel has been a rigorous ten-month labor of love. I could not have completed it in its present form without the help of several very special people:

My longtime friend and publisher, Robert Friedman, who read a few meager chapters and decided to take the journey with me;

Frank DeMarco, who helped me slay many a sentence along the way;

My cover artist, Karen Vermillion, whose intuitive cover art revealed another level of the story to me and whose love and friendship have seen me through the long months of rewriting;

And my dear friend, Mary Elizabeth Marlow, who has been a constant source of inspiration and encouragement.

"Before these events many rare birds will cry in the air. 'Now!' 'Now!' and sometime later will vanish."

– *Nostradamus*

Prologue
The Rama Journal

15 March 39. Dr. Renault was alarmed this morning. His readings indicated that I was near death. I told him to drink a cup of coffee and take a walk. All was not what it seemed. Since he could not explain the aberrant readings, he simply monitored my condition from the other room. It was the other rhythm. A memory triggered it. This state is so fragile. Give it an opening. Just a thought, and the old mechanical consciousness shifts in. The result appears to be a great disorder. The body's universal habit: death and destruction. Suddenly, the tempo changed and I shifted back. How strange. Death and immortality are notes on the same musical scale. It is a matter of conscious focus. One wonders if this world, this slaughterhouse, with its collapsed ecosystem, teeters on the edge of paradise. Can one just. . .shift it over. Renault returned and gave me more tests. I was fit as a pig. He was astounded. Of course he blamed his equipment. I said that it was the old consciousness asserting itself, and he said that was not scientific. I told him to hook me up, and I would give him more "bad" readings. He declined, but with a smile. There may be hope for him.

5 April 39. I was playing a game of chess with the attendant, when I suddenly forgot the rules. Manuel thought I was joking, and he went along with me. He explained how the pieces moved, the objective. We continued to play, but I made stupid moves. He got mad at me, and Renault had to lead him out. Memory turns personal history into rules carried out by habit. It is the way it is because of the way it was. The mind

reforms everything. Something unique is reduced to its known elements. But, when you stop the mind, everything is unique. Every moment is an adventure. Nothing is defined. What if you could erase everybody's memory of how the world operates? In that moment, the world would be born anew.

23 April 39. I had another. . .episode. The old consciousness. Everything ruled by mental dictate. So harsh. It is like a billion cells butting their heads together. And then the new rhythm. . .shifted in. I could feel the cells scramble. A nervous jitter. Without the mental glue, what keeps them from flying apart? What keeps the stars in their place? Bees in the hive? Gravity, instinct? There are orderers of life other than mental rules. Does the vegetable regret losing the solidity of rock, or the mammal the plant's ready food chain? And then it shifted. The other state. Effortless, smooth. Life as an exquisite musical composition. The cells dance to a new rhythm. Can it orchestrate the plumber and the physicist as well?

15 May 39. Renault was tired hearing me say that I dropped my mind. He gave me an intelligence test. The most abstract. It was fun. I did not treat the questions as problems. No thinking. No analysis. Something in me redefined them. I saw the puzzles as three-dimensional forms. The answers were readily apparent. My score astounded him. Renault gave me a simple arithmetic test. I failed it miserably.

Part One
The Witness

Chapter One

As in earlier years, the sky was pale blue and the clouds hanging low overhead were actually white, puffy little balls and the sun peeked between them and it was orange again and its rays felt warm on Zita's naked arm, and she looked up at it open-eyed and it was a wondrous sight, and she turned and ran down the wide beach her arms spread open totally exposing herself to the elements, inhaling the air in deep, hungry gulps until her lungs burnt; and then she saw him, standing on the cottage porch, the sun reflecting off his golden body blinding her, and she rushed to him and he turned and it was Michael, transformed in some glorious manner, his body of finely sculpted muscle, waves of heat rising off it, and she jumped into his arms, wrapped her legs around his waist, and, holding him tight, they twirled around the porch like entranced Sufi dancers, releasing themselves, losing themselves in the movement, faster and faster, and they began to expand, their cells as wide as sunflowers, to spread out farther with each turn, until their bodies engulfed the earth, could feel its molten metals move through their veins feeding their passion, and. . .

Zita awakened from her dream gasping for breath. The air in the room was heavy and stale. She grabbed the silvery thin thermal blanket and flung it aside. Struggling to sit up, she heard a telltale sound overhead and immediately sensed the problem. Zita reached up and hit the oxygenator in the wall with her balled fist. It sputtered into action, coughing out spurts of oxygen. She drew in the air with short, rapid breaths. Her lungs expanded, the breaths grew longer and deeper. Soon she had reestablished her rhythm. Zita called out, "Time?"

"5:47 A.M. Thursday, February 14, 2047," the computer chirped in its cheerful morning voice.

"Damn it," she said. Zita had reprogrammed the house system to eliminate the day, date, and year recording for time requests. But, when the message space was overloaded, it often erased her changes, reverting to its default settings. The phone program could hold any number of regular messages, a dozen coded ones, or at least two high-level cryptograms, or so she thought.

Zita rolled off the floor-level mattress and stood up. Her body was stiff and achy. She reached up, her fingertips nearly hitting the low ceiling, then bent over and circled her index fingers around her big toes, holding this yoga posture for a count of twenty. Slowly releasing it, her hands sliding back up her legs, she felt taut muscles loosen. Her morning regimen called for ten minutes of stretching exercises, but today that would be too strenuous for the room's low oxygen level.

Zita was wearing her body-warmer, the one-piece thermal jumpsuit developed for winterized apartments, where the temperature was set by law at 58 degrees, but her bare feet were cold on the wood floor. She always unzipped the booties before slipping into bed at night and could never find them in the morning. Zita tiptoed across the floor and stood on the sectional rug under the window, peering out through the thin haze over the East River to the far horizon. She hoped to spy a fiery globe rising into a pale blue sky, but found in its place the sun's diffused light spreading behind a grey cloud cover. Her forecast was another wonderful day of acid rain. Water levels were already halfway up the dike, high enough for some fish to jump over the top onto the streets of Manhattan, from the "acid bath to the frying pan."

Zita had not seen clear skies over the city since the last 200-mph hurricane had torn up the East Coast three years ago. It flooded the streets and subways of Manhattan for over a week, leaving her stranded in her apartment, but it did blow away the cloud cover. For two glorious mornings, she watched the sun rise over the Atlantic. Zita wondered if the universal depression felt by her fellow city dwellers was caused as much by the dreary weather as by the horrible living conditions. On a recent trip to the desert communities of New Mexico, where the skies were generally clearer and the living conditions at least less crowded, the people had appeared equally despondent. Since they could not venture outdoors without environ gear, the sunnier climate may have made this restriction even more confining.

Zita heard her coffee cup filling. She turned from the window and its gloomy vista and walked through the wall (a refracted light field creating the illusion) into the kitchen five feet away. The Handy-Cook oven, triggered by her time request, had brewed and poured a cup of grain coffee. Zita picked up the thermal mug and took a sip. Having recently switched to the cinnamon blend, she no longer used the chem cream. A red light flashed on the unit, and she popped open the oven door and removed a packaged container of steaming oatmeal. Zita set it on the nearby counter, pulled out the recessed stool, sat down, and began to eat.

The hot creamy grain warmed her throat and felt wonderful, and soon the enzyme-enhanced blend would speed up her metabolism and warm her body as well. While she ate, Zita stared out the window at the overcast day, trying to focus outside herself as images from her dream beckoned from within. Sexual dreams were not unusual for her, or for her friends as she had recently learned, since abstinence was a way of life after the viral plagues of recent years. It was seeing Michael younger, muscular and fit—or wishing it so—that upset her. Zita thought she had accepted their age difference and that his affection for her was more paternal than romantic, though their relationship was far from chaste. This aspect of the dream seemed compensatory. She was ignoring her instinctual drives, and they were demanding attention. Would they be satisfied by her taking a younger lover? At a deeper level, as Julia, her Jungian analyst, would no doubt suggest, Zita's dream pressed her to integrate some neglected aspect of her animus. Was it a call to action?

And then the opening image of the dream burst through, that glorious day on the beach with its blue sky and white sand, with air she could actually breathe. It reminded her of her grandmother's videos that she had watched as a child: a house on a beach with waves rolling into shore, the sun shining overhead, and people walking around half-naked with their bodies fully exposed. These pictures always upset Anna, and it was only after she had retired for the evening that Zita would sneak down to the living room of her old ramshackle house and play the videos over and over again. They were a source of endless fascination; only later did she share her grandmother's sadness for a day Zita would never know herself, for a pristine earth that no longer existed.

"It is now 6:30 A.M.," the computer chirped, breaking the spell. Zita stood up, tossed the breakfast container into the paper reconstitutor, and poured her remaining coffee down the liquid drain filter. She walked over to her home computer center recessed in the living room wall. She removed the message recording disk and slipped it into the decoder. "Hi. Need to see you in Washington tonight. Have an assignment for you. Hope you didn't throw away your winter coat. See you at Anton's at 6:00. That's right. Sorry, business only. Get a return ticket. Bye for now."

Mr. Personality himself, Zita thought. She erased the disk and placed it back into her computer system. With Michael living 250 miles away, working sixteen-hour days trying, as he would say, to "keep the egg from cracking," it was no wonder she was having sex dreams. "Well," Zita said aloud, "I'm showing signs of cracking, mister, and you had better notice it." Immediately, she wondered when she had last had her apartment debugged for listening devices.

The door of the elevator tube swished open, breaching the air lock. The air from the pressurized compartment hit her like a light breeze, blowing her hair back. Zita stepped into the tube, squeezing between two well-dressed businessmen at the front, and heard them each take deep breaths in the thinner air. The door slid back into place resealing the tube, and the air jets hissed overhead equalizing the pressure. The elevator did not appear to move, and after a moment, as was her habit, Zita looked up at the floor register as the numbers rapidly dropped from 175 to 67. Rising and dropping by the regulation of air pressure in a vacuum tube, the Air Lift elevator, with its fully pressurized compartments, making hundred-floor free-fall drops possible, also made the Super Skyscrapers of the mid twenty-first century feasible, since ride time in a 300-story building was of the utmost importance. When the door opened at the basement level, Zita walked out and stepped aside, scooting along the white tile wall to avoid the stampede, as the others rushed for a downtown car pulling into the station. She hated going straight from one tube to another; it made her feel like a mouse in a maze. Zita would wait two minutes for the next car. If she could not move about outside in the open air, or not without cumbersome precautions, she could at least refuse to acclimate herself fully to living in the world's largest indoor mall.

Zita took the next subway car downtown, heading for her office in the East Forties. It was half-filled with prosperous-looking commuters, and, as she took an empty seat, Zita was compelled by her training to examine each of them. The man sitting across from her with his perfectly tailored blue suit was reading *The Wall Street Journal*, the "underground" edition as the joke went; across the aisle was a woman fully covered in a long-sleeved dress of a metallic-fiber blend for added protection; two seats down was a man wearing dark sunglasses and gloves and holding a hat, who either had just come from "topside," or was returning shortly. He was too far away for her to see his oily skin, but she could smell the UV sunscreen lotion. The car pulled into another station, and two more commuters of a similar makeup entered and took seats. They did not appear any more suspicious than the others, and Zita was satisfied that they posed no threat to country or self, and only indirectly to the planet.

As she looked around this group of privileged people, who managed their shattered lives better than most, she did not see any monsters lurking among them. If they or their parents could have seen the results of their apathy, they would no doubt have done all they could to avert the catastrophic environmental collapse of the early twenty-first century. They may have been motivated by long-term gain over short-term loss, as one ecological economist phrased it, and not by their love for the earth and its creatures, but unlike others in her field Zita found this attitude acceptable. In her estimation the problem was not the greed and self-interest of any particular group, but the way the mind processed information. In her master's thesis on the Great Ozone Debate of the 1990s, which was later published, she showed how we had largely miscalculated the speed of ozone depletion and its disastrous results because our mental model of the earth, based on classical assumptions, predicted outcomes that were fairly accurate for isolated events but underestimated long-range patterns and their effects. This led her to propose a theory, an adaptation of Prigogine's work on Dissipative Structures, *Model Incongruence.* Zita had speculated, using the latest brain research, that the mind reinforced its conceptual models like a living organism absorbed organic resources. New raw data about the environment is broken down and its familiar concepts are absorbed and integrated by the existing structure, our 2500-year-old classical model of nature, dampening the effects of repeated disasters. However, its indigestible or incongruent data gains a foothold creating its own dynamic. As the variance grows, it reaches a threshold where it totally transforms the system or the model. So feeding this process incontrovertible facts about environmental pollution and its long-range effects was the best way in her estimation to accelerate the changeover.

Like many idealistic youths of her generation, Zita deplored the environmental mistakes of the past half-century and the resulting political instability. After she graduated from college with a master's in environmental sciences, Zita surprised both family and friends by deciding on a career in journalism. She told them that the real fight for a cleaner environment was being waged in the media, and they would have been even more surprised to known just how far she was willing to pursue those ends. In graduate school, she had been secretly recruited by Michael Parker as an undercover operative for the Department of Information. Zita felt she was aligning herself with factions in big business and government that truly wanted to correct past mistakes and build a healthier world for all humankind. If that meant campaigns of misinformation and media manipulation, she could tolerate the deception if the end results were as sweeping as she had hoped.

But, with her life insulated from the disastrous effects she was trying to reverse, increasingly more comfortable as the lives of most declined steadily, Zita wondered if she had lost the moral edge on this issue, if she were merely playing at change and not living it. Although she had become a champion for many in this field with her newspaper column read by millions daily and her Ozone book now required reading, Zita increasingly felt like one of the speechmakers of whom Gandhi had said a century earlier, how little their fine words changed the lives of the great mass of people. Zita knew she was undergoing a professional crisis, as both Michael and Julia reminded her daily. But neither realized the depth of her discontent. This was more than an issue for her; it was her reason for living.

The subway car had arrived at the next station, and Zita, lost in thought, failed to notice her stop. A stranger passing by her seat said, "Lady, it's your station." Zita looked up, saw the *World News* sign, and scrambled out the door just as it closed behind her. She looked around for her rescuer, wondering if he was merely being helpful or if he was actually watching her. The man had quickly disappeared into the crowd. Michael would call her suspicion professional paranoia and tell her that while reading the agent's report. Michael would never have a crisis of conscience.

Zita strode into the newsroom and down the center aisle past a row of firmaglass cubicles where reporters were talking to their video screens, dictating stories into audio word processors. If you couldn't talk to your wife, as the saying went, your computer would always listen. In her office she glanced out the window at the less-than-spectacular view of smog-covered mid-Manhattan before turning the screen dial on the near wall to 90 percent blockout. She preferred the natural-spectrum overhead lighting to the brownish haze filtering through the window. It was a sign of the times that the artificial appeared more natural than nature. Zita opened the top side drawer of her desk and removed her whale cup with hand-painted pictures of blue whales and humpbacks. She carried the coffee cup over to the wall dispenser, choosing the grain blend.

Back at her desk, Zita sat down in her air-cushioned chair and pulled out one of the few keyboards used at the newspaper. Most of the young reporters were never taught typing in school. Zita had had to learn the skill on her own, but she liked the feel of the keys, the letters popping up on the screen at her command. It was a slower process, but it was the quality of the finished news story that was the true test.

Zita was writing a series on the world's first cost-efficient commercial fusion reactor, ready to go on-line at Europe's CERN research facility in the Jura Mountains of the Swiss province. The "Hammer," with its two-mile-high vertical acceleration shaft, bombarded hydrogen atoms with moving magnetic fields, as many as a thousand per second, to create the pressure required to fuse the atoms at temperatures considerably less than those needed in the Tokamak fusion reactors of the early twenty-first century. The theory had been proposed ten years earlier, but since there was no way of testing it short of building the device, only Europe, with its massive energy shortage, would risk it. This had placed the country years ahead of North America, and with the contemplated sale of the technology to the international community, the world's economic powerbase had suddenly shifted again. Zita was called upon by the Department to write a series praising the fusion reactor as a research success, geared for low-yield use, but casting doubt on its commercial viability. She knew the importance of this strategy, but since the planet was in such desperate need of non-polluting sources of energy, Zita could not bring herself to discredit the reactor completely. Her attitude, as revealed in the series of articles, was noted.

"Hey, you gonna make the Far East edition?" Bernie asked, his ghostly white image suddenly popping up in the corner of her screen.

"Don't worry, I'll work through lunch."

"You've got 'til three; let me take you to lunch."

"Sorry, I've got to leave early. . .business."

"Oh," Bernie said, frowning. He assumed she meant newspaper business, but he had learned that this was his cue to back off. Zita had remarkable sources of information, and as long as they proved useful, she could go and come as she liked. "Okay, but I hope you give the Euros a break in this one. Our Asian 'buddies' are quite interested in their 'hammer.'"

"They should be since they. . .," Zita stopped before revealing "shop" secrets, "need the tech as much as the rest of us."

"You didn't answer my question," Bernie said.

"It might light up a Swiss village for a song and a dance, but can it handle Tokyo?"

"Thirty million Asians hope so."

"Bernie, you've got final say. You're the editor."

"Yeah, I'm the editor all right." The last time he had edited one of her environmental articles, Mrs. Cooper, the owner of the newspaper, had questioned his revisions and told him in no uncertain terms to clear future changes with her. Sitting in her penthouse office and watching her hand shake while she sipped tea, Bernie sensed that she was being pressured, and he did not want to know by whom.

"Look, I hope it works as bad as they do, so one break coming up," Zita said.

"Good. I like it when you listen to me."

"Yeah, just listen to you."

"Okay, okay. Get back to work."

Bernie's face faded from her screen, and Zita continued writing her story. If only the fusion reactor did work as well as they claimed, the Euros could have their monopoly and the attendant political clout. The earth and her needs were more important to Zita than the economic power struggle among the world's superstates. Of course she knew the Department's policy line: economic parity among the superstates was essential to the present world order. However, in such speeches, they always failed to note that the North American countries had dragged behind the world community in regulating pollution standards since the 1980s, and their renegade industrial complexes had greatly contributed to the environmental and economic disasters that were to follow. Europe had emerged as the leader in environmental regulation, and Zita wondered if they were now economically poised to lead the world out of the ecological disaster that was the twenty-first century.

Turning off her vid phone, including computer access, Zita worked until two o'clock, completing her article. She downloaded the file for Bernie and Mrs. Cooper to read. Zita opened her door and stepped out into the newsroom. Valerie, the group office assistant, looked up from her vid screen and slid her headphones down around her neck.

"Any calls?" Zita asked contritely.

"About twenty, and I'm not joking."

"Anybody who can't wait?"

"I've transcribed the crucials, if you're ready for a feed."

"Give me ten minutes."

"It's your dime." Zita shook her head; Valerie had been watching too many late movies. They had not minted dimes in twenty-five years. She walked down the row of outside offices to the executive ladies' room. Inside, she went over and sat down in the recliner, stretching her legs out as the chair adjusted to the contours of her body. Zita turned the dial to full massage and lay back as a thousand leather fingers gently kneaded her body. She was so tense she decided not to set the timer.

Twenty minutes later, after Zita had failed to return to her office, Valerie came looking for her. She leaned over and shook Zita awake. "Hey, if Coop catches you napping, it's *Time* magazine for sure."

"Whew, I can usually handle this." Zita pushed the arm back and slid out of the chair. She stood up and looked down at her rumpled business suit.

Valerie shook her head. "If it's dinner for two, I'd change first."

Zita glared at her assistant. "Valerie."

"Sorry, I know you said no monitoring, but I do need to know your schedule."

"You certainly do," Zita said, "and when you need to know, I'll tell you." Valerie appeared sufficiently penitent. "I'm taking the four o'clock maglev down to Philly, and should be back by ten." Zita watched for a reaction, but Valerie merely nodded her head and ambled out the door, apparently unaware of her appointment with Michael.

Zita walked into the locker room, sliding past the half-lockers to her full-length one at the end. She tapped out the combination on her serial lock. The door popped open to reveal bright yellow environ boots and coat (for her occasional outdoor assignments) and a medium-length black evening dress and top. She did not have time to return home and change. Although Michael had ruled out any romance in advance, Zita felt that she needed to engage him on a more personal level. It was certainly ironic, she thought, how circumstances had arranged for her to express that feeling in the dress she was now forced to wear to dinner. Her unconscious desires were intruding into her conscious life; this could be a good sign or a bad one, depending on her priorities. For self-growth it was positive, if she were ready to confront these desires. But, if they affected her conscious control, her feelings could interfere with her performance as both a reporter and an undercover operative. Zita found her ambivalent response to these two options interesting. Her feelings had definitely shifted.

Chapter Two

Racing across New Jersey at 275 mph and nearly one hundred feet above ground did not soften the impact of the wasteland spread out below her. Zita was riding the elevated maglev train along the Jersey turnpike, outdistancing the few electric cars on the road heading out of town. On either side were woods of sick, desiccated trees, some rotten and fallen to the ground, all dying. It was a pitiful sight, and Zita could barely hold back her tears. Over the last fifty years, average temperatures had risen one degree per decade, moving climate zones fifty miles north with each increase. Trees once suited for the Jersey countryside would thrive today only in upstate New York. It had been recently estimated that the carbon released from dying trees in the past two decades had merely replaced levels from the banished internal combustion engine. Since forests naturally move only one half mile per year, it would take centuries to replace these dying trees by migration. However, with the government's aggressive reforestation program, you could see, amid the weary waste, replanted southern shrubs taking root.

"Awful, isn't it," the man said sitting across from her. He looked to be in his early seventies, but she suspected that he was younger. He wore a tattered grey overcoat and an old-fashioned cloth hat which was no doubt lined with environ plastic. "I can still remember how green it used to be."

"I don't," Zita said sadly.

"But then you're a little younger," the man said, smiling without showing his teeth. "You're Zita Hiller, the columnist, aren't you?"

"You read me?" Zita asked.

"No, not really," he said, his voice cracking. "Your columns were often a topic of discussion in my ecology classes at Princeton."

"You've gone on to greener topics," Zita said, trying to draw him out.

"No. I was retired," the man said bitterly. This drew a sympathetic response from Zita, but before she could offer an encouraging word, he hurriedly added, "I'm writing a book."

"An ecology textbook?"

"No, for the general public, but more rigorously thought out, I would hope, than the usual pop sludge." He hesitated, nervously stroking his chin, before saying, "It's interesting I should run into you. I've always objected to your kind of pop ecology. In fact, if I may be blunt, I think your idea of Model Incongruence is pure balderdash. Good scientific objectivity is what we need to solve the ecological problem, not rethinking our thinking."

Zita tried not to overreact. "So you've read my book."

"Yes, and it would have never passed my muster, young lady."

"What did you find so objectionable?"

"Ms. Hiller, we did not miscalculate the effects of the greenhouse gases in the 1990s because of our classical assumptions about nature, that it operated like a 'Newtonian Machine,' I believe you phrased it, but simply because there was no hard evidence." He could guess her rejoinder. "The rise in yearly temperatures could have been due to any number of factors."

"And twenty-five years later," Zita said, "when the accumulated effects were five times what anybody had predicted, and the trail led to misidentified fluctuations clearly evident back then, you still can claim there was no 'evidence.'"

"Anomalous occurrences are sometimes overlooked until they suggest new theories on nature's operation that incorporate their behavior. It's the age-old scientific method."

"And that's exactly what I'm saying," Zita said. "It's

the built-in classical logic of our world view, slow to recognize anything new, different, and anomalous, that slows our reaction time and prevents us from quickly adapting to ever-changing nature."

The man shook his head in disgust. "The problem with dilettantes, Ms. Hiller, is that they divert attention from the real issues. Report the facts, lady, and leave the theorizing to the professionals." He reached down to switch on the video magazine monitor, his frayed shirt cuff sticking out from his overcoat.

Zita watched him for a moment as his right eye twitched. His was such a typical attitude, what she had been fighting these past five years. She wondered if his early retirement indicated that the new "unified" ecology was taking root, but she saw little sign of that elsewhere and doubted it here. It was more likely that his rigid thinking had made him obsolete. She looked past the professor to the other passengers on the maglev train. Their soulless eyes revealed more in one glance than the pile of survey reports sitting on her desk. Zita could have taken the underground bullet to Washington and avoided the unpleasant celebrity-encounters riding public transportation. But she needed to keep in contact, to judge living conditions for herself. What these excursions told her was that the retreat of the natural world from the daily lives of people had resulted in cutting them off from some natural part of themselves, what had once defined their humanity. Although people might be physically adjusting to their lower standard of living, they were emotionally and spiritually at rock bottom.

The environmental collapse was a catastrophe for all humanity, but its most devastating effect was in stealing hope for a better tomorrow. For despite recent signs of recovery, future improvement would be only incremental for at least several generations. In the past, with hard work, will and determination, you could create a better world for yourself and a better future for your children. The only limits were lack of desire or imagination. When class or race was an impediment to self-improvement, you picked up and moved on to greener pastures. However, today all roads led to dead ends. The human race had breached the ultimate limit: the carrying capacity of the earth's biosphere. Two centuries of uncontrolled population and industrial growth had finally taxed the planet's capacity for self-adjustment, though hopefully not beyond the point where the earth could rally back.

The express train slowed down as it passed through a station loading passengers for a commuter train on the cross-Jersey line. Many of them were casino workers in Atlantic City; their colorful outfits peeked through slick environ coats and hoods. The city itself was reduced to the domed casino strip with its sixty-foot walls, an island fortress with the new coastline three miles inland. These workers were the most cosmetically pleasing. The less fortunate had cloth coats and oiled-down skin for outside exposure, which prevented them from using makeup to mask a plethora of tumors or their excised holes. These haggard faces were, as one commentator had unkindly characterized them, "the garbage dumps of the twenty-first century." Skin cancer from UV radiation had become pandemic in the last twenty-five years. Clean, clear skin had replaced the educated accent as the new class distinction between the haves and the have-nots. And plastic surgeons had long since overtaken lawyers as the profession with the highest per capita ratio.

A little girl, barely five, her right cheek bloated with a tumor, who had seen Zita's clear-skinned face pressed against the window, raced up to the edge of the track to get a closer look at this dark-haired angel. Zita smiled at her and whispered, as the little girl waved, "Don't be fooled, my dear, by beauty bought with the coin of your misery."

The maglev train passed through the station, picking up speed rapidly until it was once again flying across the countryside. Gazing out at the dead trees, the faces from the platform arose before her: haunted faces, deadened eyes, and then it struck Zita. The little girl's eyes were alive, full of life, unlike those of the other children. How remarkable, she thought. Maybe there was reason for hope.

Michael was late for dinner, and Zita ordered an appetizer while she waited. The seaweed, sauteed in a creamy garlic sauce, was very filling and she ate only half the portion. With more protein per gram than tofu, and considerably tastier, hydroponic seaweed had become, along with whole grains, a large part of most healthy modern diets. And, as the waiter had joked laying down the plate, it was "untouched by human hands." Most commercial poultry, fish, and beef were the product of sixty years of genetic tampering to improve their natural qualities. While the meat was leaner and tastier, and the animals grew twice as fast, the popular saying, "quick to table, quick to grave," had been validated in recent studies on the availability of its protein. Natural meat was now the major export from Third World countries who had fortunately missed the biotech revolution.

"Sorry," Parker said, as he slid into the seat across from her.

Zita looked up from the newspaper and studied him coolly. Michael Parker was in his mid-forties, medium height, his black hair streaked with grey. Since he always appeared distracted, his mind occupied elsewhere, he was often mistaken for a college professor. But, when he focused his full attention on you, that illusion was quickly dispelled. The sheer force of the man with his keen intelligence and deadly personal charm was hard to resist. It was that combination that had propelled him at an early age into the upper echelon of political operatives. He had been offered the director's job at the Department of Information twice and turned it down both times, preferring a less politically vulnerable position that would allow him to build a power base which could survive from one administration to another. He had succeeded and was now in an almost unassailable position to enforce his own political agenda. It also allowed him to move about under less public scrutiny and have clandestine dinners with pretty, young female operatives.

Parker smiled, his eyes blinking with sincerity. "Got some info on the Euro's new ozone seeder, and some tech guy was. . ."

"Will it work?" Zita asked immediately.

"Well, we don't have the specs, but we know the theory, and tech feels it has an outside chance."

"That would be wonderful."

"Yeah," Parker said sourly. "They build a shield over Europe, while the rest of us gook up."

"They're a signatory to the treaty; they'd have to share their eco tech."

"For a price, and they can withhold disclosure during testing, and in this case, the test would be a working shield."

"That would be unconscionable."

Parker laughed cynically. "Yeah, we should be so lucky."

"Not while I'm working here."

"We'd start with the beach resorts, then plop one over Disneyland, reopen it," he said teasing her.

"Michael, this is serious."

"Tell me. Hell, before we duplicate it, their tourist trade will suck up half the world's available cash."

"That's not the point. Ecologically, we'd be out of the woods."

"Yes, Little Red Riding Hood, and on the way to grandmother's."

"Michael!" Zita said shrilly. "Is that how you see me? Some starry-eyed little innocent."

"It is your most endearing quality," he said and added, "and your most useful."

"And you use me well, don't you Michael?"

"Not well enough, I've been told."

Zita heard the catch in his voice. "My employment was conditional."

"I know," he said in exasperation, "but I thought you'd outgrow it."

"Did you really," Zita said. Parker gave her a sharp look in reply. It stopped her. "You are angry?"

"They're not pleased with your fusion series," he said haltingly. "But it might work out after all."

"No retractions."

"What about a follow-up?" Parker asked wearily. "The Euros love you, and wouldn't mind you dropping in and asking a bunch of questions."

"The ozone seeder?"

"An objective, but not the assignment."

"And what would that be?"

The waiter stepped over and laid down plates in front of them. "Went ahead and ordered for us," Zita said, "since I'm on a time crunch."

"Okay," Parker said hesitantly, hearing her sharp tone. He forced himself to look up from the finely textured, perfectly formed steak. Parker noticed Zita's dress for the first time. He held her stare for a long moment. "Did I tell you how beautiful you look?"

"That's nice to hear," she replied, staring back blank-faced.

"It's been awhile, hasn't it?"

"Yes, Michael. It has."

"Well, maybe you should stay." Michael swallowed, the steak's aroma making his mouth water.

Zita waited, torturing him. Finally, she smiled. "We'd better eat before you bite your tongue off."

"Hey, is that supposed to mean something?" Parker picked up his knife and fork and cut into his twelve-ounce "tech" steak. "More taste, less fat, and I can skip my hormone shot."

"Don't be too hasty," Zita said coyly.

Parker tried to reply with a lecher's leering grin, but bulging cheeks from an overstuffed mouth made him look more like a chipmunk. Zita laughed at his comical expression. She loved his self-deprecating humor, those all-too-brief openings in his iron-clad seriousness. It was what had first attracted her. She could still remember those long nights when he courted her for this job, at first in restaurants and later in bed, listening to his comical portrayals of the world's Not-So-Greats. Impressed with his stories of behind-the-scene shenanigans to epic world events, Zita fell in love with this charming, politically correct—or so she thought—world mover and shaker. Although later recognizing the calculation of his recruitment, Zita never doubted his affection for her. But the times were squeezing the life and love out of them. Glancing up from her vegetable plate, she found Michael staring at her.

"Serious, and a little sad I'd say," Parker said.

"You can add frustration to that litany."

"With what, or with whom should I ask?"

"I don't know. I miss us, back when, and I'm not blaming you—or me for that matter. But, it's more than that," Zita added with a sigh. "It all seems so hopeless: us, the world, the planet. And I don't have any answers anymore."

"That does sound serious," Parker said, his knitted brow revealing his concern. He hesitated, making a quick assessment, and then reached for his briefcase. "What you need, my dear, is a change of pace."

Parker pulled out a fifty-page file. He removed a large newspaper photograph and passed it across the table to her. She held it in the light, viewing the faded picture of an East Indian, in traditional attire, seated at a table in what appeared to be an old courtroom. Zita was forced to read the caption to identify the man: the guru, Rama, at his trial for sedition. Luxembourg, Europe—April, 2028.

"He's a little before your time, but I'm sure you've read about his trial."

"Of course. It set all kinds of precedents in international criminal prosecution." Zita looked up from the caption and examined the man's features. He was forty, had a trimmed beard, a long angular nose, and the most intense dark eyes she had ever seen.

Parker laughed at her expression. "Yeah, he was a real charmer all right. Held millions in his messianic spell. Rama was implicated, more for his ecological stance than from any direct evidence, with the psychic 'Greens' in the computer breakdowns of the 2020s, but they had trouble building a case against him. The psychic marauders could destroy whole computer networks with a single mental flash, but proving who did what was another problem. Well, in the aftermath, when the worldwide economy had collapsed and countries were forced to merge into the present territorial states, he called for a world government to stem renewed economic competition—which was, in his estimation, the root cause of the ecological disaster. Since he was backed by 50 million followers worldwide, this made him a big-time political liability. It seems silly in retrospect: the 'one planet, one people' stuff, but the world leaders, who saw competition between countries as the key to recovery, were alarmed. Rama was arrested as a co-conspirator, and using new evidential standards for psychic crimes, was convicted along with the others and sentenced to life in prison. It was a fix, of course, but a necessary one at the time."

"And?"

"And the Euros, who have him incarcerated with the psychic Greens in the Tesla Field Prison at Bernia in the Swiss Alps, are listening to calls for his release."

"Well, what threat does he still pose?"

"He claims," Parker said rather dispassionately, "that while in prison he has passed into the natural state of being, and that his soul has merged with the soul of the planet."

"Quite a claim," Zita said, catching his tone. "Are you impressed?"

"Not really," Parker said with feigned disinterest, "but there're millions of back-to-earth nuts out there, a bunch of God-freaks, if you ask me, who're waiting for a messiah. And Rama fits the bill."

"Has he shown any interest in their cause?"

"He's disavowed political movements for mystical communion with God and Earth. But his followers act otherwise."

"And they have a right to their religious and political beliefs."

"If it were merely that, we'd say fine—this isn't the 2020s—we can withstand radical leaders and their movements," Parker said as if reading a prepared speech. "But there's something 'physiological' happening to him, that our scientists can't explain. What if he ends up with extraordinary new powers? And we now know enough about consciousness and morphic fields to realize that he might be able to instill them in his followers. They could then mount another psychic assault on computer systems worldwide, and we'd be back where we started and worse off."

"And you want me to interview him, discredit him, and bolster world opinion against his release."

"Something like that."

Zita considered the assignment. "Let me read the file, do a little research, check my sources, and get back to you."

"Sure. Just be careful. We don't want the Euros to know what's coming."

Parker passed Zita the file, and she placed it in her briefcase. She shoved it out of sight under the table, and put both it and the Rama file it contained out of her mind. She looked back at Michael. "I believe we have another offer on the table."

"Yes, we do."

Michael lay beside her in bed wheezing loudly, despite the room's high oxygen level. Like most men his age, he had lungs that had breathed a lifetime of stagnant filtered air, and it had taken its toll. It also resulted in generally poor circulation, contributing to a greatly impaired sexual responsiveness. Michael rolled over and slung his arm across Zita's chest. She waited a moment, then sat up in bed, causing his arm to slide down and come to rest on her abdomen, his hand lying on her upper thigh. Passive and inert, only seeking comfort from the warm touch of skin on skin, his hand in repose excited her more than its probing fingers had earlier. More than passionate lovemaking, Zita had wanted just to have him hold her, to be cradled in his arms, breathing in sync with him, each looking deeply into the other's eyes. But such intimacy would have required a feeling response from Michael more terrifying than a loaded gun pointed at his head. And so they had made love in the only way he could sustain it, leaving her mostly unsatisfied.

In times past, if love were not an avenue for intimacy, one could always seek it in nature. To lie naked on a deserted beach, wiggling deep into the warm sand, the sun beaming down on you, the ocean breeze licking your face, or to run down a wooded path between 300-foot-high redwoods, breathing in the musky damp air, vines snapping at your heels and leaves slapping your face. . . It was this communion that Zita longed for with all her soul, snatched away from her by the age's ecological disaster. Nor would she find it in the company of family and friends. Crunched together in glass towers, underground caverns and indoor malls, people vigorously withdrew from intimate contact for fear of losing what little speck of individuality they could claim for themselves. Zita was more fortunate than most, but the private space bought with her privileged status was filled with little more than a lonely heart.

Michael rolled back, removing his arm, and Zita quickly slipped out of his bed undetected. She pulled on a wraparound robe and headed out of the bedroom into a rather large living room—one that could hold a sofa and chair. Zita jumped up on the high-cushion sofa, sinking down slightly, and gazed out tinted windows to the blurred glowing lights of Washington. She picked up the remote and thumbed the roller-dial, cutting the window tint to 20 percent and increasing magnification by 50 percent. Coming into focus, less than five miles away, was the White Dome. The twenty-story dome enclosed the old White House and the compound grounds. It contained one of the few green lawns and flower gardens in the Western Hemisphere. More tourists, they said, came to see the roses than the current resident of the White House.

Zita rolled back the magnification until the Dome blurred out in the distance. She turned away from the window and the contemplation of things mortal to the vid screen which presently showed a live satellite view of the starry heavens. This sight always took her breath away, and she could view it, as she did on her visits here, for hours on end. It would soon be available on her cable system, and she looked forward to viewing it at home. For her, the effect was not otherworldly; somehow, and strangely enough, the star vista drew out the feeling side of her nature which was very grounding. Or, at least, that was how she perceived it. Her analyst, Julia, a woman with a decidedly more numinous makeup, simply called it her "other" side.

Julia had explained that the two interpretations were not incompatible. Although the spiritual view was that of a self-actualizing "other," it could also be viewed for a mental type like Zita as the feeling component of the total self. Either way she lost control, as Julia liked to remind her. Zita could sense within her, whatever its makeup, a world as great as the one she now contemplated. Since what drew this overwhelming response was nature at its most expansive, Zita could not help but wonder if this "other" was her hidden link with that world. Could the communion denied her in the forest primeval be accessible through a journey into the deeper recesses of the self?

Almost immediately, and it was an eerie experience, the image of the incarcerated guru, Rama, flashed before her eyes. This startled Zita, but she recognized the unconscious association. He claimed to have taken a journey resulting in this kind of merger. But she could not deny the surge of interest in the man and his supposedly "natural state of being." Zita slid off the sofa and went over to the dining room table where her briefcase lay. Sitting down at the glass-top table, she pulled out the Rama file and opened it. His newspaper photo with those enormous dark eyes stared back at her. However, this was not the image of him in her vision. Zita hurriedly thumbed through the mass of pages looking for a more recent photo. Near the end was one taken last year for his five-year Red Cross physical. Here was the greying Indian in his sixties she had seen, and not the young rebel of the newspaper clipping.

This was very curious and a little unnerving. Julia would call it image projection, a form of telepathy, which Zita had studied in college psych courses. This type of phenomenon was now universally recognized. But Rama was being held in Bernia, a Tesla Field prison, that supposedly blocked out telepathic communication of any nature. It had been built to contain the psychic marauders who had played havoc with the world's computer banking system. Could it be defective? But, even if it were, how would he know of her interest in him? Could he just scan the world reading minds at will? No, that was preposterous. There must be another explanation. Maybe this natural state of his opened up a range of possibilities not yet explored. If so, he would certainly be perceived as a threat to her associates in the mind-control business.

Zita turned the pile of pages over and began to read. The story that unfolded with each new page fascinated her; the man was a living enigma. He had singlehandedly reformed one of the world's great religions to make it more responsive to the needs of the hungry masses, and then walked away when it proved resistant to his spiritual search. Rama had a following of millions whom he repeatedly told, "I can't help you," and still they flocked to him. He was a peaceful man, a nonviolent man, who had challenged the world's governments to deindustrialize along ecological lines and redistribute the world's wealth so Third World nations would not exploit their natural resources. When they had refused to listen, he supposedly led psychic commandos on an assault on the global computer banking system that brought the world to its knees. He was an eloquent man, who had refused to defend himself at his trial, meditating until the judge insisted that he follow the proceedings.

Zita looked up to see the light of the new day seeping through the cloud cover. She had read only half the file, but stopped at this point, marking her place.

"Time," she called out.

"6:05 A.M.," the computer chimed.

She could catch the 7:00 bullet to New York if she hurried. Although she set her own schedule, Zita was anxious to begin her research. She took a blank sheet of paper out of her notebook and left a message for Michael: "Buying a new overcoat today. Bill to follow. Love Z."

Chapter Three

From afar it appeared to be a giant eagle's nest perched atop the mountain's spiring peak. The turbocopter approached, swinging around to the east; with the snow-covered cliffs in the range ahead in shadow, a three-story circular structure was revealed in relief against the darkened background, its massive firmaglass windows looking out on a desolate mountain landscape. Coming closer, the turbocopter's passenger could see that the peak was actually a gigantic metal cone, the Tesla scalar interferometer, with corner disks projecting a dome-shaped shield of intense electromagnetic energy and from antennas above and below the structure, a psychically impenetrable scalar wave field. The copter was given final clearance, as the outer shell, capable of vaporizing physical objects, opened, and it lowered itself onto the world's most secure prison, what some inmates called, "Alcatraz North," and one "Gulag Mentalis," prison of the mind.

Along its outer rim, sandwiched between surveillance stations above and below it, was the cell reserved for its most famed detainee. This man, wearing a traditional white sarong and blouse for his visitor, his short-cropped grey hair and beard framing a tanned face with surprisingly few wrinkles, sat in his window perch watching the turbocopter approach. It was his favorite seat; he had insisted they pad it for his comfort and for him to knock his head against since they, "did not provide me with a padded cell." The man's peculiar humor was not his only idiosyncrasy that baffled those called upon to contain him and to study his state of being. While the other prisoners read, played chess, or watched videos,

Rama sat motionless in his perch looking out the window day after day. The scientists questioned whether he was actually observing the mountain landscape, making note of its features. They speculated that he was remote-viewing during this time, which the scalar wave field was designed to block out. In his first years at Bernia, the utter strangeness of his daily routine, under constant camera surveillance, had a disturbing effect on the guards monitoring him. Prison authorities were forced to rotate them more often, and after one religious guard had a nervous breakdown, the warden began importing them from psychiatric institutions accustomed to the behavior of the mad, be they divinely mad or otherwise.

However, today the routine was broken. After the copter landed, Rama slid off his perch and stepped over to the desk in the alcove. Warden DeWitt called this Rama's "study," and he would display it to Red Cross and World Council monitors as an example of the prison's humane treatment. After Pope Helen had complained that Rama's quarters were too sparse, DeWitt had had a wall knocked out and a recessed area built, furnishing it with a desk and bookshelf. Rama had showed no interest in the new accommodations. When he failed to supply a requested list of books, the shelves were lined with the world's great religious classics. The Dalai Lama, on his first visit, noticing the books gathering dust, asked if there were others he could supply. Rama told him that the words no longer stuck in his mind, but books of blank sheets could at least be used to wipe after him. His remark, passed around in transcript, became notorious among the guards and set the stage for a wary conviviality between the irreverent "holy man" and his scoffing keepers.

Rama sat down at the desk and turned on the lamp with its bowl-shaped shade reflecting its light off the low ceiling. The man's eyes could not focus on an overlit page of print. He opened the document awaiting his signature. It was an appeal written by a follower, an international law expert, petitioning the European Supreme Court for his release. He slowly read the ten-page brief and considered the lawyer's argument. Rama's entrance into his famed "no-mind" state did not preclude the use of his mental faculties; in fact, his cognitive powers were sharper than ever, the difference being that when he withdrew his attention his mind became "disengaged." No run-on train of thoughts constantly bombarded him. The mind was still there, ready for use, but it did not impose itself. He now grasped the key point of the brief: Rama had been extradited under then-existing international laws that permitted one country to try another's notorious criminals when doing so would ease social unrest in the home country. The law had been judged unconstitutional by the Asian Supreme Court, Rama's home country, and his lawyer proposed that this ruling—which had used Rama's case as a prominent example—if it did not nullify his conviction, at least called for a re-trial in Asian courts.

Since Rama was supposedly unbounded in this state, remaining in prison or being released should not have mattered to him. This supposition was another misconception: that he was disconnected from his human side, his feelings and emotions, and needed little contact with others. On the contrary, the diminishment of the mind and the subsequent erosion of the "I" center of the personality allowed a full blossoming of his feeling nature. It was their feeling side that had always distinguished the true masters. Rama, who could be stern when required, had a childlike sweetness that endeared him to everybody. It could be that he touched their souls, and they were fed by that connection. His presence seemed to activate people at a very deep level; those who responded often experienced surprising results.

The buzzer rang. "Gov'nor," the voice called over the intercom, "can I come in?"

"Yes, Joseph, I am just finishing up."

The cell's photonic barrier modulator, the prison's interior psychic containment field, was momentarily deactivated and the metal door swung back. Joseph Murdock, the senior guard, stepped inside the cell, leaving the door open. He had two men waiting for them in the corridor. Murdock was a short spry Englishman, a few red hairs sticking up on an otherwise bald pate, who bandied his lower-class accent while others hid theirs. When he arrived at Bernia ten years ago, within months of Rama's "changeover," the guards were still leery of contact with the holy man. His food, laundry, and personal effects were passed via a portal door that kept a photonic barrier between them and the prisoner. Joseph had said he would not treat his dog in such a coldhearted manner, much less their esteemed prisoner, and had received permission to bring Rama his breakfast in the morning. They would chat, and the two of them had soon established a rapport. But Joseph had had trouble finding a suitable form of address. He later learned—to his immense satisfaction—that Rama had aristocratic English blood from his mother's ancestry. The holy man had been "gov'nor" to him ever since.

"Your visitor is finishing her clearance check."

"No doubt another pleasant experience for all."

"She's a corker, all right," Joseph said. "Wouldn't go through x-ray again, but finally agreed to a sonic sweep."

"She says visiting me here, with all this electronic static, has shortened her life span."

"But she must be eighty at least."

"God knows why, but Mother plans to live forever, or a few days short of it."

The men exchanged a knowing look that monitors viewing the video record would not detect, but Joseph understood the reference perfectly well. When he first began serving Rama his breakfast, Joseph had arthritis and the prognosis was not encouraging. Within weeks the inflammation had subsided, his blood pressure was lowered, and he was cured of a whole list of minor ailments. This actually scared him, and Joseph scheduled an appointment with the prison doctor. It occurred to him that his contact with Rama, a legendary healer, might be the cause. He carefully probed the holy man about his "influence." When asked about the yogi healers of his native land and their miraculous cures, Rama told him that the stories were mostly true but that the cures were often undone by the sufferer's lack of faith. Joseph got the point. He cancelled his appointment and had not been to a doctor in ten years.

Rama stood up from the desk and placed the signed document in its folder. "Well, Joseph, if this is granted, I might be leaving here one day."

"Our loss, Gov'nor, but for your sake, I hope it's soon."

"I would not worry. Personally, I never overestimate the wisdom of any worldly body that calls itself 'Supreme.'"

Joseph snickered; he loved the man's irreverent attitude that spared no target. The two of them turned and walked out the door. They were escorted down the hall to the third-floor arboretum which served as the visitor's lounge. The people they passed reacted to Rama's presence with either awe or fear. One women, a cafeteria worker, wheeling a cart of empty trays, stopped and bowed her head. Rama returned the bow. She reached over and touched his hand before the guards could restrain her. One of them now took the woman to the warden's office where she would be summarily dismissed.

"I hope it was worth it to her," Joseph said. He looked at the holy man, whose only reply was a mystifying smile.

Martha Coomaraswamy sat in the wicker chair, impatiently sipping her English breakfast tea and awaiting the arrival of her famous son. Half-English, half-Indian, her light complexion was only slightly wrinkled and spotted by eighty years of living, which she attributed to a strong English constitution and her Indian heritage of meditative discipline. It also helped that she made a yearly pilgrimage to Bernia for her "prana" boost, as she described it to friends. During the early years of Rama's incarceration, Martha did not visit her recalcitrant son. She was still angry with him for renouncing his Hindu faith and for allegedly participating in the banking debacle. Then, of course, there was the trial, which she had attended and which made him a prisoner and her a pariah in social circles east and west. The accumulated effect of this family tragedy had hastened her husband's death and left her a widow at an early age. She stayed away until time had softened the hard edge of her anger, and decorum required at least a ceremonious visit. On her return five years later, she had noted an enormous change in her son, a complete transformation, and experienced an elevation of energy in his presence that had miraculous results. And, with each subsequent visit, her body and her spirit were renewed. Martha was a driving force behind the movement for Rama's release, with the hope that once freed he would return to the ashram where she could drink at his well daily.

Rama entered the arboretum and walked between the hanging plants and potted bushes, stopping to smell the fragrance of a white rose and picking a long-stemmed lily for his guest, finally arriving at the chair setting. Martha stood up and embraced her son, feeling the strange tingling sensation down the length of her spine, the light pressure between her eyes, the pounding pulse at the temples that signaled the quickening of her energy. She took a long, deep breath and reluctantly stepped back. Rama handed his mother the flower. She held it, bowing her head in appreciation and in deference to his spiritual status. They smiled at each other in silence before seating themselves.

"Tell me, Uncle Hari and his goats, how are they?"

Martha took the cue and launched into a half-serious tirade. "Well, we were finally able to grow grass under the south lawn's environ screen. It was looking very decent. Then I was called away to Singapore, and when I returned, the goats had eaten the grass to the roots."

"It is what they do: eat grass."

"Yes, I know. What I take exception to is what Hari does, meditating all day in his room, letting the ashram go to seed."

"You could move Uncle Hari's meditation mat to the south lawn."

"I could move my brother back to Bombay and let him fend for himself."

"You know what they say, 'find me a useless man, a man the world can not use, and I will show you a master.'"

"If that is the test, he should have ascended by now."

Rama laughed wholeheartedly in giggles that rose from the pit of his abdomen, with its nasal whistle blowing in short staccato notes, and reverberated in the domed arboretum. The guards standing at the entrance smiled and then laughed in return. But they did not detect, as did Martha, with her eyes closed and her pores opened, the sudden buildup of negative ions in the air, as if lightning had struck in the enclosed space. When she opened her eyes, Rama was watching her with amusement.

"And so, apart from Uncle Hari and his rampaging goats, the ashram is doing well?"

"We have guest speakers and weekend seminars, conduct courses in the healing arts, occasionally a holy man will take up residency, but eventually they leave, chased away some say by the living ghost of Rama."

"Yes, we are a superstitious lot."

"No one can take your place, my son, and everybody awaits your return."

"Even President Kataro?"

"He did send greetings on your sixty-second birthday."

"Any fool can praise a caged bird's song."

"There are calls in the parliament for your release, and the religious community, despite jealousy in some circles, has always opposed your imprisonment."

Rama took the folder and passed it to his mother. "Here is the petition. Tell Mr. Beauvoir that his argument is sound and that I appreciate his efforts on my behalf."

"Jacques will be thrilled. He is one of your most ardent devotees."

"Let us hope he is as good a solicitor."

"He absolutely thrashed our landlord when he tried to have us evicted last year."

"My jailers will be more formidable."

"But, if the Gods will, what can they do?"

"Indeed, mountains can be moved, but I doubt this peak is high on their list."

Martha would dispute this claim, but Rama shook his head indicating the subject was closed. In matters spiritual, she always deferred to him. His moral authority was recognized at an early age. It was more than his precocious grasp of religious doctrine. (He understood fine shadings scholars spent lifetimes acquiring.) His preternatural insight into the human condition—his early teachings about the division between ego and self were classics—revealed in weekly talks at the age of seven at the ashram of a famous swami, accorded him the reputation as the "wise child" of ancient lore. His father had wanted to make a religious scholar of him; Rama was sent to the university at age twelve, but he resisted, preferring the natural sciences—which soon bored him as well. It was at the age of eighteen that he experienced his first "Satori," the direct insight into the true nature of reality, that set his course and began his holy campaign to renounce and denounce all that stood between the human and the divine in ourselves and in nature. A path that led him to this lonely peak in the Swiss Alps and twenty years of imprisonment.

Martha took the folder and placed it in her briefcase, removing a folded newspaper. She handed the paper to her son. "There is another matter to discuss."

Rama opened the newspaper and glanced at the circled article. The headline cried out for research to save our "dying" forests from climate displacement. The by-line was Zita Hiller, and the columnist's photo showed a dark-haired, intense young woman.

"*World News* contacted us and would like to do a series on you, while the Court hears your petition for release," Martha said, pausing a moment. "The Hiller woman has a good reputation as an environmental advocate, and so we assume by her selection that they intend to use that angle, which could be a two-edged sword."

"And my keepers have no objection to conducting the interviews here?"

"She has gotten the clearance rather quickly."

"Interesting." Rama studied the woman's photo for

a moment, getting a "feel" for the situation. He now stared at his mother with heightened intent.

Martha could "read" her son: there was duplicity here, but they could use it to their advantage. "For many you are still a symbol for environmental advocacy, and the Europeans are particularly sensitive to these issues. It could help."

Rama could not help but smile. His mother played the game so well. He held up the newspaper. "Rather pretty, is she not?"

"Rather, but I would not think that was a consideration."

"Well, even we celibates can appreciate a pretty woman."

"Would you like to consider this offer further?" Martha asked, in the dismissive tone reserved for her son's lapses from religious uprightness.

"No. Tell them short interviews only, but as many as they will permit."

Martha nodded her head, knowing this stipulation was part of her son's strategy but unsure of its implications. She knew Rama was not manipulative in any ordinary sense, but like the Zen Masters of old, he could disarm the cunning ego in a student or an opponent by energizing the person's unconscious, creating a conflict in the less-than-pure-intentioned that could lead to their own self-undoing. He did not act but merely precipitated in others activity that they brought upon themselves by contact they initiated with him.

They sat in silence for a moment. It appeared that their visit had come to an end. "Before you leave," Rama asked, "shall we take a look at the view? It is spectacular this time of the year."

"Yes, I was rather looking forward to it," Martha replied, her voice quivering with anticipation.

Rama stood and escorted his mother around the bushes and potted trees to the window-wall overlooking the Swiss Alps. They stepped into position along the railing, a ritual enacted during recent visits, and stared out at the mountainscape. The guards watching them in person or with remote cameras observed two people standing together viewing the mountains. More subtle "eyes" would have seen a literal cascade of light emanating from Rama and engulfing his mother, greatly enhancing her life or morphic field. All they actually recorded on tape, noted in an edited stop-action replay, were the nearby plants curiously leaning in the holy man's direction.

By the time Rama returned to his cell, the sun had set behind the mountains to the west, deepening the shadows in the valley until they were absorbed into the darkness of the rapidly descending night. Rama, sitting in his customary perch, watched with endless fascination the change of day into night in his tiny mountain domain. The light of day showed the world separate and divided, but with the night all things merged into uniformed oneness. It was easier for most to see the one behind the many; Rama could also see the many in the one. And so the night was as interesting for him as the day was for most. He had requested earlier that the spotlights, which illuminated nearby cliffs making the night view scenic for the other inmates but distracting for him, be removed. They complied with his request for this arc of the circular building. If he were indeed remote-viewing, as they suspected, in defiance of their security screen, they wanted him to continue. They then tampered with the scalar wave field frequencies, trying to disrupt him, but Rama gave no indication that the different settings affected him. Eventually the scientists abandoned their efforts and reset the field. As with other invasive attempts, they were unable to penetrate his wall of silence.

Neither could vagrant thoughts arising from within gain a foothold in this most stilled mind. What it lacked was a center to hold the thoughts together. In its absence thoughts simply evaporated, their energy dissipated into the body. It had been a considerably more intense release that accompanied Rama's entrance into his famed "natural" state of being. It disrupted that center or the traditional "I," created and sustained by thought, and the massive discharge short-circuited every cell in a body dominated by thought, scrambled age-old patterns, and rerouted the flow of current through the cells transforming every bodily function.

In the months leading up to, during, and after this changeover, he experienced incredible pain. The body consciousness was in open warfare with the mind's mental conditioning. The headaches alone were unbearable. The body was fighting to unhinge itself from the mind's total domination and to establish its own natural rhythms. As a result he began to experience the world through drastically altered sense organs. All outside sound, a bird twittering in the aviary, a spoon dropping to the floor, originated within himself. His vision changed to a focusing arrangement best described as a reverse fisheye: things faraway appeared closer and vice versa, as if his being included both the center and the circumference of the circle. In time he came to understand that it had expanded to include increasingly greater territories until the culminating experience years later of himself expanded to include the entire planet within his being.

The immediate effect was the appearance of a grave illness that brought him near death. Rama was moved to a private room in the infirmary and placed under the watchful eye and care of Dr. Renault, a French physician and psychiatrist who specialized in the mental aberrations of the prison's psychic inmates. The initial prognosis was liver cancer that had gone undetected and was now inoperable and terminal. The warden had been alerted, and he prepared for the death of his famous prisoner by informing the Red Cross, whose doctors would perform the autopsy and absolve them of any wrongdoings. When Rama refused pain killers and slyly suggested all was not what it seemed, Renault began to monitor his condition more closely. What came next astonished both the doctor and his patient. On Rama's head, neck, and torso there appeared, at points the ancient yogis called chakras and modern scientists the endocrine glands, skin discolorations. But it was the activities of the glands themselves that baffled and amazed the doctor. Blood tests revealed a whole range of new glandular hormones being secreted, whose functions he could not ascertain at that stage of his inquiry.

Catholic by birth, metaphysician by choice, Renault aided the process by withholding disclosure. Under the guise of an experimental nutrition therapy—increasingly recognized in the treatment of advanced cancers—he confined Rama in the infirmary until his condition stabilized. Renault encouraged him to keep a journal, while he surreptitiously photographed the discolorations on a daily basis and kept his own journal. After Rama miraculously recovered from his liver cancer and was returned to his cell, Renault smuggled the material out of the prison and presented it to the Rama Society. Unfortunately, the devotees could not contain their excitement, passing the material among themselves until a stray copy found its way into the hands of the European security force. Renault was convicted of treason and sent to a far less hospitable prison, and Rama became the subject of an intense medical investigation.

The full moon had risen from behind the mountains to the east and lit up the surrounding peaks. This drew Rama's attention and with it came the awareness that the fluids in his body were again responding to the pull of this heavenly body. After his changeover, he had discovered that his body, without its rigid armor of thought, responded more fully to the circadian cycle of day and night, the change of seasons, to sun spots, and there were effects in which he could not identify the influence. And as his awareness expanded so did his sensitivity to all within its scope of activity. The death of a fellow inmate and an earthquake in China were felt the moment they occurred.

The effects covered a wide range, including an elevation in body temperature, a buzzing in the ear, and the reappearance of the skin discolorations. They lasted anywhere from seconds to hours and then subsided. But, slight as the effects were, the scientists could not deny them. Whatever the force, it was able to penetrate the scalar wave field, and affected Rama without significant changes in his already scrambled brain-wave rhythms. Apparently it was not mentally amplified, like all known psychic phenomenon. Although he appeared to be merely at the receiving end of this force, the prospect that he could—or did—use it to "affect" those outside the field barriers of the prison disturbed those charged with containing him and the psychic marauders.

Chapter Four

On the video screen, Rama was seen sliding off his window perch, walking over and lying down on the bed. Dr. Erik Gustafson, the Swedish brain specialist, hit a key on the console and a graph of the subject's brain wave rhythms was superimposed over the picture. Rama appeared to fall asleep immediately, and instead of the gradual four-stage descent into deep sleep, his brain waves quickly lengthened into those indicative of that stage. The scientist turned to his visitor, who appeared anxious for an explanation that was purposely withheld. Gustafson liked to dangle tantalizing bits of information in front of visiting scientists and then make them squirm for amplification. The tall Swede, his thin blond hair unfashionably long, a hard body built with costly oxygen-consuming workouts, relished the superior position. Finally, he threw out, "He does not waste time, does he?"

"That's amazing. What does it usually take, about 60 minutes?" Dr. Henry Halzack, a physical anthropologist from the University of the Americas in Quebec, North America, was in his mid-forties, loose-limbed and athletic, with an outdoorsman's rugged face tanned from outside exposure.

"Thereabouts. And there is more—or less, I should say." On another monitor appeared a video study of Rama sleeping, with a superimposed graph of his brain waves. The tape scanned at fast-forward, exaggerating the man's tiny head movements. "Look at the graph. His brain waves do not change during the entire four-hour sleep. No REM period at all. We have not recorded the man dreaming since we installed the long-range brain scanners and began monitoring his sleep five years ago."

"There are cases. . ."

"Of people who do not sleep and are not affected, but here is the case of a sleeper without any REMs at all."

"And the others?" Halzack asked.

"Pathological, diseased or otherwise. But Rama, despite his abnormalities, is neither."

"Some psychologists believe that dreams are strategies to heal the split between the conscious and unconscious mind, and that they subside in those who have unified theirs."

Gustafson stared skeptically at his colleague. "I would not know about that." He leaned over and spoke into the microphone. "Save and store image file Rama: sleep studies, and play file Rama: brain scans." The digital tape of Rama sleeping on monitor two was replaced with one showing him in their lab with the dome-shaped brain scanner above his head. The scans quickly flashed forward. "Stop, reverse, previous set and hold." An image of a brain with a dozen colored hot spots appeared. "Here we see none of the electrical brain patterns that characterize pathological states like schizophrenia. However, as you can see, doctor, there are some unique signatures."

"I'd say." Halzack studied the image for a moment. "The right and left hemispheres appear perfectly balanced."

"Unusual, but look at the basal forebrain," Gustafson said, staring in disbelief for the umpteenth time. "Active in a completely conscious subject. This is usually indicative of sound sleep."

Dr. Halzack nodded his head, thinking it over. Almost to himself, he added, "Which he enters instantaneously."

"Yes, as we just witnessed."

A concept was forming in Halzack's mind. "Without dreaming, or showing any ill effects."

"And the point?" Gustafson asked impatiently.

Dr. Halzack suddenly understood it. "Mystics claim that deep sleep and the enlightened state are essentially the same." His colleague stared back blankfaced. "I think you've just given me a scientific criteria for enlightenment: conscious sleep, which is, with brain scans, demonstrable."

"That's all very interesting, doctor," Gustafson said, his voice edged with sarcasm. "And, if you were to bring me a dozen more claimants, with the same brain scans, I might label it as such. But, for now, all I have are a group of unusual indicators that do not fit any acceptable category."

Halzack smiled mysteriously. "So, you think a dozen would do it?"

Gustafson gave the man a hard cold stare. "Dr. Halzack, are you toying with me?"

"No, I'm perfectly serious. I may be on to. . .something, a discovery of sorts, that might prove my point."

"Somebody who can duplicate these readings?" Gustafson asked with keen interest.

"That's why I'm here. To gather data, build a profile, for comparison."

"Well, we have reams of data, and I would imagine you are cleared to review it," Gustafson said invitingly. "And I would like to hear more about your own work, doctor."

"It's still in its infancy, as they say, but it holds promise."

"Could you be more specific?"

Halzack winced in anticipation of Gustafson's reaction. "I've detected readings suggestive of not abnormal, but what I call supernormal states of mind in some misdiagnosed autistic savants, and in normal children with extraordinary abilities."

The tall Swede stared back incredulously. "Curious research for an anthropologist."

"Well, when my primary research leads elsewhere, I usually follow it up myself."

"But Zischler wrote the book on autistic savants thirty years ago."

"I feel Dr. Zischler's perspective prejudiced his findings: he saw these minds, despite his great compassion for the children, as irredeemably flawed. And when confronted with displays of extraordinary ability, he saw them as a shattered mind's rallying point."

Again the presumed obvious escaped Gustafson. "And?"

"I see them as new faculties trying to evolve out of old brain structures, bolstered by the discovery that the brains of some of these children show physiological differences."

"But, unlike them, Rama is totally functional."

"Yet his sensory distortion suggests he lives in another world as well; one these children inhabit, if not to the same extent. And who is to say which is superior? To them we could appear highly dysfunctional."

"In that case I would say the majority rules."

"But just how long will we be in the majority?"

Gustafson finally grasped the man's argument and was both astonished and appalled by its perceived superficiality. "If you are suggesting that this man's no-mind state is the forerunner of some kind of evolutionary leap by our species, I would remind you, doctor, that the development of our neo-cortex with its higher reasoning functions is evolution's supreme achievement, and the further development of that capacity is most definitely the route human evolution is taking."

"What distinguishes our brain from the lower primates," Halzack said insistently, "with a billion fewer neurons, is self-reflective consciousness. We not only are conscious but are conscious of being a conscious self. And from what we know of Rama's condition, he has certainly expanded his 'self' to include more than his individual being. In fact, if we may take him at his word, to include the planet as well. That capacity, instead of greater number crunching, is the next step for our species."

Gustafson gave the man a long silent stare. "Mysticism, while welcomed in a religious leader, can be deadly for a scientist."

Dr. Halzack stared back with equal penetration. "What some mistake for mysticism in others is the intuitive sense they lack in themselves."

Gustafson stepped back and folded his arms. He had

to admire the man's mettle if not his science. "And your next stop, Dr. Halzack?"

"The infirmary."

"Ah yes," Gustafson said, smiling smugly, "even the biological sciences have not been left unscathed."

When Halzack returned to his room, night had fallen and the room was dark. He immediately walked over to the window and adjusted the tint until he could clearly see the lighted mountain landscape. It was a sight more welcomed than he had anticipated. In that moment he knew that the spotlights had not been installed for the inmates but for the scientists who were dealing with the disorienting effects of this man's condition. In the light of day, with the sheer physicality of the world pressing in on one from every corner, you could turn off a monitor, shelve a notebook, and more readily detach and reorient oneself to the customary world of the senses. At night, adrift in the insubstantiality of a darkened world, the aftereffects of their investigation were more threatening.

Jean Elan was escorting Dr. Halzack to the infirmary on the first floor. Since there were few outside visitors, the prison did not have a full-time public relations officer, and the warden's secretary usually assumed the role when needed. However, she had neither the aptitude nor the enthusiasm required for the job.

"Here we are," Elan announced with relief, as they walked up to a double glass door marked: Infirmary & Biological Laboratory. Elan ran her key-card through the scanner and the door slid open. The nurse's station was unmanned, and the monitor on the wall showed a security ward with only one patient. Elan used her key-card to open the first door in the Sally-Port corridor, but the second door required her voice identification.

"Elan, Jean 22923921."

The door opened, and they walked down the hallway. The first examination room was empty, but they heard voices coming from the next room. They went inside and found Rama sitting on an examination table, stripped to the waist, giving a blood sample. The nurse looked up in surprise. Elan stepped back.

"Where is Dr. Cherenkov?" she asked pointedly.

"He is removing the guard's hangnail," the nurse replied. She looked down at the filled tube and capped the non-invasive needle.

Rama swung his legs around to face them. This further unnerved the secretary. Reacting to her fear, Halzack stepped back from the man. Rama smiled at them, his eyes lit up like candles. He stuck out his wrists. "You can handcuff me if you like."

The nurse laughed, and Halzack was utterly charmed. Elan was unmoved. She turned to Halzack. "We have to postpone your meeting. You do not have clearance for personal contact with the prisoner."

"I'm scheduled to leave shortly. Can I wait out front until they're finished here?"

"A North American?" Rama asked.

Halzack looked back at the man leaning forward on the table, his body as loose as a baby's. "Yes, I'm Dr. Halzack from the University of the Americas."

"Tell me, doctor. It has been several years, but have the Yankees won another pennant?"

"The baseball Yankees?"

"The New York Yankees."

"I'm sorry, I don't. . .I really don't know."

Dr. Andre Cherenkov, a short broad-shouldered Russian, barged into the room. He was followed by a young baby-faced guard with a bandaged finger.

"Oh, I see everybody has met."

"Doctor, did you clear this contact with us?" Elan asked.

"What? Their meeting?" Cherenkov asked impatiently. "It just happened, and I am not rescheduling."

"Fine. You tell it to Dr. DeWitt." Elan turned and walked out of the door.

"Charming," Cherenkov said.

There was a moment's silence. "So doctor," Rama asked, engaging him with a smile, "what kind of needle-pusher are you?"

"Actually, I'm a physical anthropologist who's kind of. . . branched off."

"And what kind of branch did you climb out on?"

Halzack looked to Cherenkov for help; he had not anticipated such a sharp exchange with the prisoner, but the Russian was sitting back on his heels enjoying it. "Yes, well curiously enough, I've been investigating children, autistic savants, prodigies, and others with extraordinary abilities."

Cherenkov gave his patient a probing look. "You see a similarity in our conditions?" Rama asked.

"Some of them experience sensory distortion, if not as extreme as yours. Your brain scans, which I've just studied, show some similarities, and I'm wondering if you have physiological markers in common."

"What kind of markers are you looking for?" Cherenkov asked.

"I've detected several abnormal hormones in these children, but have been unable to identify the genes."

"Well, we have identified some 'unusual' hormones in Rama's case."

"Yes, that was the advance word, one of the 'abnormalities' that brought me here."

"If they matched, that would be interesting," Cherenkov said, thinking aloud.

"I have their DNA sequences for comparison."

Rama slid off the examination table. "Let me let the two of you. . .compare notes." He slipped his gown top over his head, stepped up and took Halzack's hand, staring him straight in the eyes. "I hope your visit proves. . .fruitful."

He was escorted out of the room by the guard. Halzack leaned back against the wall for support. "Feel like I've been hit by a. . ."

"Hundred pound feather," Cherenkov said, and Halzack nodded his head in agreement.

Cherenkov took his colleague by the arm and led him down the hallway to the computer room. It was small and nondescript with a half-dozen terminals. The walls were covered with geometric drawings of DNA molecules, arranged for comparison. Halzack stepped up to the back wall for a closer look. He was fascinated by a molecule with an elegant design.

"That is a pineal gland hormone," Cherenkov said.

"But isn't the pineal gland inactive in adults?"

"Apparently his condition reactivates it."

Halzack went over to Cherenkov at the computer terminal and sat next to the man. He laid down his briefcase, opened it and withdrew a file folder. "All I have is a printed runoff of their DNA base sequences."

"Fine," Cherenkov said. "Hand them to me page by page." He turned and spoke into the microphone, "Scanning mode." Taking the first breakdown, he flashed the sheets in front of the monitor screen. The response was instantaneous. "Pretty close, I would say."

A comparison between the two molecules appeared on the screen. "The amino acid sequences are nearly the same, indicating a similar function. The hormones differ greatly only where the DNA base sequences were pieced together from existing genes."

"That's remarkable."

Cherenkov looked up at his colleague. "It is more than remarkable." He stared at him for a long moment before turning back to the console. "I am copying our breakdowns on disk, and would like a copy of yours as well."

"Sure. Can somebody flashcopy my printout? I'm leaving shortly."

Cherenkov stood up from the computer and stretched his arms. "Maria can copy them." The Russian now spoke slowly, drawing attention to his words. "While we are waiting, would you like to get some fresh air?"

Halzack looked at him inquisitively. "Fresh air?"

"There is a fenced-in walkway on the roof for us nature buffs. It is brisk, about ten degrees today, but the view is spectacular."

Halzack heard the man's intonation and read his expression. "I've always wanted to climb one of these mountains. Sounds like a safe alternative."

"Wonderful," Cherenkov said, as they walked out the door. "We have environ coats and glasses, all sizes."

When they stepped out onto the roof, the two men were hit by a gust of cold wind. Halzack had to grab hold of the railing to keep from being blown back into the building. His glove stuck to the cold metal. Cherenkov closed the door behind them and led his colleague from the shadows of the overhang down the walkway into the bright sunlight. At the end was an outlook with wooden benches. From here you could see a panoramic view of the mountains from all sides. The sight was breathtaking.

"Magnificent. Absolutely magnificent," Halzack uttered in amazement.

"Nature at its most sublime," Cherenkov said, the depth of his feeling measured by the length of his sigh, its condensation clearly seen in the frigid air. "Gives one an appreciation for the mess we have made of it."

Halzack nodded his head. He studied the scientist for a moment. "I assume you asked me up here to share more than the view."

"Yes, doctor. It is more private," Cherenkov said, and looking back over his shoulder at the tower, "but not totally."

"I understand."

"Dr. Halzack, how do you account for the similarity of these two hormones?"

"We could never locate an individual gene, so I assumed the sequence was, as you said, pieced together from existing material."

"Doctor, you have studied genetics?" Halzack nodded. "What could do that? Cause such a rearrangement."

Dr. Halzack thought for a moment. "The collapse of an econiche: what happened in Africa when jungles gave way to grasslands, requiring an extreme adaptation for the animal life; building new functions—teeth for munching grains instead of fruit—from the existing genetic material. Or, when a virus, with only a few genes, is attacked by a new drug. It excises, rearranges, or combines the genes that make it susceptible, creating immunity."

"Well, we have discovered another force: consciousness," Cherenkov said, pleased with his colleague's unflinching and apparently open-minded reaction. "We have known for some time that the mind or mental states affect the body. What we are discovering here, in our research on Rama, is how consciousness can alter our genetic structure."

"That would explain the genetics of my discovery."

"Yes, and why you have gained such easy access here," Cherenkov said pointedly.

"I wondered about that," Dr. Halzack said, concern creeping into his voice.

"The hormone comparison suggests you have Ramas in the making."

"And look what they've done with him," Halzack said in dismay.

"The man is treated well, but they will never let him go, and as for your children. . ." Cherenkov said, his voice trailing off.

"Guess I've been naive."

"They do not give school children mandatory psi tests for statistical analysis."

Halzack studied the man for a long moment. "And your own research?"

Dr. Cherenkov took a badly tarnished silver lighter out of his coat pocket and handed it to his colleague. It had a submarine emblem: *USSR Surgut.* "We Russians have learned the futility of some allegiances." Halzack returned the lighter, and Cherenkov lit it. "You see doctor, it still works."

Dr. Halzack had flown to London to attend a conference on exceptional children, and now viewed with growing interest the video presentation by his colleague, Dr. Dana Cosgrove. It showed a half-naked, dark-skinned native boy of seven. He was walking across a grassy clearing between rows of thatch-roofed huts nestled between towering trees—whose foliage apparently blocked out the sun's UV rays. His jerky movements, twitching head, and long-legged unsteady gait caused clinical psychologists in the audience to nod their heads in recognition. And then the boy turned and stared at the camera.

A flash of light suddenly washed out the picture for ten seconds. When the video returned, the boy was standing in the doorway of a hut smiling back mischievously.

Dr. Cosgrove, a behavioral psychologist from the University of Chicago, her dark hair tied back, wearing metal-framed glasses for eyes with correctable defects, stood at the podium speaking into the microphone. "Baba can flash at a distance as well. I tried taking a photograph of his village from a nearby mountain only to have my film wash out."

The video cut to the interior of a small hut. Baba was sitting at a table studying a chart with fifty images. The shot pulled back to reveal a random electronic imager on the table. Dr. Cosgrove was operating it. Baba pointed to the image of a snow-capped mountain. Cosgrove hit the trigger button and the imager shuffled through its selections finally displaying the snowy mountain. Baba next pointed to the snake and the tiger. Cosgrove hit the start button twice, and these two randomly selected images appeared one after the other. The boy turned and talked to somebody at the back of the hut. A woman, no doubt the boy's mother, stepped over and smiled at the camera. She handed him a pencil and paper. Baba quickly wrote down a ten-number list of images. Cosgrove set the imager for ten, and the pictures, starting with a star, flashed on the screen. He was perfect, ten for ten. The boy looked up and stared intently at the camera. The next shot appeared to be a still photograph, hazy and opaque, of the camera crew shooting the previous scene.

"A rather remarkable psychic photograph, wouldn't you say?" The last film clip was a line drawing of Dr. Cosgrove. "His mother said that he drew this picture of me about a year ago. Interestingly enough, that's about the time I first heard of him."

The lights in the auditorium now came up. Above the viewing screen was a banner: OXFORD UNIVERSITY'S INTERNATIONAL SYMPOSIUM ON EXCEPTIONAL CHILDREN. The room was half-filled, and the audience appeared restless after the long presentation.

"Wish I could provide a more exotic demonstration, but this test of the boy's precognitive ability, as you saw, was off the scale, as were his scores on clairvoyance. His mother told me stories of him predicting accidents, hurricanes, even the last solar eclipse seen in that part of the world. But these are not his only paranormal abilities. He has a whole range of them; some yet to be classified. He successfully read personal items I brought with me, telling me the people's histories. He can move small objects with his mind; I had a rather entertaining video that was. . .lost. One night he came to me in a dream state and we astral-projected back to Chicago. I saw my grandmother, and was able to describe what she was wearing to bed that night."

Dr. Cosgrove took a drink of water and resumed her talk. "You can read a full account of my journey to the Australian Islands in next month's *Exceptional Children's Journal*. But I want to leave you with a story that has some rather disturbing implications, with the hope that some of my colleagues here tonight might be able to shed some light on this incident. Baba's mother, Roya, said that last year before the rainy season she was preparing to re-thatch her hut. She collected all the materials and tools, but one morning she woke up to find the job nearly completed. She had not worked on the roof herself, nor had the others in the village. Finally, since Baba seemed amused by the whole situation, she asked him what he knew of it. He told her that while working on the roof she had fallen and broken her neck, and so he had to 'change' it."

There was an eerie silence in the hall. "The territorial doctor examined her and reported that she had torn muscle ligaments characteristic of a broken neck but no bone damage." Dr. Cosgrove peered out at her audience, but there was no response. She could almost feel her colleagues shuddering, yet she was compelled to continue. "If we're to take Baba at his word, his mother fell but he was able to create a new time-line that included old elements, the thatched roof and her torn muscles, but one with no broken neck." Finally, a hand went up in the audience. "Ah, yes, Dr. Murdock," Cosgrove said.

"Well, I know a few surgeons who could benefit from new 'time-lines,' which I will no doubt need after my next grant review."

Laughter broke the tension in the audience. "And on that note," Cosgrove said with relief, "I conclude my talk." Most of the audience jumped up from their seats and headed toward the back doors. Cosgrove closed her video prompter case and headed across the stage for the stairs.

At the back of the auditorium, Dr. Halzack had remained in his seat. He had watched the film clip on Baba with great interest. It was the most spectacular demonstration of paranormal abilities in one person he had ever witnessed. There were psychics as accurate in each area, but none had as many diverse talents as this child. And yet, this demonstration was still within the upper range of human capability. It was Dr. Cosgrove's last story that captivated him. In the last fifty years, science had shown that interior states of being could exteriorize themselves in real-world events. Or, you attracted to yourself situations that mirrored your inner psychological complexes. But the ability to alter the fabric of time and space, to rearrange the physical world at will, as if it were made of malleable dream material, was an ability Halzack would expect from the members of this new species. He was still identifying these children, had tested only a few of them, and had not yet developed a behavioral model. But, he thought, laughing to himself, this was one talent he might not recall.

"Ah, Dr. Halzack," Cosgrove said, walking up the aisle, "avoiding the stampede I see." Her tone was ironic, but she seemed to expect no less from him.

"No, just letting your talk settle in."

"That's rather encouraging," Cosgrove said. Halzack stood, and the two of them walked out. There was a reception being held for Dr. Cosgrove in the outer hall, but only a few members of her audience had stayed behind. A waiter stepped over and offered glasses of sparkling apple cider.

"I do miss the real stuff, but if it'll help feed the starving masses, I'll do my part," Halzack said with mixed emotions.

"I rather like the cider, myself." After Cosgrove had taken a few sips, she asked, "So, what do you think of my find?"

"Quite a little comedian."

Dr. Cosgrove laughed. "The others miss that. They just see power, the ability to command matter."

"Diehard Neanderthals, one and all."

"Ah yes, a tiresome lot, aren't we," Cosgrove said, her eyes smiling. "I'm looking forward to your talk."

"It's been. . .I've cancelled it."

Cosgrove studied her colleague for a moment. "You've discovered something new?"

"No, I'm just. . .not going public, for now."

She unconsciously shook her head. "Your trip to Bernia?" He did not reply. "The man's all he's made out to be?"

"I got some very interesting readings," Halzack finally conceded.

Dr. Cosgrove smiled. She reached into her coat pocket and pulled out a sheet of paper. "It seems, my friend, that our research is overlapping." She handed the picture to Halzack. It was a line drawing of him. "Baba drew this right before I left."

"I've seen the boy before. In my dreams."

"You realize. . ."

"He can plant dreams? I assumed as much," Halzack said, "but if he can reach us, can he also reach the others 'of his kind'?"

Dr. Cosgrove stared at Halzack for a moment. He had confided in her, but she was still not certain where his peculiar research would lead. She knew it would undermine her credibility in some circles, but events seemed to be pulling them together. The prospect of uncovering other remarkable children like Baba was too much of a temptation for her to turn down the implied offer.

"Now wouldn't that save time," Dana Cosgrove said, nodding her head in agreement. "Look, I was planning a return visit in six months, but I could do it in three."

Dr. Halzack stared at her for a long moment. "Are you sure?"

"You bring the mosquito net," she replied, blushing slightly.

"I hear they're as big as bats down there," Halzack said eagerly, looking forward to another outdoor expedition. His expression grew more serious. "But, if we're going to work together, you need to know everything, and some of it isn't pretty."

"Why you cancelled out?"

"Yes. To start with, but there's more."

"Then let's have dinner, and discuss it," she said, her voice flat, her manner businesslike, but her eyes—they held out other possibilities

.

They met at "George's," a fashionable West End restaurant. Dana Cosgrove looked stunning walking across the dining room to the stairs as Halzack watched her from the second floor. He had dined here on previous visits to London and knew to arrive early to stake a claim on one of the popular upstairs booths. Dana was wearing a long black and gold skirt of an African design and a white blouse embroidered with a Lion's head. The waiter showed her to the booth.

"Dana, you look lovely," Halzack said as she took a seat across from him. Dana smiled and gave the waiter a drink order.

"A refill, sir?" the waiter asked.

Halzack looked down at his empty beer mug and then up at Dana. He would need more liquid sustenance to withstand this woman's charms. "Yes, why not." The waiter picked up the mug and left.

"Have I kept you waiting?"

"Came early to grab a seat up here. It's more private."

"They don't take reservations?"

"Not with this city's underground."

"Tell me," Dana said. "And I thought New York's subways were bad."

They had both been nervously leaning over the table, and they now sat back in their seats feeling more comfortable.

"I want to tell you what happened at. . .," Halzack said.

"Henry, why don't you start from the beginning. You've never told me how you discovered them."

Halzack wondered if this were meant as a recrimination. "Well, Dana, you're one of the few people I've shared any of my findings with." She reached over and touched his hand, nodding her head in acknowledgement. The waiter served their drinks, and Halzack took a sip of his warm beer. "A friend of mine, Dr. Leslie Gardner, an endocrinologist, was treating two children in a small borough about fifty miles outside Toronto. One was an autistic savant in a Government Home, and the other a musical prodigy from a prominent local family. Both were having severe headaches that common treatments had failed to alleviate. She was brought in to investigate evidence of a glandular imbalance. Leslie discovered an unusual hormone in their blood, that she traced to similarly mutated pineal glands. She knew of my work in population genetics and asked the statistical odds for such a rare mutation in a small population base. Of course they were astronomical."

"The hormones were exactly the same?"

"Very close. But, so far, we've been unable to discover the precursor genes." Dana was puzzled by this revelation. He added, "There's a theory, but that's ahead of my story." She nodded her head, and he continued. "I wondered if there were other similarities, and was given permission to conduct a thorough examination of both children. I discovered twelve similar mutations in body organs and skeletal structures. As far as I was concerned, there was only one conclusion that could be drawn: the children were members of an offshoot species of Homo sapiens."

Dr. Cosgrove blinked her eyes in amazement. "You've intimated as much, but that's the first time I've heard you actually say it."

"Astonishing, isn't it," Halzack added. "I hope you can understand why I didn't share my findings or my conclusions."

"I do have a problem with that, Henry. I know what it would mean for these children—they'd become regular lab rats—but if you're correct, think of its consequences for us as a species."

"I did, and I felt I had a greater responsibility to them as a species, and that the two might be mutually exclusive. On my trip to Bernia, that fact was made even more evident."

Dana waited for a further explanation and then conceded good-naturedly, "But that's ahead of your. . ."

". . .my story," Halzack said, taken aback by her openness. "I figured that the genetic mutations were only the tip of the proverbial iceberg, and that they must result in different aptitudes, abilities, and behaviors. I quietly began to investigate exceptional children, and in the Canadian province alone, I found ten more with the same genetic mutations."

"And worldwide?"

"I've only just begun looking abroad, but so far I've discovered another ten."

"And there could be hundreds of thousands?"

"More like thousands if the per capita ratio is the same."

"And you factored in for the overlooked ones?"

"Yes, and that they all appear to be younger than nine years old," Halzack added.

Dana sat back and studied her ingenious colleague. He was as daring as he was rugged and handsome. "And your plan?"

"So far I've just been seeking them out and collecting data, figuring that eventually a pattern would become evident."

"A pattern?"

"Call it instinct, or whatever, but new species seem

to have strategies for survival, usually against great odds."

"The parent species?"

"Yes. Despite their kinship, they've been known to kill off the new upstarts."

"Why you're anxious to visit Baba?"

"He seems to be the most advanced. Maybe he can tell us how to protect them."

"The rest of your story?" Dana asked, and her colleague nodded his head.

The waiter stepped up to the table to take their order. Dana allowed Henry to order for them, and while he was giving the waiter the order, she watched him and decided that despite her boyfriend and Henry's wife, this professional night on the town would not end with polite after-dinner chatter.

Chapter Five

Zita looked up from her vid screen and stared out the window into the fog-covered night. Illuminated by beacon lights running up the side of the building, the fog swirling in the gusty winds suddenly broke, revealing city lights that shone like twinkling stars. It was ironic that, with the night sky and its starscape blocked out by the perpetual cloud cover, humankind's more puny designs would reign supreme. It might swell our pride, she thought, but it would never feed our souls. The opening in the fog bank closed like the pupil of an eye, imploding from all sides. Zita reluctantly lowered her eyes to study the captive image of Rama frozen in the video court transcript. His black hair was longer, tied in a ponytail, his beard cut closer to his face, his brown eyes clear. He was a remarkably handsome man. All his female devotees were in love with him, or so claimed one of them in a recent interview. But, unlike others in the "Swami" business, his celibacy was never questioned. There was in this face a strange resolve that was not hardened determination, or defeated pessimism, but an unvanquished surrender to life or fate, as another "holy man" characterized it. No doubt this accounted for his unwillingness to defend himself at his trial. It must have been obvious to all that these were trumped-up charges. Any decent lawyer, if he could not gain acquittal—unlikely given the forces aligned against Rama—could have at least laid the legal groundwork for a quicker appeal. But this man, who had fought and won other battles, refused to fight for his life. This Zita could not understand.

She released the freeze-frame, and the image on the

vid screen came alive. Rama's eyes were open, and from this angle, it appeared he was watching the court proceedings. But, when the camera panned around and came in closer, his eyes revealed a consciousness that was only partially present. Some vital part of the man had clearly withdrawn. His meditative state was unnerving the judge and the jury. Matabu, an African Supreme Court Justice who had been asked by the Europeans to try this case, kept watching the defendant whose remote presence apparently distracted him. Others in the court were equally affected, giving rise to speculation from the press that Rama was psychically manipulating the court officials. Finally, in exasperation, the judge had interrupted the proceedings to question the man. Zita scanned through the video transcript to that point.

"Sir," Judge Matabu said, starring at Rama. The prosecutor, who had been cross-examining a witness, stopped in mid-sentence. Everybody in the courtroom turned to the holy man.

A close camera shot of his face showed the life in his eyes coming back, as if adjusted by a rheostat. "Are you addressing me, your honor?" Rama asked.

"Sir, are you on trial in this court?"

"I am."

"Are the charges brought against you not serious?"

"They are."

"Then why, may I ask, are you not following these proceedings?"

"I have chosen not to defend myself."

"That is your right, but do you question the right of the state to try you on these charges?" Judge Matabu asked.

"I acknowledge the state's need to maintain social order."

"Then why do you disrupt these proceedings?"

"Meditating is disruptive?" Rama asked incredulously.

"I find it so."

"And the jury?" Everybody looked at the members of the jury. Half of them nodded their heads in answer to the defendant's question. "Well, I would not want to scare the seven old ladies of the jury," Rama said, referring to the world council.

"Sir, I can assure you that this verdict will be based solely on the evidence and arguments presented in my court, or I will throw it out. That you have my word on."

"Then let us proceed," Rama said. He had followed the trial after this exchange, but he had appeared more bemused than attentive. Later, after he was found guilty, he had accepted his life sentence with the same equanimity. Was it a martyr complex, Zita wondered, or did Rama feel his influence would grow, as Gandhi's had, during his unjust imprisonment? She freeze-framed the image and zoomed in on his face, enhancing the man's dark eyes until they filled the screen. Zita stared into those eyes for the longest time but there were no answers to her questions in their bottomless depths.

She downloaded the video transcript into the central archive and turned off her computer. There were other files to review; a compilation of news articles tracing the man's career particularly interested her. However, reviewing the trial tape had triggered an unexpected emotional reaction. She would need to process her feelings and isolate this nagging voice before continuing with her review. Zita stood up and stretched her arms doing a complete head roll. She had been sitting at the computer console for only a few hours and should not be this tight. Muscle tension, said her yoga teacher, always pointed to an emotional conflict, and the stressed area was often symbolic. Zita had a stiff neck and wondered what that suggested. She went into the bedroom and changed into her workout tights, picked up her gym bag, and headed out the door.

The nearest facility was on floor 225. It was after ten o'clock on a Sunday night, but it was busy. The gyms were open twenty-four hours a day. Indoor living had blurred the line between day and night, resulting in a culture running on its own artificial time. Although studies showed that biological rhythms still followed circadian cycles, those people working nights shifts had adjusted well. In the locker room, Zita slipped on her sweat bands, stored her bag, and walked out to the Flex Machines. She started by doing upper-body twists but had soon progressed to a full-body workout. In ten minutes she was in her rhythm and began to feel her way through the block. The image that immediately surfaced was Rama passively sitting in court refusing to defend himself. Although he was making a statement, or so it seemed, with his disregard for the judicial process, she did not feel he had an emotional investment in this stance. He was neither arrogant nor supercilious in manner, and appeared only calmly bemused by his plight.

In his place Zita would have fought the prosecution to the end and then made an impassioned declaration of belief for all to remember. Surrender—to life, fate or God—was not something she would do easily. This was no doubt the source of her unconscious irritation. And, if the same fate, lifelong confinement in total isolation, had awaited her, the guards would have had to drag her out of the court kicking and screaming. Of course, she had to admit that, given his spiritual orientation, the prospect of imprisonment was more palatable to him. Apparently it offered more possibilities, considering Rama's supposed illumination in prison, than she would have ever imagined. It must be this aspect of his story, she thought, that aggravated her. He represented a mode of being whose values were totally alien to her own. It was ironic that she should be the one called on to discredit this man. Julia would say Rama's consciousness and its inherent point of view was compensatory to her own narrow conscious focus. If the road to wholeness involved absorbing your opposite, or at least acknowledging it, she would be hard-pressed to square this circle.

Zita concluded her workout with a rush of intensity. The manager had asked her halfway through to slow down her pace and then kept a watchful eye on her. The gyms were allotted a limited supply of oxygenated air for every twelve-hour period and would have to close down when oxygen levels fell below a certain level. To shower she had to charge the hot water, an equally precious commodity, to her resident credit card. In her apartment, Zita sat back down at her desk without changing clothes. It was late, and although she had an early morning appointment, she wanted to work on her article, if only briefly, to reaffirm her commitment.

They met for breakfast at an uptown restaurant. Zita had waited for nearly half an hour before she saw Allen drag himself off the elevator and peer around the room with those huge watery eyes. She raised her hand, and he picked his way through the outer row of tables over to her booth. Harry Allen, *World News*' senior political writer for thirty years, was a tall thin man with an enormous head, sarcastically called Scarecrow by both those whose political careers were cut short by one of his famous exposés and those who feared the same treatment. Although he was older than the age for mandatory retirement, management did not dare to force the issue, afraid of the electronic skeletons bleeping away in his coded files. They could only hope—those who wished to replace him and those who wished to escape their comeuppance in a future column—that one of his legendary ailments would soon dispatch him to his own information graveyard.

"Lucky you're a looker. Only thing that'd get me up this early," Harry said, sitting down and leering at her.

Zita did not flinch; she had come prepared. "But you'd walk a mile for a camel?" she said, relying on reports that he was a secret smoker.

Harry was taken aback by her rejoinder. His eyes narrowed to thin slits of dark inquiry. It was rare for him to be on the exposed end of a confidential report. Although he did not like the feeling, he could certainly appreciate the woman's methods.

"The slogan's a little before your time. Isn't it?"

"Read about it in an advertising course, used it for a psych paper on addictions."

"Yeah," Harry snorted, as if that explained it. "Bernie

said you wanted background on Rama, but what little I know is hardly of any consequence."

"I've read the record; I know the facts. What I want is subtext. What was everybody feeling? Were they afraid of him? Did they really believe he was part of the plot?"

The waiter stepped over. They both declined breakfast, but Harry let the man pour him a cup of coffee. "If it's made with beans," Harry said, and the waiter assured him that he had ground them himself.

He hurriedly drank his first cup and waved the waiter over for a refill. Feeling sufficiently fortified, he turned back to the young reporter. "You know I interviewed him years ago, at his ashram in Bombay. He was on a hunger strike, demanding more shelters for the exposed masses, or something like that. I liked him. He was real. Didn't put on any airs. Used what he had to effect political change. Totally fearless. Would stare down a tank or a verbal attack with the same equanimity. He was young then, barely twenty-five, but he had the country in an uproar. And he got what he wanted, and more. Knew he was going to be a problem for a lot of people. And, later, when he took his environmental crusade across national boundaries, I could see it coming."

"So you believe the charges against him were fabricated?"

"You have to remember the times. It was chaos. A worldwide economic collapse. You could still walk the streets, but it wasn't safe with all the falling bodies. You know what a human being looks like after jumping off a three-hundred story building?" Zita winced. "Well, you can imagine how people felt about those responsible. The psychics got off easy. They were safe in prison, safer still when they were moved to Bernia. There they didn't have to put up with the negative vibes, as they say. But the Greens got clobbered. A regular witch hunt. Run over in parking lots, dragged out of their homes and beaten to death. Of course this was before the ozone layer was totally dissipated, and the politicians were still denying the disaster claims of the environmentalists. So here was Rama, the world's most revered

Green, defying everybody's political solution to the mess: unification into competitive super states. He didn't have a chance; the trial was a joke. In that climate, nobody objected. His followers had long since disappeared into the woodwork."

"It was strictly political?"

"That's what they want you to believe," Harry said, watching her closely.

"Okay, if not that, then what?"

"They say you're pretty smart; you tell me."

Zita thought for a moment. "Well, if the psychics' reach really caught them off guard, and they didn't know what they were dealing with, they might've figured that Rama, given his legendary healing powers, was as powerful a psychic."

Harry nodded his head in agreement. "His presence always had the most remarkable effect on people. It wasn't hard to believe that, in regard to Rama, anything was possible."

"As it proved to be,"

"Or so they say."

"You think they're exaggerating his condition to keep him locked up?"

"It's not his transformation I doubt, but their assessment. It's like having chimpanzees cross-examine Einstein to determine if he's a threat to their food chain." Harry shook his head in frustration. "They're telling themselves he's different from them, but they still expect him to act as they would if they had his power. That is, control everything."

"They're afraid he'll lead another crusade, aren't they?" Zita asked, curious about the man's passion for the subject.

"No, that's not what's bothering them. They've discovered something, a potential of sorts, that's unnerved them. I'm sure of it." Zita looked at him inquisitively. "Don't ask me what. But, with your connections, you could probably find out yourself."

Zita did not respond. No doubt Bernie had shared some of his suspicions about her "sources" with his longtime friend. "Well, thanks, Harry. You've been a big help." She paused for a moment, while he took another sip of coffee. "I take it you wouldn't mind seeing him released from prison."

"Yeah, well he got a bum deal back when, but then there are those 'other' considerations," Harry said. He stood up and waved for the waiter. "You staying or going?"

"Think I'll do my notes here; and Harry, the coffee's on me."

He nodded his head, began to walk away, then stepped back. "Want some advice?"

Zita looked up. "Didn't know you cared."

Harry laughed. "Do yourself a favor and clock off this story while you can." He turned and hurried off before she could ask for an explanation.

Zita found his recommendation rather curious. She suspected that, if it did not originate with Bernie, he at least knew about it. That conclusion made it more ominous. The newspaper had an exclusive interview with one of the century's most controversial figures at an historic moment, and Bernie would jeopardize this story to protect her? It was apparent that Rama's release was the subject of an intense international debate, and some of the parties, including her country, were not willing merely to leave the decision to the European Supreme Court. Were the stakes so high that even minor players like her were at risk? It appeared that one of them suspected as much, and Bernie, who had always treated Zita like a daughter, had decided to frighten her off. It was touching, but she would have preferred a briefing to vague innuendos.

Zita's first interview with Rama was scheduled for the following week in Switzerland, but she would be flying out early to interview the world-renowned parapsychologist Cary Jamison in London. He had testified as an expert on psychism at Rama's trial, and she was hoping he would not only clarify his trial testimony but clear up some of the conflicting claims in the field of psychic warfare. Her research had proven more difficult than she had anticipated. It appeared that the government had expunged much of the early research on the subject. Books, magazine articles, and videos had been systematically removed from libraries after the psychic debacle. However, since the use of mental energies for healing and self-development had become so pervasive in the early twenty-first century, and the scientific model was very similar, it was difficult to totally erase the literature on the subject. Zita acquired books from European and Asian sources where the suppression was not as complete. And, unlike book burners of the past, DI kept theirs and added to them. It was her own department's cache of material on the subject that was to be her prime source, despite some curious deletions.

Bernie had insisted that Zita include a factual historical review of the events that led to Rama's trial and subsequent incarceration in her series on him. He now asked for a summary of her research before she left for Europe. Zita assumed Bernie was worried about the exotica she may have uncovered on this sensitive subject. They met in his office late that afternoon, as the brown haze of the smoggy overcast day bled through the partially screened windows, casting a pall over an already bleak presentation.

"In the West, where paranormal phenomenon and its research were never given much credibility," Zita continued, "the scientific establishment was taken by surprise back in the late twentieth century when visiting scientists to the then Soviet Union reported on research, at the highest levels, on some rather exotic paranormal experimentation. The research included hypnotism at a distance by telepathy, psychotronic devices (thought machines) that could maim and kill small animals, apport techniques that dematerialized distance objects and transported them back, and the more fanciful claims of a nuclear howitzer that could transmit a nuclear explosion through hyperspace to any designated location. The fact that rivals, who had already beaten them on early space exploration, gave this area serious consideration put them on the alert and sent a shudder through the unprepared military establishment."

"But it was all propaganda, wasn't it?"

"A lot of it, although some experiments, like hypnotism at a distance, had been proven. But, at the time, the reports were taken seriously here. The result was rampant paranoia: Russian psychotronic weapons were blamed for everything from the loss of the nuclear submarine *Thresher* to Legionnaire's disease. A high-level survey of the time claimed that Soviet psychics could telepathically read secret documents at a distance and even mentally influence political and military leaders. Although this alarm did not lead to massive funding, it opened the door to the first serious consideration of the field's possibilities in this country."

"We're good for that," Bernie added. "Take the Nazis' efforts to build an atomic bomb. They were way off, but it scared us into a stepped-up program that actually worked."

"Yes, but here we weren't nearly as successful," Zita replied.

"I wouldn't call it success."

Zita nodded her head in agreement. "Now the more credible experiments were conducted at the university level, and among those Project Scanate had the best results. Puthoff and Targ, at Stanford Research Institute, challenged the CIA, pitting their psychic remote viewers against satellite photography of secret installations here and behind the Iron Curtain. Merely given map coordinates, the psychics were able to identify and describe the locations with amazing accuracy. One viewer even stuck his 'head' into a locked cabinet at a military installation and correctly read the labels of a half-dozen top-secret files. Others were able to locate U.S. and Soviet submarines after seeing unlabeled photographs of the targets. Another project for the Navy on the detection of electromagnetic signatures of submerged submarines also had good results.

"However, the military's chief concern was the reliability of their nuclear weapons network. If psychics could alter the flow of current through the electronic switches in computer circuits, which had already been proven at that time, they might be able to 'push' the detonation switch on a nuclear warhead from across the country, or cause incoming missiles to misfire completely.

"This led to the investigation of low-energy psychokinesis in which psychics tried to influence a shielded magnetometer at a distance or to bend laser beams. When scientists showed consistently positive results, this research became heavily funded and went underground."

"Isn't it ironic," Bernia added, "that they use to call secret agents spooks? And that was before the intelligence community took over this whole area. A match made in hell."

"Well, historically, as well as cinematically, the most famous 'spook' was 007. John Dee, Queen Elizabeth's astrologer back in the sixteenth century, was the head of British espionage and signed himself 007. The zeros represented two eyes, and the seven, the sum of two eyes, plus the other four senses, and the mystical 6th sense."

"If you're trying to legitimize their pursuit, I'm not buying."

Zita laughed. "You're the one who wanted the historical approach." Bernie nodded his head and made a gesture for his reporter to continue. Zita looked down at her notes. "Okay, if psychics could affect matter, could they also influence minds, as some Soviet research had suggested? Professor Leonid Vasiliev of the University of Leningrad, had published an early study, 'Experiments in Distant Influence,' that suggested as much. He claimed that ESP effects were carried by electromagnetic waves like television pictures and could influence people at a distance. However, his research seemed to suggest that it was the low-level radiation that caused effects of mental disorientation and appetite loss. The Soviet military at this time began to direct weak microwave radiation at the United States Embassy in Moscow. Some claimed that the radiation was PT-modulated to carry patterns for pneumonia and heart disease. There was a high incident of illness at the embassy over the next few years, which was investigated, revealing the microwave transmissions. Protests, however, did not alter the bombardment. But, by now, word of the Soviet's paranormal research had reached the West.

"The Navy's experiments in extremely low frequency (ELF) radiation for submarine communication seemed to mirror this research and opened up some rather deadly possibilities for manipulating minds at a distance. The scientists found that electromagnetic waves, in certain frequencies, could affect the mind from a distance, slipping past a person's senses and producing a range of effects from drowsiness to hallucination. But since the ELF waves are transmitted at such low power levels, they surmised that the brain might take them for its own wave activity. In that case, it would react to changes, like interruption of a signal, as if the changes were its own."

"Yeah, I remember reading about it in school. It was the only thing in the field that sounded credible to me."

"It was the basis, along with some soviet research, for the advances in subliminal technology."

"If we had only known," Bernie said ruefully.

"Well, with the end of what was called 'The Cold War,' back in the 1990s, it became apparent that much of the Soviet claims in this area had been greatly exaggerated. It appeared, for example, that early successes with psychotronic weapons did not develop the full lethal power they had hoped. They were able to induce hallucinations, create paranoia, and generally confuse subjects at close range by neuron disruption, which became an effective tool for interrogation, but were never able to maim or kill at a distance."

"Yeah, but later?"

"Unfortunately, others were able to improve upon their research and develop a deadly array of psychotronic devices. But, at the time, the next advance, if we can call it that, was the Soviet's research on the modification of electromagnetic waves, or carrying thought-programming on radio and television signals. Scientists in this area were lured to the West, and with our combined expertise, they developed the first true subliminal technologies. By the turn of the century, governments began using it to benumb and pacify the masses with 'positive thoughts.'"

"I don't want to get into that," Bernie said, waving his hand dismissively.

"Well, without delving into subliminals, how can I present the psychics' background?"

"Yeah, you're right," he conceded. Bernie thought for a moment. "Okay, put it in a historical context. Tell how some pregnant mothers exposed to video-modified subliminals gave birth to psychic children before the governments banned their use."

"Okay, that works."

"Damn right it does," Bernie said. He stood up from his suspension chair and walked over to the window, peering out into the brown haze. He added, with his back turned, "You might mention that by contrast Rama developed his powers by spiritual discipline, which supposedly is self-limiting."

Zita arched an eyebrow. "Isn't that a little slanted?"

Bernie turned around and gave his reporter a sharp look. "Oh, you were going to be completely objective?"

Zita glanced down at her notes. She understood the implied criticism. "Let's see how the interview develops."

"Okay, I'll buy that," he said in a more conciliatory tone.

Zita gathered her notes and stood up. "Well, it's getting late, and I've got some packing to do."

Bernie walked his reporter out the door. "You're leaving first thing in the morning?" Zita nodded her head. "Well, be careful." He squeezed her arm. "This one's a hot potato."

Zita could not resist. "Then I won't accept potatoes from strangers," Zita said in a self-mocking, smart-alecky retort.

Bernie laughed. "Can I help it—once a father always a father," he said, wagging his head and stepping back in his office.

Chapter Six

The hypersonic spaceplane glided across the north Atlantic, gradually losing altitude and speed from a low earth orbit of one hundred miles and Mach 25. When it dipped down into the upper atmosphere, the nose and upper fuselage of the plane gave off a stream of friction sparks that flowed past the windows and drew some passengers' attention. Zita was oblivious to the light show, intently viewing her research on the notepad's vid screen. The speed of her page scanning belied the fact that there were major gaps no amount of re-reading would fill. Her briefing with Michael that morning in a New York hotel room, after they had spent the night together, had been unproductive. He became increasingly annoyed with her insistent questions about Rama's condition in his transformed state. Michael had decided that her interview should concentrate on the man's past association with the eco terrorists, his sympathy for their cause, and his own militant attitudes. Any admissions here would dispute his current claim of enlightened disinterest. Zita planned a more personal approach, exploring the man's history, his philosophy, and his entrance into the "natural state of being." She felt such questioning would be more reassuring and draw more incriminating admissions. Michael adamantly disagreed and in exasperation finally told his agent that there were security considerations, classified above her clearance, that underlay his objections. This had settled the matter for him, but it had only made Zita angrier.

The landing-warning chimed, and the seat belt automatically tightened around her waist. Zita gazed out the window as the spaceplane slipped beneath the cloud cover and swooped across southern England, whose checkerboard fields of private plots had been replaced, in the last twenty-five years, by uniform rows of massive greenhouses stretching across the landscape. Soon the towering skyscrapers of London appeared from behind the curtain of smog, as the spaceplane slowed down and banked to the right, making its landing approach at the airport south of the city. Zita rode the bullet train for the fifty-mile trip into London. The first half of the ride was above ground and over the green glass-beaded environmental screen, undulating in the afternoon breeze and looking like an algae-skimmed sea, that spread across the outlying area. But, as the train approached the inner hub of the city, the buildings shot upward, the boulevards widened, and the meshed screen was supplanted by slithering glassed-in sidewalks hugging their buildings and overhead tubed walkways between connecting upper floors. Her last view of a distant boulevard, before the train dipped underground, looked like a modern set of monkey bars.

There were two messages waiting on the vidphone in her hotel room. Cary Jamison had called to cancel their luncheon date, switching the meeting to his office at the University of London. The parapsychology department he headed drew the best students in the field for their doctorate studies; it also attracted undercover agents from the world's security forces to monitor its lawful restrictions. And Zita was having dinner with a DI agent, Dale Crimson, working on his master's degree at the university. The second message was from Michael asking her to call when she arrived. The request sounded more official than personal. That only made her angrier, and she decided he could wait until after dinner for a reply.

Crimson was already seated in the hotel dinning room. Zita recognized him from his photo, but the man looked even younger in person. No doubt a youthful appearance was a prerequisite for the assignment.

"You must be Dale," Zita said, as she walked over to his table. Crimson stood up and shook her hand.

"Ms. Hiller?"

"Call me Zita, and call me a waiter." She plopped down in a chair. "These weightless flights make me hungry."

"I've already ordered." Crimson put his fingertips to his temples. "You wanted the vegetarian potpie, right?"

"You're not serious!" Zita said, piqued by the man's presumption.

Crimson shook his head and smiled. "Sorry, I was just kidding, but someone did try to pull that on me last week."

"A practitioner?"

"No, she was being cute, but you never know with these loop-heads." Dale raised his hand, and the waiter came over and handed them menus. Zita quickly scanned both pages and ordered a wild-rice dish. After the waiter left, Crimson said, "You know most people would've taken the suggestion and gotten the potpie."

"You have that kind of an effect on people?"

"No. It's a psychological test we run. Invariably, the subject, thinking they're being cute or doing the unexpected, takes the suggestion."

"Just call me dense."

"No, it's called High Suggestive Resistance."

Zita immediately replied, "And Professor Jamison, is he. . .resistant?"

"He's the best. We've thrown double, triple levels of reinforcement at him, and he doesn't blink an eye."

"Which indicates. . ."

"A possible practitioner, but then you'd need a certain natural resistance to maintain your objectivity with these goings-on."

"One who prefers private offices to noisy restaurants for meetings."

"He switched on you?"

Zita noted the concern in his voice. "His office tomorrow afternoon." She watched her colleague's reaction. "That's bad?"

"Well, he's a busy man; it might be a scheduling snafu, but if he is a. . ." Dale thought for a moment. "Look, why take chances? Go ahead and wear a hair net, and a hat pulled tight over your head. Don't bring a purse, gloves—anything you could leave behind." He unfastened an elaborate silver pin on his lapel and passed it to her. "Here, wear this on your blouse."

Zita took it. "To ward off vampires?" she asked, examining the pin.

"The crystal is a minute pulse generator that flashes a light beam, a thousandth of a second, that'll wash out photographic film."

"Which. . ."

"Which, like a strand of hair, contains a person's biological pattern. The voodoo model, if you will."

Zita looked up. "Okay, let's say he's a practitioner, why me? I'm just a reporter writing a story."

"Well, there's no love lost between him and Rama. He might have a stake in whether he's released or not, and influencing you could be his hedge."

"Sounds pretty farfetched to me," Zita said, trying to hand it back. She saw fear in the man's eyes. "Okay, I'll wear it."

"Well, to paraphrase the DI slogan, 'Better dead than bled,'" Dale said with an infectious laugh.

The waiter brought their dinners, and they ate and talked about the London art scene. Crimson entertained her with salacious stories of feuds, double-dealings, riotous egos, and a little murder and intrigue. He was funny, perverse, and totally outrageous at times. Zita enjoyed being with a male her own age and even found herself attracted to Dale, but did not pursue it. In her room there was another message from Michael, and she reluctantly returned the call. They talked and she shared Crimson's concern about her meeting with Jamison. This elicited an intense endorsement of the prescribed counter-measures. Zita had wanted a show of feelings from Michael, but she now wondered if he was protecting his lover or his agent.

Zita was ushered into Professor Jamison's office by a short, rotund young man with bad skin and an extremely odd demeanor. Walking into his office, you entered another world. The walls were covered with African masks, Native American medicine shields, and spears and totems from a dozen primitive cultures. In the center of this menagerie, Cary Jamison sat on an animal-skin throne dressed in a conservative blue suit. He was an older man, in his early 60s, white-haired, with intense grey eyes and the preoccupied manner of someone not entirely present. Without introducing himself, Jamison motioned for the reporter to take a seat on the suspension sofa across from him.

"Ms. Hiller, I read your column. Very smart. But this Rama business, it's a little far afield for you, isn't it?"

"Well, Rama is—or was—the green guru."

"Your angle?"

"I'm not writing an advocacy piece, just a history with an update."

"If Einstein and Bijorsky has taught us anything, it's the fallacy of an objective observer."

"I'll try to keep it two-dimensional," Zita said in retort.

Jamison erupted in a rumbling deep-belly laugh. "Touché, my dear. Touché." He leaned forward, his chin resting on an upturned hand. "And you wanted what from me exactly?"

Zita looked down at her notes. "You testified at Rama's trial about the nature of psychic crimes, especially when there's no physical link between the perpetrator and the crime scene," she said, and glanced up at him.

"Yes, my testimony set new evidentiary standards, based on psychological profile and ability, for the prosecution of such crimes."

"Well, what I need is for you to walk me through your general explanation of psychokinesis, which was a little technical for me. It's important, since it helped convict Rama, and I have to explain it to my readers in layman's terms."

"So what is it you don't understand?"

"Let's start with what I do understand, and that is that mind and matter are made of the same. . .stuff, but. . ."

"They exist in different dimensions: matter in the third dimension, or our normal physical world, what you see around you, and mind in a fourth dimensional space that encompasses it but is physically removed from it."

"And the fourth dimension is a. . .virtual state?" Zita asked tentatively.

"Yes, one of the inner virtual states from which physical reality springs. Pure vacuum is another."

"The source of virtual photons?"

"Yes. Now all matter is charged and has an electric field, that is created by the emission and absorption of these virtual photons."

"And thought forms?"

"Are virtual fourth dimensional objects," Jamison said. "Virtual photons can be modified by thought and can affect the object or organism that absorbs them. So, we have a fourth-dimensional virtual state, giving rise to virtual photons, that are absorbed by physical matter, being modified by thought and affecting matter in turn. That's the modern model for psychokinesis."

"Can you give me an example?"

"Sure. Let's say you want to bend a spoon or burn out an electronic circuit in a computer. You concentrate on the object, focus on the desired change, and your thought energy, if of sufficient amplitude, will modify the virtual photons and carry this modification to the electromagnetic field of the object's atoms. Here it could counter its electric charge, destroying the atom and creating heat that can melt metal spoons or electronic circuits."

"Sounds simple enough."

"Yes, stripped of its physics lingo, but in practice, rather more difficult."

"But not for the boys in Bernia?" Zita paused, seeing a slight reaction. "Or for Rama?"

"No, and despite their differences, they do have something in common."

"Besides being in the same jail."

Jamison did not find her snide remark very amusing, and he continued without smiling. "Nikola Tesla discovered in the early 1900s that normal electromagnetic waves could be broken down into subunits, what he called scalar waves. He theorized, and some say proved in private experiments, that you could transmit scalar waves over a distance, then combine or pair them to create wireless electricity with no appreciable loss of energy. Now these scalar waves are the source of the virtual particle flux or the virtual photons of pure vacuum."

"So it's scalar waves which are the real energy source."

"Yes, since virtual photons create electric charge," Jamison said. "Now what's really interesting is that the interface between both sides of the brain's cerebral cortex creates scalar waves."

Zita's mouth dropped open. "Really?"

"The mad man's imbalance, or tension, and the saint's balance, or symmetry, creates increased scalar activity."

"Which results in higher photon production and its effects," Zita said, and nodding to herself, "intended or not."

"Exactly, my dear."

"It also accounts for the psychosomatic effect."

"And poltergeists, and a dozen others." Jamison added rather smugly, "It's all in my book, The Scalar Equation."

Zita glanced down at her notes. "I'm afraid. . ."

"But there is one effect that was edited out, over my objections." Zita looked up at his indignant scowl. "Maybe you can slip it by them," he said, suddenly smiling fiendishly, "one right up your alley, as they say." His eyes were staring right through her. "Earthquake faults are noted for their light and sound effects, sometimes at a distance. They generate scalar waves, due to the electrical build-up from mechanical stress. And this applies to all stressed earth formations." He let this thought work on her. "And when they link up or couple with other scalar waves, they form EM waves, photons."

It took Zita a moment to grasp his intimation. "Are you saying that thought activity of sufficient magnitude can create earthquakes?" Zita asked incredulously.

"Thoughts are transformed into photons by scalar-wave hook-ups; photons are pure energy, and when they interact with matter, they deposit their quanta of energy, which can only add to the stress in the fault zone."

"During the psychic war of the 2020s, there was intense earthquake activity."

"Case in point."

"That's rather ironic."

"Rather tragic, I'd say." There was real feeling in Jamison's voice. Apparently, he had more than an academic interest in the issue.

"But surely, nobody in their right mind, especially the green guru, would initiate such a chain of events?"

"Maybe not directly, but any use—take an assassination, what the politicals are really afraid of—can be deadly. The stray scalar waves just pass through everything and keep going until they hook up with naturally occurring scalars."

"Would that be more difficult, I mean, how much more. . . 'energy' are we talking about?" Zita asked.

Jamison stared intently at her and then spoke in a soft, modulated tone. "Less than you'd imagine. The entire body is crisscrossed by a web of subtle electrical currents. Virtual thoughts, from the conscious and unconscious mind, carried by photon absorption, continually affect body functions. Disease patterns, or short-circuit commands, of sufficient amplitude, can be absorbed and spread a disruptive influence."

"You mean it could kill?"

"Yes, a powerful enough intent could kill you, but there are countermeasures."

"Thank God," Zita heard herself say.

"God has nothing to do with it, my dear," Jamison said with a sneer, staring at her with haunted, otherworldly eyes.

The atmosphere of the room had suddenly become dark and threatening. The heaviness in the air weighed her down. Zita found it hard to breathe and struggled to rise to her feet. "Thank you for your time. It's been most. . .instructive. I'll credit you in the article if I use your explanation."

"Please don't. Last thing I need is more aspiring psychics knocking on my door."

"As you wish, professor." Zita waited for him to stand up and shake her hand or at least walk her to the door, but the man remained seated. She turned and hurried across the room to the door, opened it and let herself out.

The door to the side room swung open, and two of the professor's students walked into his office. Mick Gordon, a man in his early thirties, tall, thin and rather nervous, stepped over and held a photographic plate up to Jamison's face. He closed his eyes and psychically imprinted an image of Ms. Hiller onto the plate. The professor opened his eyes and nodded his head. Gordon slipped the plate into a foil-lined paper folder and headed out the door. He would take the underground across campus to the photographic lab, and there use his considerable talents to retrieve a faint photo from the plate. The other man, who had earlier shown Zita into the office, was younger, pudgy with a bad complexion, but his most distinctive feature were eyes of different coloration, giving him an unsettling appearance. William Edington had seated himself on the sofa, quietly preparing for his master's questions.

"So tell me, Bill. What is your psychic impression of Ms. Hiller?"

"She's definitely hiding something; she's not at all who she claims to be."

"Then who is she? Feel it out."

Edington closed his eyes, focused on the image of the woman he had studied through the glass peephole in the office wall. He switched his focus and she appeared to him as a fibrous mass. Edington peeled back layer after layer of gauzy filaments to uncover images of: an older man, an official, her boss; a city on a river, Washington, D.C.; an odd-shaped building, the Pentagon. He focused on the building, searching through its maze of hallways for her office; it was in the basement but there was an energy field, unmistakably a photonic barrier modulator blocking out his psychic prying. He opened his eyes. "She's an undercover operative for a North

American security agency."

"Very good, Bill. Very good, indeed."

"She plans to discredit Rama in her article."

"Yes, that appears to be their agenda," Jamison said, and then, wistfully, "too bad for Ms. Hiller. She's an ally of sorts, even trainable I sensed, but I'm afraid she's chosen some rather bad friends."

Edington's eyes lit up in gleeful anticipation. "Oh, let me. She'd be lovely to do."

"No, it's far too subtle an operation. We just want to slow her down; she still might be useful to us. And I have another job for you." Jamison paused to allow his protégé to switch mental tracks. "It appears we have a spy among us."

"The woman's pin?"

"Yes, you saw that. Somebody must suspect us; somebody who knows us well. Let's find them, and them you can do."

"I'll start with the North Americans."

"It would be foolish for them to plant someone here, and then reveal it so clumsily, but they're still a rather naive lot," Jamison said. "And they dress so poorly."

"And what delicious game will we play with our snoop?" Edington asked, beads of sweat forming on his upper lip.

"She wants to be daddy's little girl again, and so we'll help her keep house."

Edington squinted his eyes. "To soften her up?"

"Yes. It wasn't serious, nothing physical, just vague intimations. But the complex is there, and she's still vulnerable. I'll plant a dream, stir up some images, let the whole thing fester."

"And she'll project the complex onto Rama?"

"Very good, William," Jamison said. "He'll make a wonderful substitute, might even be able to help her."

"Making it harder for her to discredit him?"

"Yes, but we won't count on it. She has strong loyalties." Jamison closed his eyes and read his psychic impressions of the woman reporter again. He opened them. "Ms. Hiller suffers from familial Hemiplegic Migraines, the worse kind. They won't be hard to trigger."

Edington nodded his head in admiration. He looked at his watch. "You want me to take your four o'clock?"

"Yes, if you would. They're a tiresome lot, and I want to follow the woman on her journey to the sacred place."

"And tonight?" Edington asked nervously.

"Yes, Bill, that'd be lovely. I'll leave the door open."

When Jamison closed his eyes, his student quietly stood up, bowed his head with his hands folded, and left the office. By then Jamison had already departed. He watched as Ms. Hiller packed her bags, checked out of the hotel, and took the bullet train to the airport. In fourth dimensional compressed time, the journey took only minutes, and soon the young woman had boarded the air shuttle and was flying east to Switzerland and on to the prison that held those beloved of him. It was a hellish journey for Jamison, taken time and time again, but today there was at least hope that soon he would be united with his boys. The man became impatient and remote-viewed past her plane up and over the rising alps to the outer walls of the mountain fortress, stopped on his journey, only feet away from viewing them, by the hideous scalar field. They were indeed boys, many of them still in their teens, when he found them and seduced them, instilled in them his love for mother earth, and showed these fledglings the awesome power of the mind and how to use their natural gifts to protect the Mother. Together they had brought the world to its knees, made them pay the price for their awful defilement. But he had paid a far dearer price in their loss, one that could not be reconciled by those who followed. Even young Bill, the best of the new recruits, was a poor imitation. Yet soon they would be together again, and soon the world would feel the sting of his wrath.

Suddenly, through the barrier that no mind could breech, came the face of Rama, possessed of a power that eluded him, the man's eyes dark deep pools of compassion and forgiveness. Jamison shuddered under the impact of those eyes, that spied into the depths of him, that touched the sore spots, the denied parts of himself. There stirred the hideous things of a child's battered past, the monsters lurking in the cellar, clawing at the walls of their prison as the light of Rama's love shined through. The professor extended his own protective barrier, weaved from thought, but Rama's image, made of sterner stuff, easily seeped through. Jamison was forced to withdraw or surrender to this love, but he would rather die than submit.

He retreated from the barrier and instantaneously opened his eyes in his office at the university. However, the image of Rama persisted. But, in his sanctuary, surrounded by talismans and totems, Jamison was in his power, imbued with their magical emanations. Although it did sicken creatures of flesh and blood, disembodied spirit appeared impervious to its influence. Yet it fortified the magician. He now stared back at his old adversary and met his love with a fierce burning hatred. He was prepared to engage this spirit until the proverbial hell froze over. Rama soon withdrew, his message delivered. It was in effect a psychic crossing of the swords. Although the holy man was incapable of causing harm, the movement of his spirit drew reactions that could lead to one's own self-undoing. The secret in combating pure spirit was controlling your reactions, and Jamison had learned tonight that the secret of that control was meeting on your "power spot."

Part Two
The Testimony

The Rama Journal

9 June 39. I awakened in the middle of the night. My body was shaking. I could feel a great disturbance. Not here but out there in the world. And then it stopped. The next morning Renault told me of an earthquake in China that killed hundreds of thousands. That is what I felt. Later I was lying down and felt the most peculiar sensation. My body shifted again and I found myself in another. . .dimension. Not outside this world, above it, ethereal, but inside of things. The formative state. How strange.

13 June 39. I received a letter from Uncle Hari today. The warden is letting up on my restrictions. They must feel I am near death. It is obvious Hari thinks as much. It was rather funny. Here he is asking my forgiveness for any number of past transgressions—the time he beat me with a switch when I was four—that I cannot remember. I hardly remember him. My personal history seems to have been erased. However, when I look at his picture, I feel waves of love sweep over me. My feelings have not forgotten him. Without the mind and its catalogue of petty grievances, all that remains is love. It is the ego, its sense of self-importance, that suffers from these insults. When you drop it, you unload a lifetime of recriminations.

24 June 39. One of the attendants, Hans, was telling the nurse about his upset stomach. I shifted and was inside his body. I could feel the diseased organ; it was vibrating at a certain wavelength. I shortened it and immediately reversed his condition. He felt it, looked at the nurse, and then at me. Something in him un-

derstood. He practically ran out of the clinic. A memory surfaced of me healing in the old way, from the outside in. It took an enormous exertion. I can see why. The mental energies cannot tap this dimension, where the real change occurs. From here all of life springs. In this state one is an active agent, molding, changing, creating. Its potential is enormous.

2 July 39. The skin discolorations have finally convinced Renault that this is not a disease process. He has isolated me from the others, taking care of me himself. He says they are signs of new glandular functioning, and he is giving me blood tests daily. He has to make a decision. Does he reveal what is happening to me, or does he conceal the transformation? I have little doubt he will cooperate. He has already been affected. This energy is extremely contagious. Those not receptive get up and leave. Like Hans. He resigned the next day. But Renault, this French Catholic, is open to it. I need him to survive, but would never try to influence him. My will is gone. None of the old mental manipulation. You release yourself and what is needed comes in. How perfect.

11 July 39. I felt a disturbance inside the prison. One of the psychics was being treated in the infirmary. They had him contained in a weaker field, and he was able to sense my presence more readily. He directed the most hideous energy at me. I shifted out of its way. It passed right through me. Nothing here to stop it. I sensed his illness was untreatable. I went inside and changed the vibration. Later Renault told me he was monitoring him when his signals were scrambled. Afterward his readings were normal again. Renault knew it was me. But I could hear the psychic silently screaming at me and I withdrew. His was a dark soul. The will, the need to change, control, manipulate was strong in him. I could feel the whole, this magical matrix, go out to its prodigal part. Love it and leave it to its own designs. Could I do any less?

Chapter Seven

Zita was sitting in the arboretum sipping tea and viewing the great variety of plants and flowers. Since few of the inmates were allowed out of their cells, she assumed that this elaborate garden was actually cultivated for the prison personnel. Given their remote location, the restrictions on travel, and the taxing security precautions, they no doubt needed a ready retreat to normality. Suddenly, Zita felt the atmosphere in the room shift; it was as perceptible as a drastic rise in temperature. She turned in her chair to see Rama enter the arboretum. He slowly made his way between rows of shrubs and finally walked up to her. Zita was standing, and she took one step forward, extending her hand in greeting. The man appeared unruffled. He took the woman's hand in his and bowed his head. As directed, Zita bowed in return.

"Ms. Hiller, I presume?" Rama asked with a distinct English accent. He saw her curiosity. "Yes, my mother thought you could only learn proper English at Oxford, and so they shipped me off for two years. I was miserable, but I did pick up the language and the accent."

They seated themselves in the wicker chairs. "I've heard you speak on tape, but the accent wasn't as pronounced."

"I can modify it, for effect. . .you understand?"

Zita nodded her head. "I would've thought your mother, being English, would've taught you herself."

Rama reached over to the glass-topped table and poured himself a cup of tea. He was delighted to find the cream set out. "Only Hindi was spoken in my father's house." Again, as if reading her mind, he added, "He would share his life with her, but not her colonialist language."

"But it's been a hundred. . ."

"My father was born on the twenty-fifth anniversary of our independence. For him the timing was symbolic. He was always a fierce nationalist."

"Who would have his son learn English."

"It was the language of the West, and he would have his son convert the infidels in the name of the Hindu Gods."

"And when you turned from religion to eco-politics, was he. . .?"

"He did not speak with me for the last ten years of his life," Rama said with no emotion. "He died shortly after my trial." He could see she wanted him to amplify. "Despite our profound differences, he saw my imprisonment as another act of colonial aggression by the West, and he would rather die than live through it."

Zita heard the finality in his voice and did not pursue her questioning further. She looked down at her computer notepad and read through her list of questions. "Do you mind if I voice-record our session?"

Rama looked around for a recorder. "With what, may I ask?"

Zita held up the electronic notepad to show him the built-in microphone. Rama looked at it with interest, then held out his hand. "May I?"

She turned it around and handed it to him. "It's a full computer with both voice and keyboard input."

"You mean it not only records, but transcribes at the same time?" Rama asked with wide-eyed fascination. He glanced up and said, "And sends?" Zita nodded her head in amazement. Rama saw her reaction. "Ms. Hiller, turning off my monkey-mind makes me even less inclined to swing from trees than you."

"Excuse me. I'm sorry."

Rama handed the notepad back to her. "I have always been fascinated by technology."

"'Nothing is evil in itself. Just the use you make of it'" Zita said, quoting from memory.

"What fool said that?"

"'An atomic bomb, or a psychic's mind. . .'"

"Enough. Please. The sins of my youth," Rama said with mock impatience.

"You. . .think. . .differently today?"

He understood the implied question. "Yes, I still think, but fortunately not about such things." Rama smiled mischievously. "How to change a roll of toilet paper. The practical things, somewhat limited by my circumstances, but abstract speculation no longer interests me."

"You don't think about the prospect of your release?"

"Somebody hands me an appeal for my release. I read it, find the argument persuasive, sign it, hand it back, and it is gone," Rama said. "I do not remember what I read, or even when I read it."

"Out of sight, out of mind?"

"Out of sight, out of sight. Mind has nothing to do with it." Rama shrugged his shoulders. "You are asking for a definition of the natural state, but I do not have one."

"Well, can you tell me how you. . .get along—operate, as it were," Zita said, but the holy man looked puzzled. She added, "There must've been a point where you stopped. . . living in one state and started in this other."

Rama nodded his head in relief. "Yes, when I stopped questioning." Rama paused for a moment. "For a spiritual man brought up in India with its rich religious heritage, there is always one burning question: what is enlightenment, what is the state of Buddha, Mohammed, and Jesus? As a child, my father would read to me from the Upanishads, the Yoga Sutras, the Bhagavad Gita. These were my nursery rhymes. By the time I was seven, I began to experience incredible mystical states. I had glorious visions; Krishna would come to me daily, a regular playmate. My father was elated, a dream come true. His family had been blessed with a Buddha. He would stand me up in front of his friends, and I could spout this stuff for hours." Rama paused and stared back at Zita.

"Were they impressed?" she asked self-consciously.

"Yes, but mostly with themselves. And I noticed, even as a child, that most of these religious types were the worst hypocrites. They would go around babbling this high-minded stuff, and then go out and cheat on their wives or break their fasts behind the kitchen. It did not affect them; it was just another philosophy. I did not want to become like them, and so I became very bitter and cynical, took a modern intellectual attitude about it."

"You became an agnostic?"

"No, I never stopped believing in God, just his go-betweens."

"This was when you were at the university."

"Yes, and that became another problem. My seniors there were sexually active, and while intellectually I was their equal, emotionally I was still a child. Sex became an awful problem. I would think about it constantly. Remember I was still the 'Buddha-boy,' and was treated with great deference. To them I was beyond such things. So here I am giving little talks at the campus Ramakrishna Society, and I am staring at the girls' breasts and thinking bad thoughts. I was filled with incredible guilt. Felt I was no better than my father and his group.

"And then, just when I felt like exploding, something happened. I just dropped it. Everything. The desires, the recriminations, the guilt. I stopped playing the game. And then my mind stopped. Looking out at the world I saw the dance, the dance of Shiva, the perfection that is already there. It was my first 'Satori,' direct insight into the divine, and it happened on a hot, dusty after-noon, with charwomen scrubbing laundry, dogs licking themselves, and young girls laughing in the bushes. Short-ly after, I donned the orange robes of a sannyasin. I was eighteen years old."

"You had become enlightened?" Zita asked, puzzled by the abrupt end to his story.

Rama laughed uproariously. "That is the biggest crock! A totally non-existent state. Believe me, if any man tells you he is enlightened, you are talking to a dead man, or a fool, or worse." Rama turned more serious. "I stopped the thought process long enough to look out at the world and see it as it is without the buffer of the mind. That is all."

"Scientists tell us nothing is experienced but the mind."

"Because the average person, or the average scientist, never stops the mind long enough to experience the world as it is. For them everything is a mental event. They only experience their history of something, not the thing in itself. When the first sailing vessels arrived in the New World, the natives did not see them at first. They truly did not see them. They had no history for comparison."

"And the first time I smelled a rose as a child?"

"You did not smell a rose but a fragrance. The second time, you had a reference, and it became a rose. A mental classification."

Zita knitted her brow, and she asked defensively, "And how do you. . .know a rose?"

"That is asking how I 'live' and that is ahead of my story."

Zita looked down at her notepad and backspaced through the transcription to pick up the last thread. "And, after this. . .episode, the. . .question still remained?"

"Yes, unfortunately, this was only a momentary glimpse. I still had too much baggage to enter into that state, but at least I knew where I was going. But that became a problem. I made my journey my obsession. I had high ambitions for myself. Nothing but immortality would do. Buddha or bust. I was not unlike a gambler going for the jackpot and risking everything. What a delusion."

"That you could get there?"

"That there was any place to get," Rama said, shaking his head. "The real joke is that we are already there. It is our natural state, we are born into it. Everything else in nature is already there, but we are pulling up the rear, actually threatening the whole web."

"If we're born into it, what pulls us away from it?"

"Looking outside the self. Society and its instruments:

family, church and state, everything they do to us, creates a certain hunger for the beyond, fuels this search for the absolute or the jackpot, be it God or lotto. It steals us from ourselves and then enslaves us to do its bidding."

"What're you advocating: Infants in Paradise?" Zita asked indignantly.

"No, I am afraid we are genetically ill-equipped, even as infants, to accept paradise. The thought mechanism is programmed into our genes, and until nature whips up a new batch of humans, the long road home is the only game in town, as they say." Rama looked at his baffled interviewer. "Utterly preposterous, is it not?"

"But that's the point, I would imagine," Zita said warily.

"Yes, the mind can pigeonhole anything less than the truly absurd. Zen recognized this in its koans long ago. The problem is that to use the mind to destroy the mind only makes it stronger." Rama paused and seemed to gather himself. "So my questioning began. It was like one of those video games: search and destroy. Instinctively we realize that we are going in the wrong direction, away from what is natural in us, and it fuels an incredible urge to destroy all that we encounter. I became a master of it; Mr. Destruction himself. I adopted and disowned one philosophy, one psychology after another. Could knock a hole in anybody's system. When I set myself up as a guru, my laser brain would dissect the minds and hearts of my devotees unmercifully. Nothing false, nothing spurious survived my scrutiny. God only knows how many of them were broken by the process."

Zita saw the man's pained expression. It was his first real show of emotion, and it made him more human to her. "But wasn't that the idea?"

Rama nodded his head. "But we Hindus are born to the task: our ultimate goal, bred into us from our first breath, is: *samadhi,* a nothingness devoid of life. It is life that is the divine in us, not its absence. Well, my fame spread. Here was a man who could really whip you into shape. A regular yogi boxing champion.

I had them lined up in the street, ready for the old knockout punch. But, after a while, my devotees were not corrupt enough for me. I needed some really bad fish. People who really smelled of it. Of course politicians were, if you will excuse the pun, a 'natural' for it. And not just the hands-in-your-pocket kind. Every village has those. I went after the big defilers. The environmental pillagers." Rama laughed to himself. "Can you see the irony in that?"

"They're defiling nature, and you're defiling the natural state by your inquiry?" Zita asked, repeating the obvious but without conviction. "Yes," she added.

"Well, I really had my hands full. Because the bigger the fish, the more rope, or ego, it takes to pull them in. Not that you would know it. I became a super ascetic, an eco-Gandhi. A nationwide strike for more homeless shelters was worth a good month-long fast. The worldwide ban on internal combustion engines nearly killed me, between the epic fasting and the meditations. But it was effective. I told myself I was beating them with divine power. But it was my big ego that was sinking them. I was setting myself up. And, when my bubble finally burst, it snapped my mind for good."

"What happened?"

"Well, after I was arrested and while awaiting trial, I was in deep despair. Everybody was against me, even my followers joined in on the smear campaign. The newspapers were filled with one lie and distortion after another. I was accused of every crime under the sun from being a child molester to an embezzler of ashram funds. The world had crashed and everybody was looking for a scapegoat. Now, I had taken on some pretty big fish in my day, but I could not fight the whole world. My life was over, my causes were dead, and my conviction and life-long imprisonment was a foregone conclusion. The weight of it all broke my will. And that was the beginning of the end for me."

"But, at your trial, you seemed so defiant."

"I still had a little spite left, but the noose was tightening."

Zita looked down at her notepad, did a subject search and found the reference. "But you were in prison for a while before. . .it happened?"

"You must understand that this is not a gradual process. You do not whittle away at the mind until you have nothing but a big hole. It just happens. Nothing you can do can make it happen. Even when you do nothing, there is somebody there doing something. I should know. I became a master at doing nothing. Sitting here looking out at the mountains day after day. Reading nothing, talking to nobody, stilling the mind. I became a regular piece of stone, like one of those Easter Island statues. I told myself that I had finally made it, had finally arrived in that state. I mean you could not hold a heartbeat and be deader than me. But nothing felt different. It dawned on me that if there was still somebody here asking questions I was still knocking on the door. Finally, it got to me, the absurdity of it all. I just dropped it, the question, everything. I did not care anymore. And that is when it happened."

Rama nodded his head. "First, there were the massive headaches. Renault thought I had a brain tumor, and he did every test in the book, but could not find anything wrong." Rama paused, "You must understand that the body is totally thought-driven, as they say, and when the thinking process stops, when the 'I' breaks down, the thoughts cannot 'connect.' At first there is a massive electrical discharge that realigns every cell of the body. I shook uncontrollably for days at a time. The body's electrical field is polarized, if that is the word. After that every thought that comes up just discharges—puff into thin air."

"There's a total absence of thought?" Zita asked, alarmed by the implication.

"No, that is a misconception. The samadhi delusion. Thoughts arise, but they are no longer in the driver's seat. They no longer think you; they arise and you choose them. Where to put your bingo marker, when to cross the street, how to make a soufflé."

Zita looked puzzled. "You've given me a description of sorts, but. . .what happened to you?"

Rama shrugged his shoulders. "I just started operating. . .differently." Zita waited, not satisfied by this answer. "For instance, my senses began to operate independently of each other. I see someone walking down the hallway toward me, and I might hear their boot heels clicking on the floor before or after seeing them, but the two do not fit together, they are totally independent sensations. They stop; I walk over and shake their hands, feel their warm, sweaty palms, but I do not associate that sensation with the sight of them, or even their heavy breathing. And, if I smell their cologne, that is separate too."

"So you can't put a clear picture of reality together?" Zita asked, her tone sympathetic, as if talking to a moron.

"What reality?" Rama asked facetiously. "The narrow range of sensory signals you can process, or the past pictures you conform them to?" Zita gave him a skeptical look. "All I can experience is the present, five different layers of it. The classical injunction, 'Be here now,' has become for me, 'Be here now, now, now, now, now.'"

Zita stared at the man for the longest time. If she had read this description in a book or report, she would have considered him a crackpot or worse. However, looking into his clear eyes, seeing his totally relaxed body, sensing his inward peace and stillness, she could not so readily dismiss his story. If it were true—and she had no reason to discount it—then she was dealing with a man whose very being challenged her world and its way of operating. If for no other reason than that, she could see how her colleagues in the mind-control business might be threatened by his revelation and would want to bury it here for good.

Rama finally broke the silence. "It is not exactly what the people in the nirvana business have come to expect."

"No, I wouldn't think so." Zita looked down at her notepad, turned it off, and folded the cover back over. "If you don't mind, I'd like to end today's session." Rama nodded his head in agreement. "I came prepared with a list of questions that I need to review in light of our 'conversation.'"

"Oh, did I talk too much?" Rama asked half-seriously.

"No, not at all. I just didn't expect such a long and, I might add, necessary introduction. I might need, besides Wednesday's session, one or two more, if it's not too much of an inconvenience."

"Well, I believe I can fit you in my social schedule," he added.

Zita stood up. "I can well imagine," she said ruefully, and turned to signal the guard. Zita felt Rama lay his hand on her shoulder; she could feel the warmth of his hand through three layers of clothing. She turned back to the holy man.

"Before you leave, you must let me show you the view from the dome—it's quite spectacular."

Zita hesitated, but as he walked off, she found herself following after him. The window was only a few feet away, and they stood there in silence and stared at the majestic mountainscape. It took her breath away, and she identified the warmth spreading through her body as its natural response to a world set on fire by the setting sun suddenly peeking through the thin cloud cover.

Chapter Eight

When Zita arrived back at her hotel in Geneva, a quiet picturesque inn on the lake, with old painted window shutters and an outdated wooden sun deck, she booked her room for another week and informed Bernard, the manager, that she might extend the stay even longer. The hotel was nearly empty, and the man was delighted to accommodate his guest. Bernard even offered to move Zita to a suite at no extra charge. It was off-season for them, and although some tourists from the southern hemisphere migrated here to view the winter snows, most waited to flee the torrid summers for the cooler mountain air. Zita crossed the lobby, passing the restaurant, its windows etched with an old-fashioned scene of skiers whizzing down mountain slopes, to the elevators. Although it was dinner time, she had lost her appetite. This could be the result of the day's jumpy copter rides, or just the higher altitude itself, but she doubted it. Her body was unusually tense, and she knew not to feed the tension and numb it out. In the room, Zita dropped her briefcase on the floor and went over to the bed. Lowering the mattress setting to soft, she lay down prepared to focus on her tense muscles and their emotional message, but soon fell asleep. Zita slept for an hour and awakened in a cold sweat with a headache and a haunting dream fragment rapidly fading from her memory. She sat on the edge of the bed wiping her eyes clear, then went into the bathroom and drew a hot bath.

Lying in the whirlpool, immersed in her element, with the water jets foaming the soap into suds and softly buffeting her sore body, Zita felt safe enough to feel out the source of her discomfort. The trauma was concentrated in a knot just below the breastplate. She focused on the tension, which felt like fear. The jammed energy shifted, releasing itself and easing back into her body. Was it Rama she feared, or was it his supposed natural state? Zita reviewed her interview with him. Expecting a distant, self-absorbed prima donna, she had been surprised to find a wise-cracking longshoreman with the heart of a child and the mind—despite his disclaimer— of an analyst. As a reporter you learn to check everybody's story: the more outrageous the more thorough the search. In advance she had received reports from his prison doctor, Renault—himself a convicted felon, although the circumstances were certainly mitigating—that he had witnessed many of Rama's alleged physiological changes. Zita was prepared to discount the man's confirmation as the delusions of a religious devotee. And then she met Rama. Hearing his story firsthand, looking into eyes that sought neither to persuade or dissemble, she could not dismiss him outright, and that bothered her.

Zita had considered his claim tantamount to an insanity plea. But even if his entrance into the natural state were true, it did little to alter her assignment. She had come to discredit a revolutionary, whose psychic powers and philosophy threatened the fragile power structure in a world still struggling to regain its balance. However, it was already clear to Zita from his limited testimony that this man was no rabble-rouser. She could see the difference, from his speeches and from the video archives, between the eco-crusader in his thirties and the man she had just interviewed.

Whatever his powers, Zita was certain they would never be employed to enforce any kind of political agenda. She wondered if his accusers had talked with Rama recently. He was now more kitten than eco-terrorist. But, if this were obvious to her, it would be to Michael and the others. They must be afraid—and she could sense Michael's fear—of another scenario. It could be this secret potential that Harry Allen mentioned. If so, it must affect without intent, and that would be a truly scary prospect for her colleagues in the mind-control business.

Zita could easily discredit Rama; she could distort a number of his statements to portray him as a self-deluded madman. She had no doubt that interviews with cooperative scientists could also be used to verify claims of his psychic prowess. But Zita was unwilling to defame him without more proof of a tangible security threat. Zapping the multitudes into nirvana or leading more eco-crusades, as they claimed (and perhaps dissembled), did not qualify him for such treatment. The Department was already forewarned by her fusion series that she would not rubber-stamp their policy directives. Zita decided that, since Michael was so far unwilling to confide in her, she would do her own research, beginning with the medical reports describing Rama's supposed physiological changes, and uncover the man's intriguing secret potential herself.

Zita slipped into her insulated robe. The temperature of the room was already dropping; the thermostats in Europe were set even lower than in North America. She brewed a quick cup of tea in the room's Handy-Cook, walked over to the bed, slipped under the covers, sat up, and began reading the first report. The brief, entitled "The Appearance of Ash as Ionized Thought," was based on Dr. Renault's notes and his analysis of the ash-like substance that covered Rama's body at the time of his "entrance." The scientist writing the report relied not only on Renault's observations but his own chemical analysis of the substance. Rama claimed that when his mind stopped, the existing thoughts in the various levels of his being—conscious, unconscious, even in the soft tissues of the brain—burned up or were ionized into an ash-like substance. Dr. Bloch, who did the follow-up, said that the chemical structure of the substance was similar to certain neurochemicals in the brain, and he speculated that this data could be the first proof that thought had a physiological basis.

The next report was an illustrated commentary on the body discolorations that appeared up and down

Rama's head, neck, and torso. They were red and circular, and if they did not appear in proximity to the body's endocrine glands and the ancient Indian "chakras" associated with them, they may have been dismissed as splotches of an unknown skin rash. A biopsy of cell samples taken and preserved by Renault proved to be normal epidermal skin cells. It appeared that they were the side effects of an increase in glandular activity. The doctor had extracted from the various glands an unusual array of new hormones, but their production in itself could not account for the discolorations that were remarkably similar in color, shape, and size from glands that were totally dissimilar. Renault compared their appearance to reports through the ages of the stigmata, the wounds of Christ, that have appeared on Christians in ecstatic states, although he did not feel that these discolorations were in the same category: externalized delusional states. He speculated that the ionization of thought purified consciousness and allowed some primordial pattern in the morphic field to manifest. In his estimation the increased glandular secretions were not merely a biological function but that it was being directed by this conscious or superconscious design.

Zita found this speculation interesting. She was familiar with the Indian school of evolutionary thought (identified with the twentieth-century mystic Sri Aurobindo) that claimed the human was a transitional being to a supramental consciousness as far beyond mental human as it was beyond the primate. Was Rama and his peculiar transformation the first manifestation of this being, and if so what were the implications for society? Mental humans were molded and formed by the dominant beliefs of their society. They were easily indoctrinated, from kindergarten to company policy briefings. Through the manipulation of the media, the political power brokers maintained their control. But here was a man whom they could never influence, who was beyond their reach, who was free from thought indoctrination of any kind. If he were an isolated aberration, he might be useful for comparative study, but if he were the first of his kind, and could somehow trigger this process in larger populations, he was the most dangerous man alive. It was not another revolutionary idea they feared but another way of being, one beyond their control.

If this were the case, and Zita was not ready to concede that point, his revolutionary "being" must operate through some process that elevated others into this natural state. But, he claimed, if they were listening, that entrance into this state was acausal. There was nothing he or they could do to trigger it.

Sheldrake's "morphogenetic fields," based on his theory of formative causation, which had revolutionized science in the early twenty-first century, did offer an applicable model. It explained how morphic fields surrounding an organism contained an inherent memory from previous systems that habitually shaped all matter, from crystals to humans. It further stated that the morphic fields of similar organisms resonate together (morphic resonance) and exchange formative influences, not diminished by time or space. It was possible for a mutant with a new or drastically altered morphogenetic field, if of sufficient amplitude, to kindle the new pattern in others ready for the transformation. When their numbers passed a threshold, they would trip the process into the whole species, the hundredth-monkey model. Normally this would take generations. But, in Rama's case, if Michael's fear was any gauge, there might be some unknown factor that made this rather farfetched, esoteric scenario more feasible. Zita dropped the folder on the floor and picked up the next report searching for the answer.

Zita awakened in the morning with a throbbing headache agitated by the beeping vid screen and its waiting message. Crawling out of bed, she stumbled into the bathroom and was shocked by the frightful image staring back in the mirror. She doused her face with cold water, hurriedly popped two aspirin, and walked out. Zita slipped into a robe and stepped over to the screen to play back her video message. Although it was not a live broadcast, she was still too modest to watch it in the nude. She rewound the message and played it, but the picture was a mass of crisscross lines. It must be coded. She tapped out her ten-digit code and unscrambled the message.

Michael's smiling face appeared. "Sleeping in, are we?" he said in mock disapproval. "Call as soon as, or almost as soon as, you get up." The screen went blank. He was in a good mood, rare for him, and Zita immediately placed a satlink call to his office in Washington.

Michael was talking on another vid phone. "Okay, just do it and get back to me." He turned to her. "Jesus, you look like hell."

"Yeah, well that's about how I feel," Zita said, putting her fingertips to her temples.

"So, how did it go with Rama?"

"Your concern is very touching."

"I'm sorry you don't feel well, but I'm really busy." He paused. "Okay, so tell me about it."

"He's not at all what I expected, Michael. I mean, he's just this sweet gentle old crackpot with some strange ideas."

Michael frowned. "Don't tell me he's taken you in?"

"No, I can see your concern, but from what I gather, he's experienced some kind of spiritual conversion, non-psychic in nature, he claims. And, even if he could induct others, I don't see how they would pose a threat to us."

"It's more than that and you know it."

"No, I don't," Zita replied sharply. He glared back at her, and she relented. "Look, his condition is a lot more complex than I was led to believe. I'm going over the reports from the prison doctors, and maybe I'll feel differently afterwards." Zita added with emphasis, "But, I can tell you this, if his lawyer gets Rama in court, even on remote, he'll charm the pants off everybody."

"Yeah, that's what we're afraid of." Michael thought for a moment. "Okay, is he giving you anything we can use against him?"

"Everything he says is so outrageous that, if it weren't

for the modifying effect of his presence, you'd swear he's nuts just hearing him."

"Well, we won't include a photo spread with your story," Michael said impatiently. "The point is, can we discredit him?"

"Sure, and I'm only starting, but. . ." Zita hesitated, "is it really called for?"

Michael gave her his best smoldering look. "You let me decide that."

"Don't tell me that, Michael. I want to know the whole story, what this is really about, or you're getting a 'harmless old nut' interview."

Michael coolly assessed his agent. "We'll talk about it when you get back." The screen went blank before Zita could tell him she had extended her stay for another week. This was a typical ploy of his. When he could not hold a position on logic alone, Michael would pull rank on her or reduce the argument to a relationship squabble.

Zita showered and dressed. She had room service bring her lunch, and she sat down at the small dining table pushed up against the window that overlooked the lake. The water appeared hard on this overcast day and she decided against the boat outing scheduled for later in the afternoon. Zita ate her sandwich and read through the files. The numerous reports from the scientists at Bernia had still not given her a clear picture of Rama in his natural state. Zita scanned the transcript of their interview to where he was describing his sensory distortion. This gave her an abstract understanding of his state but no real "feel" for his condition. Zita remembered Dr. Renault telling her what he had witnessed in the days following Rama's first "entrance." She went back through the doctor's notes and came across a day-by-day description of the changes in the man's sensory array.

Earlier, in his notes, Renault had described Rama's entrance into the natural state and the peculiarities that accompanied it. Soon after, Rama reported that when he touched something, it felt like his hand passed right through the object, or that he was inside of it, and was able to sense its internal operation. Renault had Rama "touch" several of his patients, and he could sense which organs were impaired. He next gave him a broken mechanical clock, and he could do the same with it. The following day, Rama was escorted to the arboretum. Sitting on a bench under a potted Ficus, he was smelling all the many flower, plant, and tree scents wafting in the air, when suddenly they began to blend together into one aroma. Rama stood up and walked over to a rose bush, but all he could smell from the fragrant red roses was this single dominant scent.

The next day Rama reported that his vision had changed to a reverse fisheye: things faraway appeared closer and vice versa. Renault speculated that his being had expanded to include both the center and the circumference of his field of vision. He placed objects beyond the distant vision of normal eyesight, and Rama was able to identify them. He next placed a book within millimeters of his eyes, and they could focus on the text at this incredibly close distance. And then, on the last day, he reported that his hearing was altered, and that when he dropped his fork the sound of it hitting the floor originated inside himself, as did the footsteps in the hallway or the door slamming in the next room. He also reported hearing a book drop on the floor on the opposite end of the circular building through ten steel doors and 100 feet of stone.

Renault's speculation on the peculiar transformation of Rama's sensory array was very intriguing. He first quoted research on how infants view the world, including drawings by subjects under hypno-regression, and showed the resemblance to Rama's own altered perceptions. He further speculated that they had one thing in common. "Neither Rama nor the infant have an 'I' center to coordinate the functioning of the senses. For the infant, the center gradually forms and the senses begin to reflect the world of consensus reality. For Rama, at the other end of the spectrum, the center dissolves and the senses once again function independently and the world becomes either the madman's shattered nightmare or the Buddha's wondrous paradise." Renault called Rama's transformation, "the birth of the conscious child." At this point, he succumbed to his Catholic upbringing and quoted Jesus's dictum, "that unless we become as children we cannot enter into the kingdom of heaven."

The sheer innocence of such a state reminded her of biblical Eden, where man and beast lived in harmony. Zita knew the myth was indicative of an unconscious stage in human development, and that eating the apple of knowledge, that split off the conscious mind, had been the necessary next step in our development. But now that split threatened the very fabric of nature. Zita wondered if Rama and his spiritual adventure was showing us the conscious way back? It was becoming increasingly clear to many in the environmental movement that the mind that had created the ecological disaster was not the instrument that would rectify the damage. What was needed was not another eco-agenda or scientific breakthrough like the ozone seeder but a new way of experiencing our place in the natural scheme of things. It could be that only the conscious child could see nature anew.

Zita sat up in bed with tears rolling down her cheeks, and wiped them off with the sleeve of her silk pajama top. It was the middle of the night, and although her headache still throbbed, it was her dream that made her cry, even in her sleep. It was about her father. The two of them were renovating the basement in her grandmother's old beach house shortly after Anna's death. They were having a great time, slapping on the plasterboard, painting the walls and splattering each other. Unfortunately, it did not happen that way. Her father had hired workmen to do a job they could have done themselves. He told Zita that he was too busy, though he had plenty of time to play indoor golf with his cronies. If this had been the only rejection, she would have licked her wounds and gone on to do other things with him. But that was the summer their relationship changed. Until then, they had been the best of friends, almost inseparable. They went to basketball games together, watched football on TV. When the family went out to dinner, she always sat next to her dad.

She had turned ten that July. He did not come to her party, leaving it to her mother to give Zita his present, a dress someone else picked out for him. She was crushed. Figuring she had done something wrong, Zita went to her mother in tears asking why daddy was being so mean. Her mother told her that she was a big girl, and that "big girls weren't as chummy with their daddies." She asked why, but her mother never explained it, telling her she would soon be interested in boys and forget it. It was only much later, recalling a trivial incident that had occurred earlier in the summer, that she at least understood his reaction if she could not forgive it. Zita had just gotten out of the tub and was standing naked in the bathroom when her father accidentally walked in on her. Zita was not at all self-conscious, and even asked if he would dry her off. Her father stepped back, gave his excuses and hurried out, but not before he gave her a look she could now identify as inappropriate.

He would never fully hug or kiss her again. Her mother seemed to relish her daughter's predicament, apparently jealous of their earlier relationship. Later she would blame her mother for not managing the situation better. By then society was much more educated about incestuous dynamics. But no attempt was made to confront the situation and reconcile her father's disaffection. Her mother was right in one regard. She did discover boys that fall, but the pattern had already been set, and she had spent the rest of her life trying to replace a father's love by her involvement with older men. The most devastating repercussion was her sexual inhibition, no doubt caused by feelings of guilt for what her unconscious mind would construe as forbidden love. The result was that when her relationships turned sexual, the love seemed to leak out of them. Zita found it interesting that she should have a dream about cleaning up her basement, an obvious symbol for old issues, especially subterranean or sexual ones, on the heels of her interview with Rama, who was close to her father's age if he had lived.

The dream seemed to say that despite years of analysis she had not entirely healed this wound. Julia, her analyst, always the optimist, would no doubt point out that Zita had at least gotten down to the basement. After the rec room was finished, Zita played only one game of ping pong on the new table with her father, who rapidly lost interest in the game. In the summers to come, while her sister and her friends would take full advantage of the room, Zita could never bring herself to play there again. In fact, she generally had trouble having fun, an element missing in her relationships with men. From Noel, her English professor in college, to Michael her boss at DI, they were characterized by heavy emotionalism and the seriousness of professional people at work and in love. As Julia told her client once, "she wouldn't know a good time if it ran over her."

The joy had been sucked out of her childhood by her father's abandonment and was never reclaimed. Zita could blame its lack on the depressing world condition, but her friends, some with similar histories and all with the same concerns, had more zest for life. It was ironic that Rama, the dead man, as he called himself, of all the people she had met, was the most lively, joyful person. His childlike impishness, sweetness, his joy of living, despite his confinement and the imposition of his keepers, was so rare in her experience. She assumed that these qualities were a reflection of his natural state of being. If so, regardless of its philosophic implications, understanding his condition might also help her tap these resources within herself.

Chapter Nine

When Cosgrove and Halzack arrived back at the Baba's village in New Guinea, hiking along the last leg of the winding trail until they came to a clearing with 200-foot-high trees and their canopy of green foliage, they found the tribe of half-naked, oiled-down natives eating at a long tree-planed table. Steaming bowls of fish soup were set out for their guests. They set their backpacks up against a nearby tree and sat down at the table. Dr. Cosgrove tried to introduce Halzack to the tribe, but her speech, punctuated with gaps in their half-learned dialect, was cut short by a drawing shoved in her face. It depicted a man and a woman hiking the mountain trail; there was a big red aura drawn around the man. Cosgrove put her hand to her mouth to contain a girlish giggle from the amorous allusion, and handed the picture to Halzack. His guffaw, that sprayed the table with spittle, drew titters of delight from Baba at the end of the table and nods of approval from the tribesmen.

After supper Baba entertained the tribe with a display of clairvoyance: declaring certain facts about their visitors and asking them for confirmation. He described Halzack's wife and children along with the contents of their home in infinite detail. Baba embarrassed Cosgrove with a vulgar description of her boyfriend's physical attributes and a less than innocent depiction of their favorite game, which his mother, Roya, halted before its completion. Turning back to Halzack, he recounted a recent trip to a snow-covered world, which the natives could not readily imagine, and then the boy saw something that excited him. Baba anxiously looked around the table for a scrap of paper, becoming breathlessly excited.

Hutan, the chief, sitting next to the boy, grabbed his arm and questioned him. He now ripped off his shirt and spread it on the table, cupped his hand, as if holding a pen, and waved it at the two scientists. Cosgrove rolled a pen over to the chief. In a frenzy the boy sketched a portrait on the shirt. He held it up for them to see. It was a drawing of Rama. His mother told them that the man was her son's inner teacher. The boy was so overwhelmed with emotion that he raced around the table and jumped in Halzack's lap, throwing his arms around him.

The next morning Baba led the two scientists to his sacred place in the nearby jungle. Two trees had grown together, and their combined trunks had been carved out, leaving a circular temple with two benches and an altar. A charcoal portrait of Rama hung above it. The three of them sat inside, the adults hunched over in the confined space, and talked. Baba was anxious to learn of his teacher. With Cosgrove interpreting, Dr. Halzack narrated as much of the holy man's biography as he could recall. When he attempted to gloss over some unpleasant details, Baba sensed the evasion and insisted on complete honesty. After hearing him tell of Rama's twenty years of incarceration, in nearly total isolation, Baba wept openly but asked him to continue. When Halzack concluded his account, he tried to mollify the boy's distress, telling him that Rama appeared in good spirits, but Baba was so badly shaken that he asked to be left alone. He directed them down the path that led back to the village.

Roya met the scientists at the well and brought them to her hut. She spent the remainder of the morning showing the two outlanders Baba's impressive portfolio of drawings, some of which she could not identify, such as the spaceplane or the face of a world-famous "pop" singer even Halzack recognized. Baba returned shortly before noon and appeared to have recovered. While Roya prepared lunch, Halzack took a stack of photographs out of his valise to show the boy.

"Baba, look through these and see if you 'know' any of the children," Halzack said.

Cosgrove translated, and Baba readily agreed to "sense" them for him. The fifth photograph drew a strong response from the boy. "I see his face many times, in the well, with the others," Baba said and picked up the photo, delighted with it.

"The well?" Cosgrove asked.

"At the bottom of the earth," Baba said, and he added mysteriously, "and in the center of. . .things." Cosgrove tried to question him further, but the boy put up his hand. He looked down at the stack, and Halzack turned over the next photo. It was a pretty blond-headed girl of twelve. Baba made a comment that caused Cosgrove to blush. Roya cleared her throat in the kitchen. "Baba, do not speak of such things, ever!"

"Yes, mama," he said, and turned to Dr. Cosgrove. "I am sorry."

Roya brought a tray of sandwiches over and placed it on the table. "Let my son fill his mouth with more than nasty words," said the woman in her native tongue.

Appearing penitent, Baba picked up a whole sandwich and stuffed it into his mouth until both his cheeks bulged out. Dana Cosgrove glanced at the others, trying to restrain herself, and then laughed out loud. Roya said, shaking her head, "How do you correct such a child?"

Baba stared back at his mother, his face turning ageless. "Who is the child, and who the master?" Roya bowed her head in acknowledgement. Baba smiled broadly, his mood switching again, as he pulled two coins out of his shirt pocket and entertained them with magic tricks. The scientists were surprised by the boy's sudden change.

While Roya was clearing the table, Halzack asked if he could conduct a test on Baba. He explained that, while the boy had food on his stomach, he wanted to give him a harmless liquid dye, which, when absorbed into the blood stream, would allow him to take scans of her son's internal organs and soft tissues.

"The regional has taken x-rays," Roya told Dr. Cosgrove.

"It's not the same. This procedure will allow us to

see his liver and heart and soft-tissue organs, see if anything is. . . different."

Roya was confused. "You believe he is ill?"

"No, Dr. Halzack thinks his organs may have 'differences' that would help us identify others like him."

Roya nodded her head. "Ask the boy, he can say for himself."

They turned to Baba, who had been listening to their conversation. "And what will you do with these others?"

"Help them develop themselves," Halzack said, rather hastily.

Baba stared back at them; his face turned ageless again. Cosgrove translated. "No, you are wrong. We will help you develop yourself." He continued to stare, and they were soon compelled, like Roya earlier, to bow their heads in acknowledgement.

Baba drank the dye, making a wonderful, funny face. When the liquid had settled, Halzack began the test. The boy stood still while a doughnut-shaped scanner, a circular tube two feet in diameter, moved down his body from his head to his upper thighs in a series of quick passes. Cosgrove and Halzack, along with Roya and Hutan, watched the green screen as the data from each pass was processed by the computer to produce an increasingly sharper image of the boy's internal organs. Roya and Hutan were amazed by the technology; the two scientists were astonished by what it revealed.

Turning from the screen and watching the scientists, Roya finally asked, "You see something. . .different?"

"Yes, I'd say," Halzack said, his voice bubbling with excitement. Sitting down at the console, he typed in a series of instructions, and the screen showed several angles of the boy's brain, from the front, side, and top. "Baba's cerebral cortex seems to have an added 'ring' of gray matter, which is hard to tell given the poor resolution, but that's my guess."

"This is good?" Roya asked tentatively.

"It's probably what accounts for his extraordinary abilities."

"Greater intelligence?" Roya asked.

"Yes, but of a different kind," Dr. Cosgrove interjected. "Not just number crunching, but image-making and processing. It could even be where the 'eyes' of his sixth sense lie."

Halzack typed in new instructions, and a picture of the boy's chest and abdominal cavity appeared. He pointed out several unusual growths connected with the circulatory and digestive organs. "These soft-tissue growths, probably indicative of advanced energy processing, could be mistaken for cancer. Don't be alarmed. The resolution doesn't make a fine distinction possible. Offhand I'd say they're new organs." Roya strained to understand the scientist. Halzack added, "There's speculation that eventually our species will feed off. . .energy in the air."

Roya was concerned. "But, you do not know?"

"No, you'd have to consult with an internist or an oncologist, and they'd probably want to do a biopsy."

In alarm Roya turned to Dr. Cosgrove. "Doctor, what do I do?"

"They should definitely be checked."

"I will talk with the regional; we could go to the hospital in Port Moresby."

The scientists showed misgivings. "But, if they're as I suspect. . .," Halzack said.

"Then he would be well?" Roya asked, noting the obvious. The others did not respond. "You are concerned, why?"

Dr. Cosgrove took her hand for reassurance. "If they turn out to be new organs, your son will be identified as a. . .mutant, someone different. It will get back to the government, in Australia, and they'll be alarmed and want to 'study' him, and the two of you will no longer have a life apart from their research hospitals and centers."

Hutan immediately understood the threat. "You go back to your world and do not tell of him."

"I'm afraid it's too late," Dr. Cosgrove said, distressed that in her enthusiasm she may have placed Baba in jeopardy. "I've already shown the videos I took on my last visit."

Hutan was frustrated by this admission, but he tried not to show blame. He turned to Dr. Halzack. "Can you keep him from harm?"

"I've got good government connections in Canada. If I took Baba and his mother back with me, to my University in Toronto, they would be left in my care but subject to the same concerns from the government."

Hutan thought for a moment. "You leave in the morning, and not take any videos, or these. . .pictures," he said, pointing at the console screen. "We will burn the village and move deeper into the jungle."

Halzack shook his head. "If they want him, they will find you and take the boy."

Hutan looked gravely at the two outlanders, his anger finally showing. Baba had come over to listen. He put his hand on Hutan's arm. "I will ask my teacher, and he will know."

Hutan gave a deep sigh of relief. Of course, this was the only solution. He bowed his head, apologizing for his silent accusations, and he walked out of the hut.

"My husband was killed while hunting with Hutan." Roya lowered her voice. "And, he honors the boy's 'medicine.'"

Baba said, "And he likes the dreams I give him."

Dr. Cosgrove, realizing the boy's personal powers were his own best defense, also sighed in relief.

Three days later, in the middle of the night, Roya stuck her head into Dr. Cosgrove's tent to wake her. Finding Halzack in her double sleeping bag did not faze the native woman. She stomped her foot, and the two sat up and wiped their eyes. "Baba had a bad dream. The tribe will meet, and you must come, please." Roya pulled her head back from between the tent flaps and waited outside for them. They slipped out of the sleeping bag and into their khaki pants. Halzack only had his pajama top for a shirt, which he hurriedly buttoned up to Cosgrove's amusement. When they stepped outside, Roya was talking with Hutan, who had apparently gone to Halzack's tent. He motioned for them to follow him, and headed off between the huts swinging his lantern. At the common grounds, most of the tribe had already gathered around the table. Hutan and Roya sat in their customary places, leaving the outlanders to find seats for themselves. Baba spoke, and everybody listened. Dr. Cosgrove translated for Halzack.

"I saw men with dead eyes coming. Two day's walk." He pointed to the scientists. "They saw me in your pictures, but they are different from you. They are bad people, and I will not go with them."

Hutan was disturbed by the boy's dream, and treated it as an actual event. "Do they mean to harm you?"

"They have no souls, and could do anything." Baba reached over and touched Hutan's arm to quiet his distress. "I have asked my teacher, and he says that the man doctor will know what to do." The tribesmen turned and stared at Dr. Halzack, whose disheveled appearance did not inspire their confidence.

Halzack was stunned by the boy's charge and could not immediately reply. The tribe patiently waited in silence until Cosgrove finally elbowed her colleague in the ribs.

"Are they coming from one direction?"

"Yes, the path you walked," Baba said.

Halzack turned to Hutan. "Is there another path out of the jungle?" Hutan pointed to the southwest corner of the village. "Can you get us to a city with an airport?"

"One day south, half-day west."

Halzack thought for a moment. "Are there villages where your people could hide?"

"Yes, there are friendly tribes to the north," Hutan said, "but we cannot hide forever."

"Once the boy's safe, I'll have the paper carry it, and they'll give up the hunt," Halzack said reassuringly. "If you can get the boy and his mother and us to the airport before the. . .bad people arrive, we can fly to Sydney, and take a plane that glides through space, back to Canada."

"They would not be at the airport?"

"No. They have shields against psychic prying, and would never suspect Baba could see them coming."

Hutan gave the doctor a grave look. "If you are wrong, the boy is lost."

Baba again reached over and touched the chief's arm. "I saw us flying among the stars with them."

Hutan bowed his head; the boy's visions were always respected. He gave the orders, and the tribesmen got up from the gathering and began making preparations to leave at first light. The two scientists, unnerved by this sudden change in plans, remained seated at the table with the boy and his mother. Roya was upset at the prospect of leaving her village, this jungle, the only world she knew, for one that filled her with fear. Baba appeared delighted by the coming adventure. He finally broke the silence by asking, "Dr. Zack, could I get such a shirt there?"

Dr. Halzack regarded this impish boy, the mutant child of a new species, whose psyche he could not fathom, whose potential could alter history, and whose life and fate were irrevocably bound to his own. "I believe these pajamas come in children's sizes."

"We must get some for Ma and Dr. Cos. The 'Baba Gang,'" the boy snickered.

The two scientists looked to Roya for an explanation. "At the regional library, he saw videos from your country, gangster films." They were startled. "The buddha child is still a child," Roya reminded them.

"Yes, you're right, of course," Halzack said, wondering if he would be able to separate the two.

The tribe set out at sunrise. Abandoning the village, they left behind their belongings and signs that they were off on a seasonal group hunt. Rifles were cleaned, the oiled clothes hung to dry. Target practice was held under lantern light, the spent cartridges left on the ground. Medicine shields were painted with wild boars, and the preliminary drawings remained nailed to the walls. Food stores were nearly emptied, and the well was boarded up. The tribesmen hiked out along the main trail, to disperse hours later in different directions. Hutan led his party south heading for the Torres Strait.

The path was badly overgrown, forcing them to cut their way through the dense bush. By noon they were already two hours behind their schedule. The tribe camped for lunch, and Hutan went from one grouping to another checking environ hats and goggles that they would need later in the day when the jungle thinned out, allowing more sunlight to filter down to ground level. The pace had already worn down the two out-landers, but neither of them showed the strain, lest they slow down the tribe. Baba brought the scientists a cup of water, but they were already drinking from their thermos caps. Baba smiled and stuck his finger into his cup, then drank from it. A dozen cups of water were suddenly thrust on him. He stuck his finger in each, and the tribesmen guzzled down the holy water. The boy turned around to find two outstretched thermos caps.

The tribe arrived at a village on the edge of the forest at noon the following day. It was a short distance to the airport in Merauke. From here they could ride a taxi into town. It was now time for Baba and Roya to bid farewell to their tribe. Around the camp fire the previous night, the tribesmen had carved a wooden doll nicked once for each of them. They presented the doll to Baba, who was delighted with it. The boy walked down the row of kneeling warriors tapping each between the eyes and giving them their sacred names. Hutan accepted this benediction and gave Baba a father's hug. Roya, their tribal sister, was given a piece of cloth the women had woven.

At the airport Dr. Cosgrove, claiming a medical emergency and using her local government connections, was able to arrange passage for the two natives to the capital in Sydney and from there on to North America. Baba sat in the window seat on the jet flight to the mainland. His initial amazement, at seeing the rapidly passing landscape far below, was soon exceeded by the spaceplane's scramjet engines accelerating the vehicle from Mach 6 to the orbital speed of Mach 25, the G-force pushing their bodies back into their padded seats and then releasing them into the weightlessness of zero gravity. Lifting up off his seat, restrained only by the safety harness, Baba crossed his legs Indian-style and placed his hands together in mock prayer. "Ma, the jumping Buddha." Unnerved by the experience herself, Roya could only manage a strained smile.

While Dr. Cosgrove reassured the boy's mother and Baba stared out the window at the heavenly array of stars, Halzack placed a call to Malcolm Beaton, the university president, at his personal residence in Toronto. It was six in the morning there, and Beaton, an early riser, was sitting at his kitchen table drinking a cup of coffee.

"Henry, is that you?" Beaton asked, seeing his colleague's unshaven face on the vid phone. "Where are you?"

"We had to make a mad dash out of the jungle. I'm on the spaceplane heading home."

"Cannibals?" Beaton asked facetiously, but received only a deadpan stare in return.

Baba leaned over and looked at the vid screen. "No, Baba. I'm talking," Halzack said, and the boy pulled back.

Astounded, Beaton said, "You're bringing the boy home with you?"

"Malcolm, you're friends with the governor. Can you have him meet us at the airport with an escort?"

He stared back blank-faced and finally said, haltingly, "With an escort?" Halzack nodded his head. Beaton replied, "Henry, that's the most extraordinary request."

"Yes, I know, but it's the Crown Jewels."

Beaton looked puzzled, then it dawned on him. "Oh, I see. Grave robbers?"

"Yes, Malcolm. Our friends south of the border."

"It's short notice, but Morgan does have a nose for national treasures."

"Good, then you'll be there?"

Beaton took one last sip of coffee. "With your bloody escort. Just stay put when you land." He added more softly, "Is Dr. Cosgrove all right?"

"She's fine, Malcolm."

"Well, give her my best."

Halzack nodded his head wearily and turned off the phone, collapsing back into his seat. He sat there enjoying the sensation, letting his arms float free above the armrest. It was the first time he had fully relaxed in two days. Dana Cosgrove looked at him. "They'll meet us," he told her. "Everything should be all right."

She reached over and squeezed his elevated hand. "Rama was right. You saved us all."

"Merely to fight another day, I'm afraid," Halzack said, adjusting the straps on his harness.

It was five in the morning when Michael Parker and his commando team arrived at the boy's village in New Guinea. They spread out along the overhanging ridge, and Parker began scanning the village with his infrared night viewer. There were no signs of life, and he assumed the tribesmen were still asleep.

Jerry Cowan, the team's tech expert, crawled over to the lead position. The parabolic dish, sticking up out of his backpack, adjusted to the movement, remaining aligned with its target. "Been listening, but not picking up anything. No whinnies, no snores. Quietest sleepers I've ever heard."

Still scanning the village, Parker said, "Your call."

"Nobody's home."

Parker whispered into his collar mike, "Possible dead target. Move in with caution."

"Should I shut off the photonic modulator?" Cecil Cairns asked.

"Yeah, if the boy hasn't seen us coming, it's too late now."

The six commandos slowly edged their way down the hill, their water-inflated shoes silently squishing down, to where infrared goggles showed a ground clearing. Two hundred yards from the target they fanned out to approach the village from three sides. Arms expert Terence Kapnuk came up on the first hut. He tapped out a message and received a go-ahead reply from Parker, appearing on the inside of his visor. Kapnuk checked the gas silencer on his assault rifle. He slammed open the door, his helmet lamp flashing the inside of the hut with a blinding light. There was nobody visible in the one-room hut. The man kicked over the bed and pulled open the closet, but did not uncover anybody. "Nobody's home," he said into his mike.

"Let's try the other huts," Parker said cautiously. "These guys could be sleeping over."

They found all the huts empty. Parker walked over to the tribal table and plopped down his heavy backpack. "Okay, check'em out. I want some answers."

Lear, their utility man, came over, quickly perked a thermos of black coffee, and laid down a stack of breakfast rations. First light was seeping through the dense overhead foliage as the commandos came back with their reports.

"Okay, what do we have?" Parker asked.

"Food stores are nearly empty, the well's boarded up, no firearms anywhere. Preparations for a hunt evident. I'd say that's where they've gone, or it's what they want us to think," said Mark Owens, his operational analyst.

Parker turned to Kapnuk. "What ya think, Terence?"

Kapnuk walked over to a shooting target nailed to a nearby tree and marked the hits with his ink gun. There were no center hits, and the spread was very wide. He stepped aside so the others could see them. "From the hit pattern, they're either the worst-shooting natives still hunting for game, or they were shooting in low light without infrareds."

"In other words, when we landed two nights ago, somebody 'saw' us, and they took off with the boy, making it look like a group hunt."

Cairns shook his head. "But how could he? The photonic modulator cancels out clairvoyance."

"Well, apparently he has more than second sight."

Jerry Cowan came over and set up the portable vid screen on the table. "As soon as we broke radio silence, I did a satlink and scanned breaking news stories. Catch the headline for the Toronto *News Daily* for today." The bold headline read: SCIENTIST BRINGS HOME NATIVE PRODIGY.

"Well, I'll be damned."

"And, you have a call waiting," Cowan said, making a face. "It's the chief." He switched channels, and Peter Zandar appeared on the screen. He was in his early sixties, impeccably dressed, every hair in place, and perturbed.

"Yeah chief," Parker said.

"Michael, what the hell happened?"

"The boy scoped us out, and Halzack got him out."

"Is he an operative?" Zandar asked. "That was pretty slick."

"Some of these field scientists can think on their feet."

"Michael, that's not good enough. I'll see you when you get back." The screen went blank, and Parker's men let out a collective groan.

"Well, at least he's in our backyard, and the Euros don't have him," Owens said.

"The Canadians are worse. With them we've got rules," Parker replied. He looked around at his ragged men. "Okay, let's set up camp on the ridge, get four hours worth, and call in the copter."

"What about the village? Trash it?" Kapnuk asked.

Parker thought for a moment. "Break a few things, make it look like we threw a fit, but leave the place intact. If this thing's genetic, we might want to come back for more samples."

Chapter Ten

The prison's turbocopter shuttle was hangared at a small heavily guarded annex at the city's international airport. Zita was late for her morning flight, and the two guards traveling with her were annoyed by the long delay. As she stepped inside and took a seat, smiling apologetically, one of the guards closed the door behind her, slamming the bolt-action lock with the heel of his palm. The loud pop sounded like an exploding cannon to her aching head. Adjusting her seat belt, Zita turned to say a word to them but the guards were staring out the side window, commenting on the foggy conditions. The copter lifted vertically 500 hundred feet above the platform; the blast from the turbojets drowned out the thought and left her head jammed back into the headrest for thirty seconds. After the initial thrust, the copter throttled down and continued on its twenty-minute jog across Lake Geneva and then upward into the Swiss Alps and on to Bernia at the top of the world.

It had been three miserable days since her first meeting with Rama. Although the follow-up research proved intriguing, Zita was plagued by severe migraine headaches that medication prescribed by her New York specialist did little to assuage, and by several unsettling dreams about her father. She had thought of cancelling today's interview, but reckoned that Rama's endearing presence would be a tonic to her jagged nerves.

Zita overheard one of the guards telling his companion in Italian that American women have the most gorgeous legs; she immediately reached down and pulled her skirt over her knees. The man stopped in mid-sentence, glancing away in chagrin. He switched to German, but his companion, seeing the woman following the conversation, interrupted him with talk about the World Cup soccer finals. Zita reminded herself to wear a slacks suit for her next flight. She turned and stared out at the mammoth mountains rising upward on all sides. It was disturbing that even at this altitude the trees were dying and the brush brown with hardly any grass. The desolation outside, she thought, had its perfect complement within herself. Then, in the distance, its Tesla Shield shining bright, like a diamond against a granite setting, the prison suddenly came into view. How odd, she thought, that such an awful place could appear to be an oasis in the desert.

The energy field blinked out long enough for the copter to dart through its hazy afterglow, hover above the landing platform and set down. The scalar wave field, which formed the prison's impenetrable psychic barrier, was never turned off. To the eye it appeared as an intense electrostatic field. Unlike her traveling companions, Zita could tell exactly when they passed through the barrier; her headache ceased its dreary pounding instantly.

The platform lowered itself into a small brightly lit hangar, where the copter and its passengers underwent thirty minutes of mostly electronic screening, with laser weapons trained on them the entire time. When she finally arrived at the arboretum, Zita glanced down at her watch to find that she was nearly an hour late. From a distance, she could see Rama sitting in his chair, and she stole over to him and spied on the holy man from behind a potted tree. He looked perfectly peaceful and contented with no signs of impatience. It appeared that, if left undisturbed, he would remain seated in position for eternity and not feel discommoded. She grew restless just watching him. Zita stepped out from behind the tree and came over.

Rama peered at her as if looking from a distance himself. "Ms. Hiller from. . ."

"*World News*," said Zita with a smile. "So you don't forget everything."

"People I remember because of their feeling centers, but do not ask me what you wore last time."

"I won't," Zita said crisply. She seated herself in the wicker chair. "All people? Or do you, or something in you, discriminate between, let's say pleasant and unpleasant people?" Zita turned on her computer notepad.

"Remember," Rama said, smiling playfully, "the mind experiences things based on its past knowledge. I merely take note of their existence. Of course, if you had spit up on me last time, it might have made an indelible impression."

"But you would think no less of me?"

"I might wonder if your toilet training was as poorly handled as your table manners, but would not judge you on either count."

Zita goggled at him. "Don't mean to be a prude, but that's a little racy for a cleric, isn't it?"

"I have since resigned. Now I am just a simple man who makes no claim of holiness or enlightenment. But, in my day, you never met a more self-righteous prig."

"This is getting us nowhere."

"Where is it you wish to go?" Rama asked, smiling sweetly. He watched as the young reporter tried to compose herself. "Impossible," he conceded, "is how my mother often referred to me. Personally, I preferred. . .incorrigible."

"I guess I have some preconceived ideas," Zita conceded with a shrug.

"I never knew one that was not."

"Nor one that didn't wish to 'connect,'" Zita said, scanning through her transcript.

Rama nodded his head. "That is when they become dangerous."

Zita found the reference. "That they drive you."

"All the way to the sanatorium."

"'Where you will find more buddhas than in the parliament,'" Zita said, quoting him.

"Speak of incorrigible," Rama said in mock frustration. "Please, you must, what do you say, 'let sleeping dogs lie.'"

"But you still think buddhas and madmen are alike?"

"Unfortunately, as your quote would indicate, comparison is usually made by neither of the two." Zita laughed. "At the time, I had followed the traditional path that suppresses thinking and calls the resulting emptiness nirvana. That state could be compared to a madman's, whose mind is shattered by an exertion of the unconscious. Both are dead and lifeless. After my changeover, when every cell of my body polarized, thought could no longer gain a hold, it just dropped on its own."

"What—and I'm not being impudent—is the advantage of this state?"

"Freedom of action," Rama said and smiled, "even for those behind bars, or behind scalar fields. You are so conditioned by everything that has gone before, that you cannot help but repeat the mistakes of the past. It is how the mind operates—everything is first compared to a past experience or condition. Mental human cannot create something totally original. They can only act creatively when they put the mind aside, leaving themselves open to inspiration, allowing life to fill in the gaps between the brain cells. And that is because the mind is collective, what one person thinks, the rest hear. Although this feeds our conformity at one level, it also allows for collective change. A great thought, like equal rights, is quickly spread."

"And a great experience?"

"Yes, like washing sweet potatoes before eating them."

"The old hundredth monkey example?" Zita asked. Rama nodded his head. "And a Buddha's illumination?"

Rama gave the reporter a cagey look. "Yes, but not in the same way."

This was an essential distinction both for her article and for her report. When Rama appeared disinclined to elaborate, Zita took another track. "So are you suggesting that people can change the world more effectively by changing their consciousness?"

"I would say so."

"In all situations?"

"I do not lay down rules for people," Rama said. "I would only say, question if you are reacting to past conditioning or not."

"Then you would not condemn a heinous act of violence?"

"I would not make a moral judgment, but I will say that a person in the natural state could only do what is right."

"What's right for them, or right for society?"

"To be in touch with life at such a deep level leads one to act with respect for all living things."

"I don't mean to be rude," Zita said, hesitantly, "but that doesn't answer my question."

"Ah yes, the question. There is always the question," Rama said, mimicking Zita's frown. "What separates us from each other is the mind's constructs. In the natural state, there is no separation. What is in harmony for one is in harmony for all."

"And for the rest of us, you have no advice?"

"'Get you to a nunnery,' to quote Shakespeare," Rama said. "Actually, you could not find a worse place to develop. But, since what happened to me, if this is what you are looking for, was not causal, there is no right path, and for you maybe it is the nunnery."

"Then you don't have any regrets about what you've done?" Zita asked, regretting her phraseology.

"But I've done nothing other than challenge the social mindset. I do regret that many of my followers have suffered from their advocacy of my position."

"But that was their karma?"

"Ms. Hiller, what are we to do with you? Karma, indeed," Rama said sternly. "And we were speaking of mental constructs. Of course, it is all very logical, cause and effect, a neat little scientific formula, which may in fact be an accurate description, I do not know. But it has been used for centuries to tolerate the most inhumane treatment imaginable: literally billions of untouchables left to live in abject poverty, to die by the millions from overexposure, because they are paying off their karma. I tell you, wolves would be kinder. But mental human can justify anything with their wonderful philosophies, even genocide."

"And if we all passed into this. . .state of yours, there would be universal peace and harmony?" Zita asked, with a modicum of sarcasm.

Rama shut his eyes, and when he opened them, they had the glazed look of a man peering into the future. "There would be a lot less mess and noise, that is for sure. What we are talking about is egoless people. So, since they have nothing to protect or anything to add to, you would not have all this mad running about, all this need to accumulate things, to protect them with, what do you call them, 'personal alarms.' I remember visiting London early on. You could not walk half a block without somebody's alarm going off. A most frightful situation. That is not to say these people would be placid little buddhas with smirking faces. Again, to be in touch with life at this level, would stir wonderful passions. In fact I would imagine that feelings would be the dominate motivating force. So you might have something like you see in nature, a stampede of elephants that unfortunately kills off the mouse population of a particular field, and everybody is really sorry about it, but it is a fact of life."

"What about the savagery you find in nature, animals tearing each other apart over a kill?"

"I am sorry, I did not mean to imply that humans in the natural state would be little better than cavemen or hyenas. Animals are nature's children, driven by pure instinct, and kill merely for survival, because they are competing for limited resources, not for sport or over ideologies. Even in our world, or the one I left, there was plenty of food to go around, but millions starved because millions of others would hoard everything they could get their greedy hands on. But people in the natural state would take only what they need and forget about their next meal. I know what you are thinking, people who do that end up either starving or relying on charity, but the freeloader can be as out of touch with the flow of life as the corporate president. And possibly even more so.

"Let me see," Rama said, reaching for an apt metaphor. "I would imagine their lives would be something like an odd ballet: people moving according to spontaneous impulse but somehow meshing together in some kind of synchronous dance. Synchronicity would be the ruling principle of such a life. A person is suddenly hungry; he walks around the corner, and there is somebody with an extra sandwich that he shares with him. This gentleman tells his acquaintance that he wanted to attend the opera that evening but could not get a ticket. The man says he has a friend whose wife is ill and would gladly give him her ticket. This happens to people all the time, but the next step would be organizing your life around it in the natural state."

"But how would anything get done, with everybody going off in a thousand different directions?"

"How does anything get done now? A group of people have a goal, and they collectively work to achieve it. What keeps them together? Getting a pay check or even a salary raise? Pride in accomplishment? Fear of failure and loss of status and income? The thing is, they want something out of it. That is how the ego sustains itself, and when it does not get what it wants, it drops out and looks for something else, without considering the collective interest. Now a thousand of our egoless people might come together to do the exact same project, solely motivated by an inner prompting, a wanting to do it for the joy of doing it, not expecting or wanting anything from it. The motivation of an artist and not that of a stockbroker. You might ask, how do they support themselves? Let us assume they have financial needs. Energy begets energy, all activity creates its own vibration. They would naturally attract from a selfless universe what they are selflessly putting back into it. They all might find a thousand-rupee note in the streets every week."

"And all the indigent do-gooders in history don't count?"

"The key word is *selfless*. Thoughts, by their very nature, even the most sublime, build up your ego. Unless you drop the thinking, you're bound to it."

"So this is what you're advocating for the world, a kind of synchronous social ballet?" Zita asked, utterly bewildered.

"Good lord, no," Rama objected. "I am not advocating anything, least of all an utopian model, which people would turn into another grand obsession. And this would be worse than most, because it would require so much unnatural effort. No, unless this happens naturally, thinking falling off when it is ready, it would cause the worst kind of mental illness."

"So, for these people, everything would just run along smoothly with no problems?"

"No, there is a natural. . .tension in nature, in life, I mean death and decay are part of the scheme of things."

"So how would they solve their problems? Would they have advocacy groups, political parties?"

"Which are based on self-interest, people sponsoring solutions they get something out of," Rama said. He sat in silence a moment, awaiting further inspiration. "A problem is created when something is out of harmony with the whole. Now, in nature, there is the tendency to maintain a balance between forces: dry weather followed by wet, winter followed by summer. These people would be in touch with the whole, be moved by it, as naturally as you are by thought. When a problem arises, too much negative feelings from people in northwest North America, a lot of cheerful people would suddenly decide to move there. They would all have their own individual promptings, a grandmother who needs looking after and what not, but they would be at a deeper level responding to the needs of the whole."

"Okay, if living in this natural state is the next step for us, which I'm not ready to concede, what can we do to help initiate it?"

"Nothing."

"What about telling people what you've experienced?"

"I am talking with you."

"And when people read your descriptions they will be naturally interested and want to know more."

138

"I am willing to talk to people, but I am unwilling to educate them. All I can explain is how I am operating, and if they can get something out of it, that is fine."

"But you're not interested in teaching people?"

"Teach them what? How to be nothing?" And, with a glint of mischief in his eye, Rama added, "I could stand at the podium and say nothing for two hours, and we could practice our nothing exercises. That should be worth a rupee or two."

"It's more than that. There is a philosophic point of view in what you've told me."

"Are you hearing what I am saying? I do not want to present people with another impossible ideal, another philosophy to inflate the thinker in them, and make it all the more harder for them to come around."

"And, what if nobody heard of your unique 'experience,' of this natural state of yours, would that be the end of it?"

"I believe Ramana Maharshi, a twentieth-century yogi, said it best: 'Have you not heard of the saying. . .that if one but thinks a noble, selfless thought even in a cave, it sets up vibrations throughout the world and does what has to be done, what can be done?'"

"Which brings us back to changing yourself and you change the world," Zita said, and Rama nodded his head. She paused for a moment. "You realize this format is just a way of drawing you out without asking a lot of obvious questions."

"Which you are rather good at," Rama said, and, seeing her reaction, added, "The roundabout questioning, I mean."

"Which brings us to the end of our questioning today." Zita turned off her notepad and folded it back over.

"So how are we doing?"

"We're getting there." Zita stood up and slung the strap of her notepad over her shoulder.

Rama escorted her through the arboretum to the waiting guards. "Well, I was not sure. This is the most I have talked with anybody in twenty years, and the first time since my. . ." Rama scratched his head, "Seems awkward to keep calling it my 'entrance.'"

"Frankly, I'm not sure people will understand this experience of yours, or what it says about our possibilities. They're mostly interested in their next meal."

"And you are interested in. . .?"

Zita stopped, as the guard stepped forward to escort her away, and looked up at him. "In objectively telling your story."

"Good," Rama said, and bowed his head in farewell. Zita found herself bowing deeper and more reverently than the form prescribed.

She followed the guard down the hallway. He informed her that Dr. Gustafson was unable to see her today, but that Dr. Cherenkov was waiting for her in his lab. This was a relief. She found Gustafson pedantic and boring, always citing his experimental results but with little real understanding. Dr. Cherenkov, however, had read and thoroughly absorbed the notes of his predecessor, Dr. Renault, and was sympathetic to Rama's spiritual journey and used it as the context for his own continuing study of the man's physical "transformation." She trusted his more heartfelt assessment of Rama's condition over the mere phenomenology of the other researchers. Zita even found a sense of awe in the scientist for his most peculiar subject, one she was beginning to share. But today, she hoped to extend her stay at the prison for her own personal reasons.

Zita had recently discovered that while passing through the scalar field her headache had stopped. She knew the field blocked out exterior thought patterns, but she wondered if there was something in that collective thoughtsphere, as some called it, that was actually causing the headaches. If the media, including her own, was any indication, negative thinking did predominate today. Was she becoming increasingly more sensitive and thus more vulnerable? Whatever the cause, she would soak up the relief and hope that it returned on her subsequent visits.

Chapter Eleven

The meeting was set for the London Museum of Natural History. Jamison had picked the particular exhibit for its symbolic import. Behind a firmaglass wall, there was depicted a progression of ancestral human habitats and their fossil remains. Beginning with Australopithecus afarensis, it was followed by Homo habilis, Homo erectus, Archaic Homo sapiens and finally Modern Homo sapiens. Jamison recognized that the Rama Society, as well as other New Age or millenarian groups, was predicting the birth of a new species of divine children and interpreted Rama's transformation as a harbinger of that coming. He trivialized such speculation as vicarious redemption for those too lazy to save themselves. In his mind, it substituted Christ or Buddha with angelic children, who would redeem humanity and usher in an age of utopian peace, which had been neither earned nor deserved. For Jamison, the next step was for humanity to develop its full psychic potential and expand its mastery over the physical world. His war was with those who would suppress the mental technologies, or in Rama's case make them obsolete in his natural state of being. Jamison had demonstrated the awesome power of the psychic mind, and with the release of his comrades, intended to annihilate those who would keep humanity from claiming its rightful heritage.

Jamison spotted Ananda as he slithered into the galley through a side door. He watched from the second floor balcony while George Bates, an international criminal operator, who was acting as his intermediary, tarried in front of the exhibit awaiting his contact. Bates wore a well-tailored gray suit that amply displayed his muscular build, which was as much of a status symbol as a Rolls Royce but even more intimidating. He saw the Indian but gave no sign of recognition. Ananda walked over to the exhibit and studied it. He was a short, pencil-thin man with dark eyes and a bushy mustache. As head of a militant branch of the Rama Society, he had spread the word in the criminal underground that, if the courts rejected Rama's petition, he was willing to arrange his master's release at any cost. The group had enormous financial resources and had recently succeeded in bribing journalists around the globe to present Rama's case in the public relations' battle being waged over his release. Zita Hiller's series was in response to this campaign. Bates had gotten word of his threat and approached the group with a plan to break Rama out of prison for a price. Ananda agreed to pay a substantial down payment to develop the plan as a contingency.

Ananda moved down the line, stopping beside Bates. They both looked on in silence for a long moment.

"Did you bring the card?" Bates asked.

"Yes, Mr. Bates, as we agreed," Ananda said in heavily accented English. "And you the tape?"

"I don't like this. If you decide to cancel, I'm giving away my inside contact."

"We need assurances that you can do what you say. You can understand that." Ananda handed him the bank card.

"How does this work?"

"When we verify the authenticity of your contact, we'll release the money. All you have to do is present this card at any bank, and the money will be transferred to your account."

"And afterwards, if you cancel, what happens to our man?"

"We would not want the psychics running about again. So I suggest you retire him, or we'll give him away."

"That wasn't part of the deal," Bates said gruffly.

Ananda handed him a second card. "Here is an extra million pounds, held in reserve, to cover that contingency."

"You're paying me not to break the others out?"

"Yes, if we free our master otherwise."

"But, if it's a go, I snatch everybody. I'll need them to pull it off."

"In that case, the money is yours if he is returned unharmed."

Bates nodded his head. "That I can do." He handed Ananda the video disk. "We've got expenses, you understand."

"It should not take more than a few days. We have people everywhere."

"Yeah, tell me," Bates said abruptly, walking away from the man and out the door.

Ananda turned back to view the exhibit. He thought this was certainly an appropriate place to meet with this goon. When Bates had approached them, it was obvious that he was already planning to break the psychics out of the prison. This had alarmed his inner circle. They had wanted to inform the International Police, but Ananda had insisted that they leave this option open. He assumed the elusive leader of the psychics was masterminding the breakout, and he had great faith in the person's evil genius. He did not share Coomaraswamy's faith in their legal appeal; he had read Dr. Renault's journal and knew that knowledgeable people—the world security forces had them—would appreciate the threat the holy man posed to their control. In fact Ananda felt that his master's life was in grave danger. If his release were imminent due to political maneuvering, the security people might kill him, or even fake his death and hide him away at another facility. He could only imagine the type of hideous experimentation they would conduct without Red Cross monitoring. If he had to deal with these devils to assure Rama's safety, he would gladly suffer the humiliation and potential ostracism. His master would be disappointed, but hopefully his presence outside the hideous Tesla scalar field would trigger the desired changes and all would be forgiven.

When Bates returned to his warehouse in East London,

Jamison and his two freaks were waiting for him. "Hey, if I'd known it was a party," he said, as he walked into his office and hung his environ coat on the door hook, "I would've brought doughnuts." He laughed nervously at their deadpan stares.

Jamison, who was seated in the man's swivel desk chair, stuck out his hand. "The card will be enough." Bates took the bank card out of his inside coat pocket and handed it to the "professor."

Jamison ran his thumb over the plastic surface as if he were reading Braille. "Yes, the instructions are clear enough." He now looked the man square in the eyes. "And the other card, George."

Bates was taken aback, but he quickly recovered. "That's my bonus for bringing Rama back alive."

"That's part of the plan, isn't it?"

"I'm not sure, professor. You don't seem to like this guy very much, from what I hear. Personally, I could care less, but for a million pounds. . ."

"George, let's agree we'll return him safely, and split the bonus." Jamison was still distrustful. "And you keep the card."

Bates nodded his head. "So why don't we get on with it?" He stepped over to his wall safe, tapped out the combination, opened it and removed a long plastic tube. He pulled a set of blueprints from the tube and laid them out on the table. "This arrived yesterday. The prison layout."

"Excellent, George. Excellent," Jamison said. "Walk us through it, please."

Bates pointed to the control tower, that had been marked with tape identification. "Once the copter lands, the platform lowers down through the scalar field. Takes about thirty seconds. At ground level, you're inside the field. At this point, there're three more levels of security before we get into the prison proper. We're dead in our tracks unless you can psychically neutralize the system the way you claim. That means guards as well as computers. I've heard a lot of talk, and your remote surveillance was impressive, but I'm putting my ass on the line on your assurance that you can do something I don't even know is possible."

Jamison smiled and turned to his two students. "I believe Mr. Bates is asking for a demonstration, boys." He thought for a moment. "George, how about driving us home?"

Edington laughed, "Yeah, a limo would be great."

"Well, I don't happen to have one handy, guys."

"That's what makes it more challenging," Jamison said. The three of them turned in sync and stared at Bates across the table. Their eyes turned glassy.

Suddenly, Bates felt very tired, struggled to keep his eyes open, and fell asleep. When he woke up two hours later, he was driving a limousine across London on one of the few remaining thoroughfares. He was startled to find himself behind the wheel of the car but his reflexes took over without any loss of control. Jamison was sitting next to him in the front seat, and his two students were in the back seat. He looked over at the professor.

"You're doing just fine, George. Keep driving and I'll explain."

"Electric limos aren't cheap. Tell me I'm not paying for this?"

"No, we charged it to Itel. They use them all the time," Jamison said with a smirk. "Using telepathic hypnosis, which is just as effective over long distance as short, we hypnotized you without the swinging pendulum or the spooky voice. And we did it in five seconds, not five minutes. We had you call the limousine service, where we simultaneously had an order placed in their computer, and which you were able to call up using Itel's code. The limousine was delivered, and you've been driving us home for more than an hour. And, as you can see, you performed your task, which required using your faculties at a high skill level, under complete telepathic control."

"Impressive. How many can you handle at once?"

"The half-dozen in the lower security center. And once we gain access to the computer and deactivate the local fields around the inmates' cells, the place is ours."

"Good," Bates said, encouraged by the success of their test, even if he was the guinea pig. "I've got a line on all the Red Cross doctors."

"Give us their names and we'll start monitoring them."

"Okay, but we need a backup plan. I mean, what if the court doesn't let him out? His next Red Cross physical isn't for another four years." Bates watched Jamison consider this possibility. "You know they ship guards in and out of there on a regular basis."

"No, we've monitored them, and their ID implants make substitution impossible," Jamison said, frowning.

"And all the staff have them?"

"Everybody we've checked. No, it has to be civilians. That's why the Red Cross doctors are perfect."

"I'll work on it," Bates said, "but that just makes Rama's release all the more important."

"I know, George. We're clamping down on everybody."

Bates had turned off the thoroughfare and was making a series of turns. He stopped on a side street in front of a Victorian mansion with an environ canopy over the entrance walkway. "Thanks George, this is home." Bates looked around in bewilderment. "We planted the route in your memory. You shouldn't have any problem finding your way back." The two men opened the rear door and stepped out. "Ring me when he calls, and I'll transfer the money into both accounts. And George," Jamison said nonchalantly, "don't lose the card."

The woman's photograph, developed from Jamison's psychic impression gathered at his interview with the reporter, had been placed in a holder in the center of the square table. On each of the four sides sat a psychic whose hands were held upright on the table, pointing to the right and left and forming a circle within the square that surrounded the physical key. They were able to tap into the woman's etheric or energy body as she slept. This field, composed of virtual photons (prana) was drawn upon by the physical body to energize its matter at the level of the individual atoms. They modulated the virtual photons to carry a disruptive thought pattern that triggered the woman's one-sided migraine headaches, resulting in roiling waves of nausea and hallucinatory auras to her blinking eyes. Once this had taken effect, they used the technique to plant a dream sequence in her unconscious. It was the archetypal stalker, depicted in fairy tales through the ages, the complex that possessed actual stalkers, but who would now chase Zita through a nightmarish world where harm awaited her at every turn.

In Geneva Zita rolled over in her sleep. She could feel the pulsating headache, the discomfort spreading through her body, setting it afire and causing her to sweat profusely. She unconsciously moved away from the dampened sheet to a drier spot, but she could not outrun the force pursuing her without leaving the body itself. Zita dreamt that she was being chased through an ancient black forest with impossibly tall trees by a pack of wild, vicious dogs. At every turn were more bloodthirsty hounds, jumping up and snapping at her, until they had hunted her down. Zita stumbled to the ground, pulling her body into the fetal position, as they swarmed around, their sharp teeth biting into warm flesh, her blood. . .

Zita awakened from her nightmare dripping with sweat. She tossed off her thermal blanket in the cold room. Her head was throbbing, her mouth dry, the sounds and smells of the room amplified tenfold, and her vision was blurred; she could barely see the nightlight in the wall. Zita struggled to sit up in bed, her hands pushing down on the hard bed, but collapsed from the effort and fell back onto the bed and into a light sleep. The dream came swiftly, the unconscious responding to the outside threat, but also showing her the way out of the ongoing attacks. Zita was in a dark jungle of a city, the skyscrapers as high as the forest trees, chased by hideous street urchins down a maze of alleys, one after the other. These bruised-faced kids with their swollen eyes and vicious gap-tooth smiles were vaguely familiar to her. But now they had cornered her in an alley, and then the little monsters closed in, taunting her, grabbing at her with their grimy little hands. . .

At Bernia, high in the Swiss Alps, the white-coated young intern, his inflated sneakers resting on the control board, was sitting back in his chair reading this month's edition of *Scientific World*. The article described in great detail the method used to seed rain clouds in the African deserts. One of the monitors suddenly registered a sudden shift in Rama's waking brain wave pattern. (His conscious range spread from low theta to high beta, mainly attributed to greater whole-brain integration.) The monitor was triggered when his brain waves jumped from one to the other and the burst was sustained for three minutes. The mid-range alphas set off a red light on the control board. It flashed for thirty seconds before the intern noticed it; Wilhelm sat up and noted the change on his computer log. He glanced up at the surveillance monitor and saw the subject still sitting in his window perch and staring out into the dark night at two o'clock in the morning. Abruptly, the intensity of the wave burst doubled and then tripled. The gauge needle on the scalar wave monitor swung past mid-point of its stress range. Wilhelm assumed that Rama's heightened brain wave activity was somehow affecting this critical field barrier. He punched out Dr. Gustafson's phone code on the internet.

In fifteen seconds, Gustafson called back, yawning. "Wilhelm, this better be important."

"Well, Rama just shifted up into alpha, real intense bursts, and it is stressing the scalar field." Wilhelm looked at the field monitor as the needle swung farther to the right. "Doctor, it is breaking down."

There was a moment of silence. "Okay, transfer power from the defensive shield to the psychic scalar field. If anybody yells, tell them I authorized a Code 33. I'll be there in five minutes."

From his window perch, with his eyes closed and his etheric body spread out through the inner plane that infused all life with its energy, Rama had sensed the woman's distress. This had been the worst attack yet, and it drew an unaccustomed response from him: he felt personal concern for her. In his expanded state,

Rama could feel the injury and death that pervaded the web of life at every level, from the microcosmic to the stellar, and he would usually release this life on its transformative journey to its next form. He had healed others, a kind of intercession, but it was not of his own volition. Rama would focus on the person, and the divine energy would or would not act. This energy now reached out and raised the vibratory frequency of the woman's etheric body, allaying the effects of the attack on its physical counterpart. She began to revive, and he was pleased.

Rama followed the etheric trail of energy back to its source and found the distorted ones who were directing the attack. He felt compassion for them, sensing the pain that compelled their misguided efforts. And he appeared before each of them in their mind's eye. Rama wished to reveal, in his own embodied image, their soul selves, that once tapped could heal their awful pain. However, they rebelled against this revelation, unable to love and accept the greater self, and breaking the contact, severed the link with the woman in all the psychics but one. Their leader Jamison, the one most twisted by his childhood pain, maintained contact and escalated his attack.

Rama immediately withdrew to his prison fortress hoping to placate the man, but this retreat did not slake Jamison's thirst for more blood. Stirring deep within Rama, a singular vibration gathered force. The energy was not a stranger to him; it was part and parcel of his embodied humanity. Since his "entrance," Rama had watched thoughts arise within him countless times, only to dissipate. Now his personal concern for the woman allowed them to press further. He heard the voices of his feelings in these thoughts: "don't let her die," "you will never see her again," "you will die here and never know love." The thoughts gathered an incredible momentum, like wild horses kicking at a corral gate, threatening to overwhelm him. But, when the gates were thrown open, Rama let the feelings rush over him but the thoughts, with no ground underfoot, no ego reactions to sustain them, fell off into the silent abyss. Rama had fully released the conflict, and remained sitting in his window perch looking out into the night.

In London, Jamison broke the link connecting him to the woman. He opened his eyes to find the others staring at him. Edington finally spoke up, "How did he know? Is he in direct contact with her?"

"In his state," Jamison said, holding his hands up and nervously tapping his fingertips, "he can apparently spread out into everything, which is pretty amazing."

"Which is different from. . .seeing, clairvoyance?" Edington asked.

"Yes, and did you see how our attack was offset?"

"But, if their scalar field blocks out. . .?"

Jamison shook his head. "It's not thought-generated. He must be able to alter frequency, or shift things to a higher vibration, as he attempted with us. A much more pervasive and insidious talent than ours."

"How do we contend with that?" Edington said in alarm.

"I sensed some intense mental activity in him when I didn't break off. Maybe he can't direct the other response."

"He wanted to protect her, that's obvious," Mick Gordon added. His forehead was beaded with sweat from the mental exertion of the psychic attack. A drop now splattered on the table. The professor stared down at it disdainfully.

"Yes, Mick. That's his weakness. The man cares for her."

"Can we use that to our advantage?"

"With her in tow, and under direct threat, we might be able to control him. Maybe even utilize his special talent," Jamison said.

"You're not thinking of bringing him back with the others?" Edington asked, alarmed by this prospect.

"Don't worry, Bill. We won't put him in your room." Jamison snickered. Mick Gordon smiled, amazing himself and the others.

In Bernia, Dr. Gustafson and his two top assistants

were analyzing the data from Rama's alpha episode earlier in the morning. The man was asleep, his brain waves registering theta rhythms.

"Look, whatever he claims, this is a classic set-up for psychic transference. Gathering energy from deeper parts of the psyche, indicative of theta and delta brain waves, and then projecting from the alpha state," Dr. Gustafson said.

Dr. Emil Jomini shook his head. "But what does this tell us?" He looked around at his colleagues, who did not have a ready reply. "That he still has the desire to affect things, and probably does, through an as-yet-undetectable force—and this was some kind of spontaneous eruption."

"Or it shows the desire that the barrier keeps contained," said Dr. Kesserling, licking his lips and backing the senior doctor's opinion.

"Yes, that is the more likely explanation, Emil," Gustafson said wearily.

"If I am wrong, it is just a bad theory, but if I am right, and these readings come out. . ."

Dr. Gustafson, aware of the political fallout from such a scenario, nodded his head. "Yes, let's make note of it, for the record."

Sensing an advantage, Jomini pressed on. "I would like to test my theory as well."

Gustafson laughed. "But this 'force' is, by your own definition, unmeasurable."

"And that is exactly how they characterized telepathy before the scalar wave connection."

"Then go ahead, devise your tests, and let me get some sleep," Gustafson said, standing up and stretching his arms.

In Geneva, Zita rolled over on the bed, turning her head and laying it in a stream of sunlight that peeped through a parted curtain. She opened her eyes, blinking as she saw the hallucinatory auras and geometric images characteristic of Hemiplegic Migraines. Zita pulled her head back. She felt awful; her head was throbbing, her body sore and achy. Typical post-migraine fallout. But, at least for the moment, she forgot the yelping horror of her nightmares. Lying on her side, propping her head up with an air pillow, she attempted to orient herself to the outer world by fixing her attention on its contours: the brown curtains, the red stripe in the chair pattern, the light reflected off the brass drawer handle. She blinked her eyes again, seeing little halos around the handles. The sunlight shot through another part in the curtain, spraying her face with light. Zita rolled over and gazed into the darkened side of the room. The white wall, softened by shadows, was inviting. And as the dream world beckoned, and she rapidly slipped away through the wall into its depths, Zita saw Rama's image and could feel his sweet presence comforting her. She fell asleep with a smile on her lips.

Chapter Twelve

It was snowing when Rama awakened. He sat up in bed, clear-eyed and present. He wrapped his brown Indian blanket with its golden mandala around him—a gift from Joseph Murdock on his sixtieth birthday—and walked over to the window. The jagged peaks of the mountains were molded into shapely cones by a thin cover of dry, fine snow, that the blustery wind would soon strip bare, only to clothe again in another silky layer. Rama was amused by the suggested image; he thought of Zita and smiled. Such urges no longer bothered him, but it did remind him of his treks to the Himalayans as a young sannyasin, when he was still struggling with them. Here he would receive instruction from "one of those crazy mountain yogis," as he affectionately called Sri Boghan. The holy man lived by himself in a small wood hut at an altitude where it still snowed six months of the year. Rama had fond memories of sitting at his tree-stump table sipping a cup of cocoa, his master's one vice, the snow falling outside the window, as they talked or merely listened in silence to the wind. His master never addressed issues—claiming that they were all the same. For him being in the "divine space" was all that mattered. It was only fitting that forty years and many lives later he should have to await this woman's arrival here in his mountain domain to develop the neglected feeling side of his nature.

She would once again call him, if the inclement weather had not grounded the copter, from his perch to ask her tedious questions, while he engaged her at a deeper level. Given the circumstances of their encounter the previous night, Rama was certain she would fight the elements to come. She must sense, if only at an unconscious level, that the only relief from the vicious attacks would be found here. He had always had a strong feeling nature and had deep heartfelt relationships with people, both men and women. But his imprisonment had cut him off from friends and family—only his mother was allowed to visit and he received only one letter a month—and gradually these ties were weakened. However, in his present state, without the mind's protective barrier, his feelings were even more insistent. Rama sensed that, despite religious tradition—or at least in regard to holy men—that feelings were the path of greater expansion and awareness, and if the universe had placed a woman on that path, he would not deny her.

The woman reporter was waiting for him in the arboretum, dictating into her notepad. Rama stepped over and she stood up to greet him. Her eyes were red and watery and a little puffy. "Ah, Ms. Hiller, you seem to have beaten me here this morning."

"Yes, I arrived early. Did some research in the library. Ironically, this is the only place my migraines let up."

"Libraries give me headaches."

"No, I mean the prison itself."

They sat down and Rama poured himself a cup of tea. "The scalar field screens out the world's mind chatter." Rama took a sip of tea and said, with a peculiar emphasis, "You might be particularly sensitive to its currents."

"Ah yes, the collective mind, what would we do without it."

"Actually," Rama said, smiling broadly, "quite well."

Zita laughed. "Doing our individual pirouettes, if I recall our last conversation."

"Yes, unless the mind is dropped, we cannot do Shiva's dance." Rama cocked his ear in the air and added, "Am I being redundant?"

"Only for emphasis," Zita replied, again taken with the man's charm. "Of course this is contrary to our whole intellectual history, the idea that mind is what distinguishes us from the animal kingdom."

"It is not how we differ, it is how we are alike. It

operates like instinct, blindly, mechanically, but with more choices."

"I could debate this issue, but that's not my purpose," Zita said. She shifted in her chair. "Okay, you've said previously that you're not advocating a movement. But wouldn't your presence in the world, your very existence, be a statement, encouraging people to rally around you?"

"Not unless I open my mouth," Rama said, and in mock exasperation, "Ms. Hiller, what would you have me do? Crawl under a rock?"

"No, of course not. I'm merely exploring the consequences of your release."

Rama asked testily, "Is that what they fear? That I will whip up a new batch of super psychics, some no-mind warriors, and steal a few more shillings?"

The directness of the question startled her, but at least they had finally addressed the main issue. Zita gathered her composure. "I would assume that some, given the current political instability, fear a return to the advocacy conflicts of the past."

"You see? The mind can only cast things in terms of conflict, of conquest and acquisition; it cannot see the value of simply living in the moment, or of allowing others that privilege." Rama stared at her for a long moment. "Of course, I can understand them; it was how I saw the world for most of my previous life." He said, smiling, "I mean the one before prison. See how our histories: religious. . .intellectual, constrain us."

"So, if released, you would just want to be left alone?"

"Yes, I would return to my ashram and help my Uncle Hari tend his goats."

"That is your sole ambition, to be a goat herder?" Zita asked incredulously.

"No, I would not call it an ambition. I like goat's milk, and since my uncle is not very good at it, I will probably have to help him out."

"You wouldn't feel compelled to give talks, to enlighten others, as other buddhas have?"

"Most of whom were mental men to their eye teeth."

"You don't have an obligation to do so?"

"Not that I know of, but I have not read my Buddha contract lately," Rama said. He could see the woman's impatience. "One is compelled by one's history, personal and cultural, to repeat the past. Since I have dropped mine, I feel free to do whatever I choose."

"And if somebody asks you a question, or a series of questions, or moves into your ashram and questions you repeatedly. . ."

"I would move to North America, but only after I have answered some of their questions."

"Not all of them?"

"They only ask one question in many different guises. 'How can I change myself without changing myself.' People do not want transformation. They want to be prettified, spiritualized, homogenized versions of their old selves. If they knew what I went through, just the physical pain alone, they would want to be movie stars instead. Believe me."

"And you tell them as much?"

"I do, or will, when I am free to speak, but that is another problem." Rama closed his eyes for a moment. "By incarcerating me, they have made me into some kind of martyr. People have been idolizing me, projecting their stuff on me for twenty years. No doubt they will be disappointed if, upon my release, I do not fly out of prison on my own power. I will probably have to wear sunglasses and disguises, or really go to North America, to get away from them." Rama paused for a moment. "And I doubt if they will hear what I have to say through all the projection. I can see how those in the guru business get puffed up, think they are the Gods they speak of, and act abominably."

"But not you?"

"No, I'm just an old fart without a history, but I wonder, if I had been elsewhere, having to fight off this mental projection—would what happened to me have happened? Maybe I should recommend the prison to other no-mind candidates."

Zita could feel a little twinge of pain. She closed her eyes and waited for the throbbing pulse that accompanied her migraines, but it did not come. How interesting, she thought, a normal headache.

"I am afraid all this is not helping your headache," Rama said contritely.

"No, actually, it's not a migraine, but something more benign. It could be from drinking tea on an empty stomach."

"And the others?"

"They're genetic. My family's suffered from them for generations."

Rama smiled. "The human race has suffered from them since our ancestors dropped out of trees." Zita smiled. "There is no magic pill for them?" he asked.

"The medication offers some relief, but the side effects are as bad."

"How often do they occur?"

Zita started to reply but thought otherwise. "I appreciate your concern, but my personal problems aren't the issue here."

"Then what is?" Rama asked. Getting no reaction, he added, "Nothing happens by accident, all of life is symbolic, and your headache, benign or otherwise, defines this moment in time as much as anything I have to say."

Zita relented, "Not often, in fact. My doctor thinks it's the change in altitude, but I'm not sure."

"But they disappear, the severe ones, when you step inside the prison?"

"Yes, that is curious," Zita admitted.

"And what is different between the inside and the outside of these walls?"

"As you said, the scalar wave field blocks the world's mental chatter."

"And since mind affects the body, and yours by itself is not causing the headaches, something out there is."

"And nobody in here gets headaches?"

"The guards constantly complain about headaches; something to do with the scalar frequencies. Your relief appears to be unique."

Zita focused on the problem. "Okay, then what's affecting me?"

"It appears you are under attack," Rama said with emphasis, "by some element of the collective mind." Again he waited for her reaction. "It may be directed by somebody with a personal agenda, but they are responding to its dictates."

"Attack!" Zita said with alarm. "That sounds a little anthropomorphic to me."

"No more than archetypes," Rama said with a dismissive shrug of his shoulders. "The collective mind, like the individual mind, has one agenda: survival. And it destroys whatever it cannot absorb. Any movement away from its sanctioned confines is condemned and attacked unmercifully. It brings down the wrath of the gods. Or, in regard to our institutions, religious and political, it dictates the ostracism of the nonconformist. Our mythology is about the yearning to break away, to experience true individuality, and the penalties for doing so."

"What have I done to draw its. . .wrath?" Zita asked in alarm.

"Getting at the truth is not a sanctioned activity."

"And that's what we're doing here. Getting at the truth," Zita said in defiance.

"That is what you are doing here. I was just minding my own business before you came along."

"But I thought you didn't have any great truths to give us?"

"I do not have any words of wisdom, if that is what you mean." Rama paused for a moment. "But, what has happened to me, this passage into the natural state of being, is a great threat to the collective mind. Since it is not mental in nature, it cannot be modified or diluted or homogenized. It is totally outside its influence and its control. It cannot be absorbed. That is why my keepers, under its influence, will go to any length to keep me contained."

"But they've let me interview you."

"Yes, they have," Rama said candidly.

Zita looked into the man's eyes and turned away, feeling guilty. "So, let me get this straight. I'm being attacked because I dare to tell your truth?"

"It is not my words they fear. Most people hearing my story would probably laugh themselves to death. It is my release that frightens them. And you may be of help there."

"I'm confused," Zita said. "If all you can do is tell your story, which you admit is rather unbelievable, how will your release change anything?"

"Finally, at the end of our interview, we come to the real reason for my continued incarceration, long after my political agenda has any relevance."

"Well, I'm listening."

"I would hope so," Rama said, staring back at her. "You have heard of the term *buddhafield?*"

"Yes. It is the formative field—or morphic field, I believe they call it—around a master."

"They say, the religious pundits, that the changes a master makes on his spiritual path, a road map to en-lightenment, are fixed in his field, or aura."

"And anybody coming into direct contact with it gets accelerated."

"Yes, but more than that. This field, this buddhafield, like an archetype, grows stronger with the entrance of each person into this state."

"Do others, not in direct contact, get affected as well?"

Rama nodded his head. "At some point, says the theory, when enough people have entered, be it ten or ten thousand, nobody really knows, it trips the process into the general population."

Zita could almost hear the man's keepers, here and elsewhere, turn up the volume on their listening devices. "And they're afraid that your presence outside the scalar field would, as you say, 'trip the process'?"

"Yes, that is why they wish to extend my stay."

"But the question is, will it?"

Rama laughed. "As if the so-called contagion were spread by a psychic virus." He shook his head. "A force in me, under my control, can heal or transform you? This is just another mental conceit. We are back to cause and effect. Now that is not to say that healings do not take place. They happen all the time. But what is the transmitting agent? Is it the heat in my hands, or my positive thinking, or the 'changes' in my aura?"

"But, surely, if it happens in relationship to the healer or master, even at a distance, there must be a connection," Zita said.

"I remember a yogi master of mine, back in my searching years, whose devotee living some distance away experienced a healing and wrote that he had appeared to her at the moment it occurred. He wrote back and said he was watching a American cowboy movie at the time."

"So you are saying it was self-induced?"

"I am saying that we live within a matrix of energy grids. On a smaller scale, the human body, for example. What we do—eating unenergized food; what we are—worry mongers—affects the whole body, the master matrix. We can treat individual symptoms—take an antacid for your stomachache—but unless you shift the energy matrix of the whole, the body, partial remedies will not cure you for long."

"So it is the whole, the master matrix that really heals," Zita said.

"Does a healthy, radiant liver affect the unhealthy heart, or does it charge the body's energy matrix, that heals by redirecting the flow of energy, the acupuncture model."

"I see. Or the difference between the mystic and the occultist, however benign."

Rama arched an eyebrow. "Yes. Healers may lay on hands, or send energy, but are they affecting the person—or are they shifting the overall matrix, the context within which they both operate?"

"You're saying the transmitting agent is not mental or psychic?"

"It is dimensional. And therefore, it is not contained by their scalar field."

"So your 'entrance' could've already shifted the. . . matrix and tripped others into the natural state?"

"Yes, there is that possibility," Rama said, smiling mischievously.

Zita shook her head, reaching over and turning off her notepad, stopping him before he tightened the noose around his neck any further. "Okay, I think that does it. I certainly have enough material, and I want to thank you for being so patient, and putting up with my awful questions." Zita lowered her eyes and said self-consciously, "I know I must sound like a real heathen."

"Like many others in our secular society, you have confused spirituality with religiosity, and that cannot be further from the truth. I had to learn that myself. This is not about allegiance to any particular dogma or any particular image of God, or to any set rules of moral conduct. This is about reclaiming our true individuality, our true humanhood. It is about stripping away the conformity of the mass mind and with it our emotional conditioning and the automatons it has made of us. If you are a heathen, so am I."

"Thank you, that's very kind of you," Zita said. She closed her notepad and gathered her things. They stood up together. "I certainly hope it works out for you. I must warn you that in my article I will try to present both sides of the story, and it may come out, given editorial changes, sounding more critical than I would like."

"Ms. Hiller, I am sure you will do your best to be fair, and I wish you the best of luck with it. I can imagine how strange all this must sound to you, to your audience, and to those you answer to. I consented to the interview knowing full well what use could be made of it. But, ultimately, your designs, or those of others, including myself, are mere shadow plays. I have done what I could; do what you can do, and let it go."

Rama was allowed to walk her under escort to the holding area for the turbocopters. They stood at the window and looked out at the mountainscape for a long moment. Zita felt the warmth of his presence standing next to her, and as they parted, he held her hand in his with his light, tender handshake, and her body was suffused with energy, her eyes momentarily dazzled by the light.

Part Three
Initiation

The Rama Journal

10 August 39. I was shaving in the bathroom when I shifted out again. Renault looked in on me and found me holding my razor in mid-motion. He watched for a moment, then left. I returned and found myself looking at my shaved face in the mirror. How strange. Who finished it? The other me? I am no longer looking in but inhabiting this other dimension. A mirror image of this one. And yet different. And me switching back and forth so easily. There, with nothing out of place, things move so harmoniously. No struggle. No effort. Like waves of light music. But, in the next moment, I am here. Death and destruction on my doorstep.

27 August 39. The episodes are becoming longer. Sometimes, when I return, things have changed, are different than they were. I must exist in two places at the same time. Earlier the shifts were just short lapses of consciousness. A musical movement of sorts. This is different. More like an interlude. Renault has become alarmed. He thinks I am losing my mind. I reminded him that was impossible. He did not find this funny. He talked to a scientist about dimensional physics, and found that I am not so crazy after all. Since my ills do not follow me there, I am calling it "Healing Universe Number One." I am sure the sick of the world would be glad to shift over.

7 September 39. I am trying to remain conscious during the shifts. Lucid shifting. I am remembering more. But I still have lapses. If I am to operate freely, take advantage of this other state, I must remain conscious. I have had Renault stay close by, and after one shift,

he said he noticed only a brief pause. I looked puzzled for a moment, and then continued talking to him. Otherwise he said he would not have noticed the difference. I wonder if, in time, I will permanently shift over, or remain switching between two dimensions or two dozen dimensions.

12 September 39. I woke up feeling poorly. Why do I go on with it? Renault tried to minister to me, but I was a poor patient today. But, by noon, I had experienced another shift and felt much better. This is almost too much for me. I cannot imagine how Renault withstands the assault to his common reason. What this is showing us is the mutability of the so-called natural laws. If I can shift out of my cancer or diabetes or heart condition, why should the sun come up on time or smog hang in a windless sky?

23 September 39. Renault had the nurse walking me to stretch my leg muscles after my long bed rest. I shifted out while we were walking. When I came back, we were just finishing up. I asked her how I was doing. She said halfway through my legs seemed to limber up, and she could hardly keep up with me. Apparently I received some immediate benefit from my stay in the other world. Maybe there is an exchange between the two. Hopefully, some of its harmony will bleed through. And maybe this world grounds that one, thus allowing its harmony to exist.

5 October 39. For the first time, I was totally conscious during a shift, remembered living in both dimensions at once. My perspective was different. I saw the beauty in the apparent ugliness of this world. It was an illuminating experience, but once I had returned, was again grounded here, I felt less kindly about its deficiencies. How mutable we are, even me with my mind on hold. The world and its specific gravity, if I can call it that, must have an immense impact on our consciousness. There, only a wavelength away, I feel light and clear.

Here, at least for now, it is always a struggle. Maybe my stays there will feed my transformation here. I can only hope.

Chapter Thirteen

When the turbocopter approached Geneva, the cloud
cover was so low and the copter descended so quickly,
stirring up a white whirlwind, that Zita could not make
out the depth of the snowfall. She was surprised when
she stepped off the ladder into a two-foot drift; the
snow, higher than her boot tops, soaked her pants leg.
The drive into town took nearly an hour over icy road-
ways strewn with disabled electric cars—that proved less
reliable in bad weather than their counterparts. At the
inn the bellboy, a red-haired country boy named Eric,
wearing his father's oversized snowboots, watched for
arriving guests through the glass inserts in the double
wood door. When the prison van drove up, he hurried
out. Gripping the railing, his gloves sticking with each
handhold, the boy inched down the steps and opened
the van door. Eric held Zita's arm as she stepped out,
and the two of them, holding onto either railing, helped
each other back up the steps and into the inn.

Bernard, the hotel manager, was leaning against the
front desk, shuffling through the afternoon mail when
Zita walked over. "Ah Ms. Hiller," he said, glancing up.
"I am afraid I have some bad news." He saw her gloomy
expression. "It has not been a good day?"

Zita tried to shrug off her ill humor. "The flight
back was pretty bumpy, and my. . ." She closed her
eyes and winced in pain.

"Your migraines," Bernard asked, "they are not better?" She shook her head. "At least you did not have
to stay in that hideous place overnight," Bernard said
encouragingly. He added more gravely, "I do not understand why they did not bury those things in a hole

ten miles deep. See if they can transmit through that."

"Actually," said Gretchen, the desk clerk, "the earth is a good conductor of scalar waves." She was young, pretty, and cheerful. Zita had been taken with her when they first met earlier in the week.

Bernard snorted. "My daughter the genius."

Gretchen ignored the slight and turned to her guest. "Your messages are on your room recorder."

"And has my bill been totaled?"

Gretchen looked to her father. "Ah yes," Bernard said, "your flight has been cancelled until the storm clears."

"What's the weather forecast?"

"At least two feet of snow," Gretchen answered.

Zita turned to Bernard, and he replied, "They are not prepared anymore. In two days, maybe three."

"I assume. . ."

"As long as you like."

"Well, at least the rooms are nicer here," Zita said, less cheerfully.

"Yes, but I hear they have a nicer warden," Gretchen said, striding away from the desk. Bernard threw his hands up and said in mock despair, "With all that I do for her." He shook his head. "Do not have children, Ms. Hiller. They will be the sorrow of your life."

Zita smiled, the effort causing her another twinge. She headed across the lobby toward the elevator that would lift her to her room and plop her down in a pile of unwelcome messages. She stopped halfway across, leaned over and felt her pants legs. They were almost dry. Zita decided to eat lunch first and nurse her headache before reentering the bleeding wound that was her life these days. She turned and walked back to the restaurant.

The few remaining guests in the hotel were seated at window tables overlooking the freezing lake. Most were sipping tea and watching a snowfall so heavy and steady that it looked like sheets of snow instead of flakes. It was a spectacular winter scene they most likely would not witness again in their lifetimes. (With milder winters, snowfall averages were drastically down worldwide.) Zita sat down at a table, setting her computer in the other chair, and peered out the window. There was nearly a foot of snow on the lawn which extended out to the water's edge. The lake with its warm water was gradually freezing as the temperature fell, forming ice floes that collected the snow. They looked like snowballs floating in a giant punch bowl.

The waiter took Zita's order and quickly served a cup of tea and a bowl of black bean soup and cheese crackers. Her stomach was slowly recovering from the jumpy copter ride, and she did not want to test it any further. A spaceplane flight in her condition would have been disastrous. She wondered if the scramjet acceleration into orbit, or even the brief period of weightlessness would trigger another migraine attack. Zita decided to fly home on a transatlantic jet instead. For now she would be content to remain here holed up in a snowstorm in her lakeside inn nursing her ills. They were innumerable. The list included more than her aches and pains, the discomforts of the flesh, but also comprised all the petty mental grievances, a thousand voices, that clamored to be heard. It was almost too much for her to bear. Zita now noticed that the heavier snowfall had finally obscured the view of the mountains in the background, reducing the world to a hole in a shimmering wall of ice.

Zita's personal world did not seem much larger, with its walls ready to collapse on her. She felt trapped by her assignment. Michael was pressing her to discredit the holy man, but she genuinely liked Rama and did not wish to harm him in any way. From what she had gathered, although her inquiry was incomplete, he did not threaten world security other than by challenging its mindset. This case showed that Michael and the Department were interested in suppressing global ecological change rather than managing it, as they had previously claimed. To champion her cause, she needed to leave their ranks, but extricating herself from this shadowy world would be difficult. And yet she was not ready to exchange it for the even more frightening world Rama opened to her. Zita realized that her brief, tantalizing glimpse into his natural state had clearly shown her own deficiencies. But to enter this world, or one with more of its qualities, she would have to surrender too much, including her fears and insecurities. Rama might be the most liberated prisoner in history, but she was still an inmate of the mind shackled by desires that only bound her further to the world's anxious bedlam. Zita was temporarily immobilized by the circumstances of her life and the weather's mutual assistance.

The wind had picked up, swirling the twisting white sheets of snow, slapping the window and obscuring the lake, and then revealing the mountainscape with the next pass. The waiter stepped over and picked up her empty bowl, scraping the cracker crumbs into it.

"The snow looks like it's picking up," said Zita.

"Yes madame, it is turning into the worst blizzard of the century."

"Oh really, what are they predicting now?"

"The latest estimate is three feet." He looked over at the next table, then back down at her. "Would you like another tea?"

"Well, since I'm stranded here, why not?"

The waiter hurried off and returned with another teapot. She usually liked the European waiter's traditional reserve, but with the prospect of a longer layover, she would have loved the comfort of a more personal exchange. Zita turned back to the harsh storm from the equally inhospitable human world.

In the distance she heard a tree crack like a shot and then a moment later a hollow thud as it hit the snow-softened ground. The wind moaned in retort. Nature so easily displayed its tumultuous upsets, its outbursts of raw indignation. Did it seek to whip the immobile earth into life? Her own body required daily stretching exercises to loosen its predisposed stiffness. In her personal life, Zita knew that only strong emotions seemed to affect behavior. Was stagnation life's preordained condition? Physical matter was so intransigent, moved only by raw power. It trapped in its numbing confines the very spark of life that could free it. Did it court disaster to liberate itself? Was this blizzard in response to a thousand cries for help? As the wind moaned, Zita could hear it echo deep within her. There stirred sullen flesh floating in its liquid grave, warmer than the ice that froze the lake but as fixed and static. It could feel the upset around it and wished for a moment that it knew a way out, a freer mode of being.

The windblown snow and the dimming late afternoon light had wiped out the view and sent most of the guests back to their lunches or on to their rooms and the entertainment opportunities therein. Zita picked up the check and signed it. She had delayed the inevitable long enough. The world and its screeching messages beckoned, and it was her duty to answer. But the storm had stirred up a restless dissatisfaction with the staleness of her life, and she yearned to venture into livelier territory.

In her room, Zita pulled open the thick curtain to reveal the darkened landscape. Although the hotel no longer lit the beach at night, she wanted to hear the driven snow tapping the window. She stepped over to the video unit, beeping with its messages. Zita would return her calls before changing; wearing her business clothes reinforced the battler in her. It buzzed with an incoming message. She clicked on the screen to see Michael's smiling face.

"Oh, you're back," he said with relief. "Been calling all afternoon, thought you got stranded some place."

"No, we flew out before it got really bad," Zita said, but he wanted further explanation. "Took about an hour to get in from the airport, and I've been holed up in the restaurant since."

"Must be quite a scene?"

"Never seen so much snow in my life."

"Well, get used to it," Parker said. Zita frowned in response. He smiled. "Walther Kauss, the Euro security chief, called this morning. He was listening to your conversation when Rama dropped the bomb."

"Which bomb was that?" Zita asked cautiously.

"Seems our boy said, in so many words, that our scalar field's not containing him."

"Yes, he seemed to imply that, but do we have any proof?"

"We've always suspected he's been doing more than viewing the mountains day after day." Parker saw her dubious expression. "No, we haven't turned up more Ramas, but they wouldn't be as forthcoming as him, would they?" When she failed to respond, he added, "But, with a more detailed explanation, we might get something to go on."

"Be kind of obvious sending me back asking that, wouldn't it?"

"Right," Parker agreed. "So, write your article from there, run it next week, and when they dig you out, go back saying your audience wants more."

"Just like that?"

"Why not? From what I hear, he likes your company, and he talks up a storm."

Zita considered the possibility. She would have loved to write a follow-up, but not quite this soon. Yet, given the Supreme Court's hearing on Rama's petition next month, why wait? "Only way I can justify a follow-up is with a more evenhanded approach. Nobody'll want to hear the continual ravings of a mad man."

Parker frowned. "If you make it incriminating enough."

"Don't know if I can do both," Zita insisted.

"Okay," Parker said in exasperation, "then slant it. Can you do that?"

Zita nodded her head contritely. "I'll run it by Bernie, but this is pretty short notice."

"Get him to ask his boss; she'll approve it, trust me."

"Well, we need a certain amount of lead time, or the articles will come and go before people realize it."

"A week's worth of promo tied in with your readership will do it."

"I would guess."

"Good," Parker said. "Send me your rough, and we'll see what we've got."

"No, Michael. You're not my editor. You see it when it hits the street."

Parker scowled at her. "Do it." He now hung up.

Let Michael be petulant with her, Zita thought, as long as he allowed her to write the article the subject deserved. This would not be the muckraking smear Michael had originally wanted, nor would it be a glassy-eyed endorsement of a revered religious figure. The man was charming, and she did not doubt the genuineness of his testimony, only its relevance to the age. Michael and the politicals were worried about Rama's threat to their control, which was nonexistent as far as she could tell. Zita was more concerned about presenting people with a religious panacea. She did not think we could solve today's problems by sitting around meditating all day. But the mind's old solutions were not the answer either. People would need to tap their greater resources, she thought, to overcome fixed mental attitudes, and in that regard, Rama's experience by extreme example might open people to other possibilities.

Zita checked her messages. She deleted two earlier ones from Michael. The last one was from her editor, Bernie. She tapped out his number at *World News*, and Valerie, her group office assistant, answered.

"Zita, are you all right?" Valerie asked with genuine concern. "We heard the sky fell in over there."

"We have two feet already, and it's not letting up."

"Well, I hope it clears fast," Valerie said. "Things have really been piling up."

"Well, don't expect relief any time soon."

"No, don't tell me."

"Patch me through to Bernie," Zita said, and Valerie rolled her eyes.

She transferred the call, putting Zita on hold and spitefully punching up the beach vidsac scene. It was soon replaced by her editor's harried face.

"Hear we'll have to pull you out of there on a sled," Bernie said.

"Thanks, but I'll stay put until spring."

"I'd miss your doting on me."

"The secret of my meteoric rise. Maybe my absence will quell the rumors."

Bernie frowned. "Seriously, when are you getting back?"

"Three, maybe four days," Zita said, and Bernie winced. "Why don't I just finish writing here, and send it along."

"Can you do it by week's end?"

"Nothing else to do, except watch the vid."

"Okay, wouldn't want you to get brain rot."

Zita paused and, with a catch in her voice, said "Look, today, as we were wrapping it up, he opened a whole new can of worms. Might want to go back in, see what he says."

"A follow-up to an as—yet—unwritten series?" Bernie asked in astonishment.

"Well, he's telling me he's not contained by this field of theirs, and that just maybe he's been affecting people all along."

"He said that with them listening?"

"Yes, isn't that something?" Zita said effusively. "I mean, that's what everybody's up in arms about."

Bernie gave her a long, hard look. "Thanks for figuring that out for me," he said sharply. "And you can get back in there that easily?"

"I can give it a try," Zita said, so nonchalantly that it had the opposite effect.

Bernie understood. "Sounds interesting. Let me run it by Cooper. See what she says. Personally, with all the papers chiming in, I don't know if we can do more."

"I'll start the article, make some inquiries. Let me know what you want to do."

"Okay, let me see some pages day after tomorrow," Bernie said.

"You've got it, and I'll see if I can't send some snow your way."

"Just what I need, another weather day around here."

Zita usually began her articles by visualizing the totality of her subject as a ball of light suspended in mid-air.

She would envision herself feeling it and gathering symbolic images, giving her an intuitive grasp of the subject. The image that flashed before her eyes was Rama's silver, doughnut-shaped prison atop its lofty mountain peak, isolated from the outer world by towering walls of granite and from the inner world by its unseen scalar field. Next came a picture of Rama, grey-bearded and disembodied, floating in the center of the doughnut, at the heart of the structure, his emptiness balancing the ferocious mental activity around him. The opening lines of her article formed: "In a prison on a mountain peak high in the Swiss Alps, its desolate setting a reflection of its hard purpose, to contain behind its scalar field the psychic marauders of the '20s and their lethal projections, sits a man. He is a different kind of man, implicated in their crimes and yet removed from them by his alleged transformation, during his incarceration, into a no-mind, natural state of being."

Thus began her article. Using his own words, she narrated Rama's early history, his search—an odd curiosity in this secular age—leading up to his first satori or enlightenment, and on to the middle years of his life and his growing environmental activism. Here she stopped and introduced another history, a different view of those years. She appeared to first present the young sannyasin to offset the effects of the self-absorbed green guru. There was a brief chronicle of the era leading up to the environmental collapse with corroborating stories from contemporaries who reflected on the man's idealism and the nobleness of his cause and also on the utter ruthlessness of his methods, both spiritual: making himself deathly ill with his protracted Gandhiesque fasts, and physical: orchestrating the militaristic strategies of his global strikes, sit-ins, and walkouts.

She next presented the issues and portrayed the events of the environmental conflict of the '20s: the extremists on both sides, their increasingly violent tactics—deplored by Rama, who seemed to be the only sane voice for moderation—and then the devastating psychic attack on the world's banking system by the green psychics. Zita explored the connection between Rama and the marauders. Although investigators could never establish a direct link, one was a devotee of his and others had contributed to his eco-fund. The government claimed that psychics did not need physical contact to conduct a conspiracy, and prosecuted Rama on circumstantial evidence alone. Ironically, it was the ecological collapse shortly thereafter, which Rama and the others had predicted, that, in her opinion, caused the mass hysteria and allowed such a lame defense to succeed. Zita finished this part with a brief summation of his trial, striving to be impartial but clearly presenting the weak case against him.

The next segment of the series began with Rama's reaction to the verdict and the prospect of lifelong incarceration in Bernia. Here she showed a man at the end of his psychological rope: his causes swinging in the wind, his reputation dead and buried, his followers blown to the four quarters. Zita told how, having lost everything, Rama finally gave up his will and entered what he termed "the natural state of being." She briefly described his condition in this state, relying on Dr. Renault's corroborating evidence, and included the more skeptical assessment of the scientists studying him. She quickly sketched the portrayal of a man who had been totally transformed—there was no doubt that something physiological had happened to him—into a state whose potential neither he nor his keepers clearly understood. Zita concluded this segment with Rama telling of his transformation—his famed no-mind state—and then speculating on the prospect of a whole society living in the natural state.

Anticipating a follow-up supplement, she wrote the last part as less a definitive summation than originally planned. She needed to draw a thin line between Rama's natural state as a potential threat: with possible unknown lethal effects, and its benefits: with what it revealed about our mental conditioning. Although she did not suggest emulating him—faithful to Rama's injunction—Zita showed how his entrance into "the natural state," by extreme example, revealed the mind's pervasive influence, often at the expense of feeling and intuition. Rama's exhortation, by inference, was for us to utilize greater parts of ourselves in tackling today's pressing problems.

As Zita was completing the series, the creative process slightly shifted her perspective. Reviewing this man's life, and especially his words, with more subtle implications than she had at first perceived, she had an intuition. Maybe this diehard activist had found a more effective tool for change. If Rama was indeed, as he claimed, affecting the world from the other state, his influence could be more pervasive than they had supposed. In the last ten years, great progress had been made in many areas of previous concern to him. Had he had an impact? And, if it were wide-ranging, what could a thousand Ramas accomplish? Zita was always searching for more effective methods to implement her environmental agenda. If Rama, who once had had similar ambitions, had opened an avenue for effective action, Zita was compelled to explore it. Rama had implied that this state could not be used for one's own limited purposes, whatever the mental ideal, or even because of it. Still she wondered if just stirring this pot could wreak more change than grudgingly slow governmental policies. Maybe the outcome would be the desired one but the route totally unexpected.

Chapter Fourteen

The circular building rose upward for fifty stories, its scientific labs and classrooms, its libraries and offices arranged around the inner space. In the center was an atrium with a square blue-tiled fountain; a metal fish's bloated mouth was shooting a stream of water that arched high in the air and fell like raindrops splashing the pool water. Radiating outward were paths with granite steppingstones twisting between bushes and around trees, each turn having its own wooden bench hidden under the green foliage. On one sat a young boy, his feet tucked up under his thighs, his cupped hands resting on his knees with thumbs and forefingers touching lightly, his eyes closed and his mind stilled. Slowly, pulled like metal filings in the grip of an overwhelming magnetic force, people gathered at the inner windows, scouring the treetops for an opening and a glimpse of the boy whose energy wafted through the building like sweet-smelling flowers. The fragrance quieted some jittery minds and nervous fingers, moving some to cry and a few to close their mental pores.

Dr. Halzack was standing at his window staring up at the others, his eyes moving from floor to floor. Malcolm Beaton, the university president, stood beside him, nervously shifting his weight from one foot to the other.

"Henry, if he keeps this up, we're never going to get any work done," Beaton said half-seriously.

"I would think quite the opposite."

"Really Henry, can't he. . .meditate at his quarters before coming here?"

"He does," Halzack said and added, "I believe he balances the energies wherever he goes."

Beaton arched an eyebrow. But, before conceding defeat, he furiously tried to wave the others away. They either did not notice, their eyes fixed below, or ignored him. Halzack took his colleague's cup and walked over to the coffee maker. "Plain?"

"Yes." Mortified, Beaton shuffled over and plopped down on the suspension sofa, churlishly grabbing the offered coffee cup from his friend. He took a sip, and then leaned back into the soft cushions that gently wrapped around him. "Are the results in?"

Halzack slid the blue folder across the coffee table to the administrator, who thumbed through the report, glancing at the graphs but not actually reading a line of it. Beaton glanced up impatiently.

"Sorry," Halzack said, seeing the man's baffled look, "but it's pretty mind-boggling." When he first picked up the report from Genetics, he had been absolutely amazed by its results. Seeing them neatly arranged in colored columns and spelled out in print shocked him further. "Appears that the boy's entire genetic structure is affected, and not just the cells in the mutated organs."

"And his mother doesn't show any signs of it?"

"No. She's perfectly normal, and I'm sure the father was the same."

"How can that be?"

"Well, it seems to be an ongoing process, that starts with minor mutations and spreads throughout the body. Some of the children I first detected show considerable change, although Baba is the most affected."

"So we're talking about a new species, right?"

"Two dozen a species does not make, Malcolm. But it's enough for a theory."

"And how many to prove it?"

"I really don't know. Maybe a thousand worldwide."

Malcolm Beaton did understand the implications of this conclusion. "Well, maybe we should go public to find the others."

"With what?" Halzack said in alarm. "Wild conjecture?"

Beaton held up the blue folder. "This and the other reports are enough to present your theory."

"Yeah, and create the biggest witch hunt in history."

"No, I don't think people would react that way," Beaton said with the reasonableness of an accountant.

"Personally, I don't want to take the chance."

"Well, Henry, the university's been footing the bill for your research, and the board wants some payback."

"I'll pull my research out of here, if they pressure me."

Beaton could see the hard glint in the scientist's eyes, and he knew enough to back off. "Okay, I'll tell them you need more time, but you're going to have to give them something soon."

"Look, when I've got the other reports, I'll make a presentation, update them on our progress."

"Headlines is what they want, not progress reports." Beaton stood up and said warmly, "Has Dr. Cosgrove arrived yet?"

"She's coming in this afternoon."

"Oh, good. Why don't you bring her to dinner at my house."

"Thanks, but we'll be working late tonight. She hasn't seen the report."

"Okay," Beaton said with the patience of a shark, "then bring her to my party Saturday. Some board members will be there, and rubbing shoulders with them can't hurt your funding."

Dr. Halzack nodded his head. "We'll be there," and before Beaton could ask, "but without the boy; he doesn't do parlor tricks."

"But I heard he does wonderful parlor tricks," Beaton said in disappointment. He walked to the door. "Saturday at eight." He opened it and left.

A moment later, Dana Cosgrove slipped out of Halzack's private bathroom. "That was close."

"Yeah," Halzack said in disgust. "Can't believe I've got to hide my female colleagues from Malcolm."

"It's just me, I'm sure."

"Absolutely doesn't look at another woman," he said, sarcastically.

Dana stepped over to the window. "They're still looking for him."

"Looking doesn't bother me; wanting a piece of him does."

"In light of your conversation, not to mention our jaunt out of the jungle, I wonder if actually finding the others is wise."

Dr. Halzack thought for a moment. "I've been afraid to ask myself that."

Dana lightly squeezed her colleague's arm. "Let's do that now." She stepped back, sitting on the edge of the desk. "I know we're scientists on the trail of a discovery, but is that all that's at stake here?"

"No, if this is a new species, I'd rather see them make it than see us collecting Nobels for discovering them."

"Agreed," Dana said adamantly.

"But can they survive if left alone? I mean, can they go undetected and surface later, when they can better defend themselves?"

Dana considered this scenario and shook her head. "No, we monitor our children too closely. They'd never escape the net."

"Not to mention our friends in security."

"What are our choices?" Dana asked. "Eventually they'll be discovered and either identified as freaks and studied, or put away if the security people get them—more likely given Baba's exposure. So do we make it known and press for governmental protection?"

While they were considering their alternatives, the boy walked into the office and came up to them. He was closely followed by Roya and their bodyguard, Sabu. Baba stood on his tiptoes and looked out the window. "What are they doing?"

"They feel your presence, and are looking for you below," Cosgrove said softly, and then translated for Dr. Halzack.

"Why do they not seek me in their hearts?"

The others had no response to this question. Roya said, "They will, my son, when their hearts are opened."

Baba nodded his head and looked up at Dr. Halzack. "Do not worry, Sabu will fight them off."

"Yes, master, until I am without breath," said the East Indian, bowing his head.

Baba smiled at the two scientists. "There is another way. You tame a tiger by changing his stripes."

The curtain had been pulled across the window in Halzack's office, the lights turned off, and a single candle lit. Baba sat cross-legged on the suspension sofa, meditating. A voice recorder stood upright on the coffee table. Halzack and Cosgrove were sitting across from the boy, waiting in anticipation.

"I am in the well," Baba announced, and Dr. Cosgrove translated.

"Are the walls of fire?" Halzack asked.

"No walls, and it stretches forever."

Halzack looked at Cosgrove. "Can't be the molten core."

"It is of your world, and beyond," Baba added. His expression suddenly changed. "My friends have come."

"How many, Baba?" Halzack asked.

"Ten times ten," replied the boy.

"And everybody has come?"

"Yes, doctor." Dr. Halzack was noticeably disappointed by the low number. Baba laughed. "Why more?"

"No, Baba," Dr. Cosgrove said hurriedly. "That's fine." She looked down at her notes, "Tell them it's important not to let anybody know about them. Not to show off their abilities. And, if they become ill, they must try to heal themselves. No doctors, or hospitals."

"This is to protect us from the people with no souls?"

"Yes, Baba. It's important they don't discover you," Halzack said firmly.

The boy was silent while he worked at the inner level. "Do not fear for us," Baba finally said; his voice had a different timbre, the group oversoul. "We are few, but there are many seeking the change."

"And they would replace you?" Halzack asked.

"Yes, in time, but much could be lost."

"So it is critical that this take hold?"

"It is a choice you must make, not us."

"And who are you?" Cosgrove asked, startling the others with her audacity.

"We are who you are in your innermost self," Baba said, blinking his eyes.

Halzack was poised to ask another question but waited.

"That is all we wish to say," the boy said, and added, smiling sweetly, "but I will talk to you."

"Are you thinking as a group?" Halzack asked.

"Not in the way you think," Baba said, and seeing the pun, "and I am not making a joke."

Cosgrove added, "You are one and many at the same time."

"Yes, you understand."

"Will the others take the precautions?" Halzack asked tentatively.

"We do not fear physical death, as you do, but we do wish this in. . .'God's speed.'"

Halzack sighed in relief. "We were asking ourselves what we can do to help."

"Follow your heart, Dr. Zack, and you will do right."

The two scientists glanced at each other, and Dr. Cosgrove turned back to Baba. "You must be hungry?"

"Does a monkey eat bananas?" said the boy, his eyes lighting up.

Roya looked cross at her son. "And this monkey eats too much. . .bad food?"

"Okay, only good food today." Dana looked to Dr. Halzack to join them.

"No, I've got work to do." He said to Baba, "And light on the desserts, young man."

The boy smiled. "Dr. Zack reads minds and makes jokes. He is doing fine."

After they left, Halzack sat down at his desk to complete the paperwork that had accumulated during his expedition to Australia and in the aftermath of his return. As head of the department of anthropology, he assigned routine administrative tasks to his assistants, but matters like hiring staff did require his attention. A teaching professorship had opened, and the applications were backed up on his computer. But, after his morning session with Baba, and its disquieting residual effect, Halzack glared at the blue screen and turned off the monitor. In the hallway, he headed for the elevator that lifted him up to the doomed observation deck on the roof of the building.

There were several people sitting on the wooden benches eating lunch or standing at the observation ports looking out over Lake Ontario, what little could be seen through the smog. Only a few people, amazingly enough to him, sat staring at the Japanese rock garden that rimmed the interior of the circular platform. In minutes the Zen effect of the layout had placed him in a meditative state. Soon the image of Baba and the others—in the boundless dimensional space—arose before his inner eyes and drew him into a contemplation on their fate. It was obvious from his talk with Dana Cosgrove that they could neither ignore nor protect these fledglings. But, as the image persisted, Halzack wondered if there were not another option. What if they could accelerate the process, bring it to fruition before its suppressors could act?

Speciation was the fundamental process of evolution that had produced the great variety of plant and animal life since the first one-celled creatures. From the first appearance of these children, with their slightly differentiated organs, indicating the usual adaptation scheme, Halzack had assumed it was a speciation process. However, it appeared that the changed organs were for processing a finer energy source than solid matter. Scientific thought had speculated—though few took the subject seriously—that such a species would have organs that processed the higher levels of environmental toxins, following the classic model: environmental change (toxins) leading to behavioral shift (supply processing) to anatomical change (new organs). But these mutated organs appeared incidental to another evolutionary aim. This dimensional space, where the children gathered, intrigued him. Could they be adapting to life in an inner world instead of our polluted outer world?

Halzack thought about Rama's state, and how Dr.

Glazunov claimed that his physiological changes, initiated by new genetic functioning, was the result of consciousness acting as an adaptive force. This would explain not only the genetic anomalies within one generation but their progressive nature. It appeared that some inborn consciousness in these children, not environmental conditions, was precipitating the emergence of this new species. The process had apparently begun with Rama's breakthrough. Perhaps it opened a doorway in consciousness for others to step through. If, as was now accepted, life or morphic fields that surround living organisms contained the equivalent of an etheric genetic code that directed the development of the organism, then a change in the collective field, the programming for Homo sapiens, could result in emergence of a new species, or a drastic change in the existing one. To accelerate the process, they needed to affect this collective field. If, as he surmised, Rama had precipitated the first breakthrough, could he now quicken the pace? It would be imperative to contact Rama and discuss this matter with him. There were children he could examine in Europe, and while there he could request another visit to Bernia.

It had been a particularly frigid winter in northern Norway. Snows were three feet above the average for the last twenty-five years. However, the inhabitants of Tromso, located within the Arctic Circle, expected an early spring and an extended growing season. Dr. Halzack had traveled to a small village twenty miles outside of town where the Lapp population of the area resided. Christina, a well-known child psychic, had helped support her family with the money taken in from her readings. (Halzack found that many of these children were from aboriginal populations like Baba or the Native North Americans he had identified.) Christina's psi scores, as well as scans of her internal organs, confirmed that she was one of the new species' children. Halzack had a private session with the young girl and discovered, to his immense delight, that she was as aware as Baba. She understood the importance of secrecy and restricted her readings and healings to the common psychic variety. He congratulated her anxious parents on Christina's remarkable gifts and hurried off, leaving their readied questions hanging in the frigid northern air.

At his hotel in Tromso, there was a message for him from Dr. DeWitt, the prison warden at Bernia, denying his request for a visit. He cited a number of reasons, which were obvious excuses. Halzack surmised that the security forces, knowing he had absconded with Baba, must know the connection between Rama and the children, and were denying the scientist access for that reason. Halzack considered how to circumvent them and gain access, but he could not think of a plan. Dejected, he packed his bags and reserved a seat on the evening train to Oslo. It was six hours by rail (they did not run mag levs this far north), and he refused to fly the smaller commercial jets. At the station, he picked up Saturday's edition of *World News*. The lead article was the first installment of Zita's series on Rama. Halzack checked his baggage, found his seat in first class, and began reading it.

He found Rama's early spiritual struggle oddly relevant, in light of his recent discovery, but once the article moved on to the man's ecological agenda, Halzack became fascinated with his story. He recollected the 2020s well. In college at the time, he was himself an armchair activist—too absorbed in his studies to be more than a petition signer. Reviewing the man's life, finding himself inspired by his causes and outraged by the injustice of his trial, Halzack felt a strange empathy for Rama. But he sensed that his reaction could be attributed as much to the compassionate tone of the article as to the holy man's plight. Halzack put the paper down and looked out the window just as the train passed through a small station with its lighted platform. In a moment, he was staring at the darkened landscape. If he could not gain entry to Bernia, he thought, maybe this reporter, Zita Hiller, could act as his go-between. She was evidently concerned about the man and his causes and would surely be interested in hearing of Rama's latest brand of activism.

Halzack did not know if he could trust her, but with no other option, he would have to risk it. Using the train's satlink, he contacted *World News* in New York, and, through a science writer who had once written a profile on him, Halzack obtained the name of the hotel where Hiller was staying in Geneva. In Oslo the next morning, he phoned the woman in Switzerland. Mentioning his contact's name got him through to the reporter, and piquing her interest with a reference to Rama's undisclosed activities got him a meeting at her hotel later in the day. Halzack booked his flight, making reservations at her hotel. In the lobby, on the way to breakfast, he picked up the morning edition of *World News*, and devoured, along with his toast and hummus, the next part of Hiller's series.

Though it had been over two weeks since the snowstorm of the century blasted Geneva, the city was still digging out from under the remaining snow. But the roads were cleared of the stalled vehicles, and Dr. Halzack's ride in from the airport was slow but uneventful. He checked into the hotel and phoned Ms. Hiller. She agreed to meet in the restaurant for tea at four o'clock. Halzack was sitting at a window table when Zita came up and introduced herself.

"Ah, Ms. Hiller, I was just reading your article again. A superb job," Dr. Halzack said, as they sat down.

"He's a very colorful character," Zita replied, in gracious acknowledgement.

"But, given the circumstances, a delicate subject, nonetheless."

"Yes, there are those who find it too evenhanded."

The waiter stepped over to the table, and they ordered. The brief interlude allowed Halzack to study the woman. Her eyes were bright and intelligent, but her face was etched with troubled concern. She turned back to him.

"Had my newspaper send me your profile, and I'm wondering what your connection to Rama could possibly be," Zita said frankly.

"Before I proceed," Halzack said firmly, "I need to know whom I am talking with. A newspaper, or a human being?" He paused and stared at her, and she bristled at the insinuation. "Can I then assume you can keep a secret?"

"If you have doubts, why confide in me?" Zita retorted.

"Because I need you to get to Rama."

At least the man was forthright, she thought. "Well, if it will compromise him, your secret's safe with me, and if it's hogwash, as my father would say, I wouldn't print it anyway."

Halzack nodded his head. "Two years ago I discovered two children with the same widespread genetic anomalies. I have since uncovered. . .more, and I believe there're hundreds on the planet." He paused for a moment. "They represent, I believe, the emergence of a new species of humans, like us in many ways, but also very different."

"Shouldn't you be speaking to our science editor?"

Halzack shook his head. "Six months ago I ventured to Bernia, where I reviewed the research data on Rama, and did a comparison between unknown hormones found in these children and those discovered in Rama. They matched."

This revelation grabbed Zita's attention. "And the other. . .changes?"

"Not yet. Nor have they entered 'the natural state,' as he describes it. It could be that it'll happen in time, or another round of mutations may be needed to birth some future generation in that state."

"Is Rama aware of them?"

Halzack paused. "They say he comes to them in their inner world."

So he is affecting, Zita thought, without laying on the hands. How interesting. "And what do you want from him?" she asked.

"I feel they're in jeopardy, and I want to know how to speed up the process."

"Well, you know they listen in on my interviews."

"There must be a way."

"I don't see how, but if it should develop, I'll ask," Zita said, figuring she could not deny the impossible.

Chapter Fifteen

Zita was four years old, her black hair pulled back tight in a bun, with holes in the knees of her pants, the white skin punching through as she ran down the narrow path in a forest with impossibly tall trees, their green foliage the sky, chasing Jane and Mark until she found them climbing a tree, the rungs of its rickety wooden ladder tottering with each foothold; and as they slowly ascended, Zita grabbed hold of the bottom rung and climbed upward, kicking them off with each vault, and soon the ground below was a distant speck and her friends had disappeared into the green sky above, and she came to the tree's highest branches, woven together with other trees to form a thick green mat, and discovered that this sky was actually the ground of yet another world, and she poked her hands and head into the black dense sod and became stuck in this telluric border between two worlds, and Zita began to suffocate, the earth filling her nostrils and mouth and stifling the air's passage until she expired, her body drawn up into its tomb, but then animated by another force, Zita arose and walked through this dark world, its matter passing through her unimpeded, and she saw a shaft of bright light, came to it and pulled herself up into the world above, which was a park with shiny glass buildings, and the trees and grass and animals had lights inside them, and she found Jane and Mark, who looked odd but felt good, and they had lights too, were taller and much thinner with different eyes, and together they ran through the park, and the buildings swayed in the breeze and felt alive, and they went into one and rode an elevator to the top, and from there she could see the whole world, and it was green with trees and blue with water, and all the plants and animals were clear, and she could almost see through them, and she knew that this was her home, the one she had been looking for all her life, and she was happy. . .

It was not until later, as the turbocopter flitted between the canyons of this snow-covered world, her headache blurring her sight, and Zita glimpsed the glass prison, looming above a distant peak before the copter banked out of sight, that she recalled her dream about the new inwardly lit world and the children with the strange eyes. While suffering the endless indignities of their security check, Zita mused about her dream and sensed that these were Halzack's children and that she was attempting to break through to their private world and to an understanding of them. The key, it appeared, was hidden in Rama's glass prison. She now faced the problem of questioning him about the children without the world listening.

They were to meet again in the doomed arboretum. As she drew near the table with the wicker chairs, Zita spotted the tea service for two with one cup half-filled, but Rama was nowhere in sight. Finally, from beyond a row of Rhododendrons, she heard him call out, "Ms. Hiller, come see my world from here. The view is spectacular with the snow."

Zita stepped around the shrubs and over to the walled window. Rama stood there staring at the mountainscape. He took her hand between his and gently squeezed it. The man was evidently excited, and she dared not speculate as to its source. He released her to the viewing. Zita peered out through the moist haze of the melting snow across a chain of alps rising like a staircase into the mist, each more snowy than the next. Suddenly, a pain shot up the back of her neck and exploded in her head. She reached with her fingertips to touch her temples, and then heard a voice speaking inside her head.

- *Ms. Hiller, excuse me for barging in, but you wanted to speak in private.*

"Yes, but what. . .," she said aloud before catching herself.

- *Just think the thought, and I will hear you.*

- *Dr. Halzack came to me about the children. He needs to know more, if he's to help.*

- *Very well.*

"Breathtaking, is it not?" Rama said with a sly smile.

"Yes, it's. . .it is," Zita replied, stumbling over her words.

"Perhaps, we should sit and begin." Rama took the young woman's arm and led her back to their seats.

After Zita had set up her computer notepad, poured herself a cup of tea, she anxiously glanced at the holy man waiting for him to start.

Leaning forward in his chair, Rama said with an edge to his voice, "I must say, I was surprised by your request. . .," and added "although pleasantly so."

"You read the article?"

"Yes, my keepers made an exception in this case," he said. Rama paused, taking a breath. "You did let me talk too much, and I sounded like the world's biggest fool." Zita shook her head. "But I thought you presented both sides of my case fairly, and I was impressed with how you treated my 'entrance.' I would have thought it too religious a subject for your readers."

"Well, it's what brings me back. Since we ran the first installment, we've gotten a ton of mail. Everybody seems fascinated by your natural state. I'm sure it sounds like a super headache cure for your average pill-popper, but at least they're interested."

"And you want to do an article on me living in the natural state?" Rama asked incredulously.

"Look, despite the hardships of your imprisonment, you're neither bitter nor cynical, and you sound a lot happier than they are."

"Well, that's simple enough, and I could tell you that rather quickly."

"Okay, I'm listening."

"The Buddha tells us that unhappiness, if you will, is caused by desire, fueled by the mind's restlessness. Eliminate the desire by quieting the mind, or in my case dropping it, and you have the secret of my success."

"I'm sure it's more complicated than that," Zita said. She suffered the splitting pain in her head and felt the shift again.

- *When actually you wanted to talk about the children.*

Zita watched herself talking with Rama sitting in their chairs, while also participating in an interior dialogue.

- *And we can go on like this, having two conversations?*
- *Yes. To understand these children, you must understand that we live in many worlds at once. Are in fact, what you would call, multi-dimensional.*
- *You mean the physical world intersected by spiritual dimensions?*
- *All of us have aspects of ourselves, like our mind, in one of these other dimensions, which vibrate at different wavelengths, like notes on a musical scale.*
- *So they can intersect without being visible to each other,* Zita thought.
- *Yes, and these children, as physical as you and me, have larger parts of themselves in the spiritual dimensions around us. As their numbers increase, they will raise the frequency of our physical world and allow it to merge with other dimensions.*
- *And your entrance into the natural state began the merge?*
- *So others more naturally attuned to the higher vibration could come in.*
- *And this merge, what you do that brings in the children, is ongoing?*
- *Yes, but soon, as their numbers increase, the shift will occur.*
- *Dr. Halzack would ask what can be done to quicken the pace.*
- *Raise your own vibration, and you feed the process.*
- *I don't know if I understand all of this, but I'll pass it on to him.*
- *Allow yourself and the understanding will come.*

Zita watched herself from this other dimension sitting in the arboretum with Rama listening to his long explanation and feeling perfectly comfortable situated in both worlds at once.

". . .and besides the animal kingdom, the other little worlds that intersect our own, like the plant kingdom, that of insects, even bacteria, all operate outside the mental realm. They all get along very well without it. So, is it so difficult to imagine ourselves, or children born less adapted to our world, moving beyond its confines?" Rama asked.

"Okay," Zita found herself responding, without will or intention, as she continued to watch her conversation with Rama.

- *Welcome to the world of the Watcher*, Rama thought.

The other self paused and looked quizzically at the holy man, sensing the parallel contact.

Downtown sections of old Geneva had been razed after the environmental collapse. A two-hundred-foot-high environ roof had been constructed under which the town's schools, municipal and office buildings, shopping and entertainment complexes were built. The enclosure was in actuality a three-mile-wide mall with natural light streaming through filtered sky lights, and Zita strolled down cobblestone boulevards under potted trees and felt like she were outdoors on a cool, overcast day. At the next real-grass park and children's playground, she sat on a bench under a tree and watched two ten-year-olds playing on the swings and slides.

Zita had not yet recovered from her last interview with Rama. She sought out the company of others, unusual for her, especially in a foreign country. She found herself walking the mall daily. If she had not been panicked by the revelations and experiences of that encounter, needing time to sort out their implications, Zita would have been conducting another interview with the holy man this morning. Immobilized, out of sync with the flow of her life, she discovered that part of herself was still fixed in that interior world, as she now acknowledged, of her greater self. As she flew out of the safe confines of the scalar field, the split perspective had continued and her headache did not return. It was only hours later, in a dispute with a waiter, that she became reabsorbed and felt the splitting pain. When, in her room, Zita was able to will herself back into that objective space and the headache let up again, she was more panicked than if the pain had continued.

Zita had called her therapist, Julia, in New York for a phone consultation. Julia assured Zita that she was not losing her mind, and that she had experienced similar episodes in her spiritual journey.

"I told you about the time I was working with Raoul, the shaman in New Mexico, and he split me into a dozen selves, each with its own issues to resolve."

"Yeah, I remember, I almost dropped you after that, it scared me so much."

"Zita, this is basic psych these days. You must've taken courses that covered this material in college. The multi-personality phenomena of the twentieth century, where they discovered how cancer, diabetic, and even heart patients were perfectly healthy when another ego-self surfaced, revamped the single-self theory of personality, as Zimmerman sarcastically called it, a long time ago. Today the normal psyche is considered multi-faceted until it integrates itself."

"But, I didn't feel this. . .self, had issues. It seemed. . . whole."

"The Watcher, as he calls it, might actually be Jung's Self, the totality of the psyche, or some would say, more religious types, that it is the Soul."

Zita told Julia about her incestuous dreams. The therapist, who had previously dealt with her client's memories in this area, reminded her of Zimmerman's work with incest victims, or in her case, disproportionate guilt. "He shows that our perceiving self, especially a child's, sheds itself like a snake skin as it grows and is replaced by a succession of such selves. In trauma cases, they split off and become self-contained, able to assert themselves later. Normally, the perceivers live on, like old scar tissue that new skin re-forms—and usually as innocuous."

Julie extended their session and conducted several more in the days that followed, helping Zita access that child self that had sustained the injury, treating it as a living being. She had her client, who had tapped into the ten-year-old little girl self abandoned by her father, feel the child's feelings, the awful guilt over Zita's innocent provocation, feeling lost and unsupported. She began to heal her inner child. The incestuous dreams slowly diminished, as did her headaches with each Watcher episode lengthening the time between, until they finally ceased.

Zita realized that it was this process of healing, extended by her own self-examination and self-nurturing, that had brought her to this park bench on each of the last three days. Watching the children playing on the seesaws, swings and slides, she felt the freedom of their reckless abandonment, the exhilarating thrill of their joy. Seeing them scamper about on the playsets reminded her of her recent dream. Climbing the ladder into the upper kingdom. Was this an invitation to the lost world of her childhood, a reclaiming of her free spirit? Zita stood up and walked down the hill to the playground. A little girl, whose mother had grown tired of pushing her swing, was begging to be pushed higher.

"May I?" Zita asked the woman in German.

The mother gave the young woman a quick glance. "Not too high," she said.

Zita gave the swing a firm push. "And what is your name?"

"Heidi," said the little girl.

"That's a pretty name." The swing flew back into her face and she gave it another push.

"Do you have a little girl to swing?" asked Heidi several passes later.

"No. I've not married yet, but I may some day."

"You should. You are a good pusher."

Heidi jumped off the swing on the next low pass and hurried over to the carousel, calling to Zita. "We can ride this together."

Zita walked over, grabbed hold of the upright bar and pushed it halfway around the circle before jumping on, her leg dangling off the side and kicking the ground on each turn around. It was great fun. And, as she went from one set to another, losing herself more fully on each ride, Zita could feel the child in her breaking out. Letting go and riding the energy, uplifted by its golden glow, safely bouncing over, sliding under, twirling around each encounter with disaster, she knew in her heart that she must give herself over to the energy welling up within her, releasing herself to a journey with no set destination, letting go of her agendas and goals, knowing that there were other ways of birthing progress, and she must trust her feelings and allow them to open the way for her.

They met at the aquarium located at the center of the downtown complex. It was built underground to take advantage of the earth's natural insulation, and the passageway down to the first level was dark and humid with green paint peeling off the walls. Although it was mid-week, early afternoon on a school day, there were a few adults and their children viewing the exhibits. Boxed up indoors and blocked out from the natural world, people tried to substitute the missing contact through visiting zoos and aquariums—which also acted as wildlife preserves. (Each aquarium concentrated on a certain variety of marine life, as did the zoos for animals, and the aviaries for birds—usually not indigenous to their area.) Dr. Halzack had escorted Zita from one tank of tropical ocean fish to another, viewing the moray eel, striped butterfly fish, cuckoo wrass, Devilfish, blue-banded goby, and angelfish. As they walked, Zita reported Rama's discourse on the children and their fourth dimensional perspective. The scientist was mostly puzzled by the revelations.

At the exhibition pool, they sat on wooden bleachers and watched the handler feeding dolphins. Their entrance—there were others viewing the spectacle—seemed to excite the mammals, who raced about the pool jumping in the air flipping their tails and splashing water over the side. The handler, sitting on the end of a long firmaglass plank, his legs wrapped around a bucket of fish, looked over his shoulder into the stands for any obvious disrupters—kids jumping up and down. He did not find one. A dolphin scooting past him half out of the water caught his attention, and he tossed it a fish.

Dr. Halzack waited while Zita, who had glanced away, turned back to him. "I'll have to admit, Zita," he said, as she insisted he call her, "that I don't really understand this metaphysical. . .stuff."

"I know. It kind of throws me as well."

"I do remember talking with a physicist about Bijorsky's Unified Field theory, which is based on a multidimensional world view: all possibilities existing in split-off dimensions."

"Professor Jamison uses it to explain psychotronics as well."

"So we both agree there is a basis to what he's telling us, but I don't know how it helps me."

Zita felt the shift take place and found herself in the split-off space from which she viewed the world as the Watcher, and she instantaneously grasped the subject in its totality. "I think the key is wavelength. If they vibrate, as he says, at a different wavelength, the same as the spiritual dimension, by matching it, you could speed up the process or the changeover, as he calls it."

"Yes, of course," Halzack said. "The university has an electronic modulation lab, where we might be able to. . .gauge the wavelength or something. The place is crawling with new-science types, one in particular, a guy name. . .Burke, Benjamin Burke, would probably eat this up." Halzack looked over at Zita in amazement. "That was brilliant. Do you have a science background?

"In ecology," Zita said dubiously.

"Yes, it's a strange new world for both of us." Halzack caught his overstatement. "I guess 'both' is a stretch."

"Maybe not," Zita replied, catching him by surprise. "I'm not making a lot of progress writing articles. Everybody reads them, nobody does anything about the problem. I'm coming to believe something more pervasive is needed. But I really don't know what." She paused for a moment. "I'll keep your secret, but before you enlist me, I have a secret to share with you."

"Great, more surprises," said the shell-shocked scientist.

Zita did not smile. "The man with no soul, as Baba called him, the one who came for the child in his village. I believe I work for him."

Dr. Halzack turned completely around and stared at the woman in horror. He had to resist the great urge to jump up and race out the building. "You're an undercover agent for DI?" he asked incredulously.

Zita nodded her head. "When they recruited me, I was convinced that working inside the government was the best way to effect change. I was mistaken."

"And your article on Rama?"

"Was intended to discredit him."

Halzack finally cracked a smile. "They must be disappointed?"

"Yes, they're not happy with me."

"And their interest in Baba and the others?" Halzack asked tentatively.

"I was unaware of this operation, but it has their signature. I do know they keep tabs on psychics, monitor children for the gift."

"Why they want to keep Rama imprisoned."

"Yes, but your children pose a far greater threat to them. They're afraid that if they release him, he might be able to jump others into this 'natural state' of his, and it might spread into the main population. Consciousness is contagious, as they've discovered, and used to manipulate the public for decades."

"Well, what do you recommend?" Halzack asked.

"I really don't know. But, whatever you do, do it fast."

Chapter Sixteen

It was a circular room with small glass booths along its outer rim that were lit by artificial light in the lowest visible light spectrum. At first glance one might mistake them for broadcast booths for a radio or television station. However, a closer inspection did not reveal microphones hanging from the ceiling, nor did the broadcasters wear headsets or read from video speech prompters. In fact, their eyes were closed and their lips did not move. They were focusing their mental energies on the electronic screen of the strange device on the table in front of them. The Psychotronic Spectral Image Enhancer exposed the thoughts of the psychic sender to a stream of free-floating photons that passed across the screen in a medium that separated them individually, making them more susceptible to modulation. The pattern of thought, or the modulation, could be anything from cheerful, positive re-enforcement to disease and death instructions. The PT-modified photons were then gated and became the electromagnetic carrier wave for a television or radio signal. Exposure to this wave and its photons, viewing a television program, would result in the body, at the acupuncture points, a procedure identified by Soviet physicist Adamenko in the 1970s, stripping off the modulation pattern and introducing it to the human nervous system. There it would be kindled or amplified and carried to the body's electromagnetic fields to effect the desired change.

This top-secret underground complex in the mountains of West Virginia was shielded by five hundred feet of granite rock and a series of metal and crystal beds from the stray radiation that could interfere with the sensitive psychic work conducted here. Michael Parker strode off the elevator at the twelfth floor, hurried across the heavy carpet to the command center, and stepped inside. He came over to the window, tinted to prevent the white-spectrum artificial light which squelched the psychotronic effect from bleeding into the room below, and viewed the booths on the outer rim. It was a busy morning, and twenty-five psychics were working this shift. He looked at the operations board and ran down the list of the targeted areas. There were several cities in the Midwest province where recent flooding had driven tens of thousands from their homes into community centers. (Broadcast signals were first routed through one of four centers located around the country. The West Virginia complex covered the Northeast and the Midwest provinces.) Those signals were now carrying subliminal reassurances: "the dispossessed would be well provided"; "don't worry about loved ones"; "the waters will soon recede." In Buffalo, a late winter storm had collapsed the downtown environ roof, killing thousands. The signals droned: "winter storms are rare"; "environ roofs are still safe." Parker briefly scanned the remainder of the list and was satisfied that all emergency situations were being handled. He glanced up at the overhead plaque: "We Don't Influence Minds. We Calm Nerves." The man laughed; others may need such justifications but not him.

Subliminal Persuasion Behavior Modification was the official title for this program, which Parker had taken over early in his career at the Department of Information and had expanded and developed far beyond its original intention and even civilian comprehension. As long as it worked, the politicians had not wanted to know the details. After the psychic wars of the 2020s, and the economic and environmental collapse that followed, the country had been in chaos. The intelligence community was directed to pacify the general population by whatever means possible. All earlier forms of subliminal modification proved inadequate for the task. However, further research led to a series of diabolical breakthroughs. The government was no longer restricted to flooding the airwaves with stultifying alpha waves but could now actually tailor messages for specific purposes. This led to laws prohibiting the broadcast of television signals: cable transmission was a considerably more effective carrier, as were radio signals—covered in the same law—when their bands were widened.

During the last five years, this program under Parker's direction had spread its influence into every level of society. The political trend had been to lessen the restrictions and social controls implemented after the crisis and gradually to phase out the behavior modification programs. A case was made that conditions were still too unstable, and the time required to restart the program would leave them vulnerable to social chaos in future catastrophic breakdowns. When this argument was categorically rejected, the politicians were bombarded with subliminals that just as gradually modified the consensus opinion and slowed down the program's termination. This program was carried out by the most advanced cadre of psychics in the world, who were more than a match, Parker bragged, for the lunatics in Bernia. To assure the World States continued population control, while they dug out from under the environmental collapse, these programs were essential. What Parker needed—and had convinced most of the security chiefs—was another global crisis to rally political support.

Parker turned to the facility's director, Dr. Jan Van Horn, who was busy calibrating the frequency feed for the riot-prone Philadelphia area. "What's happening in P2?"

"Well, the Court's getting ready to hear another Freedom of Information case, and we're piping in subliminals through computer, vid screens, and even the elevator music."

"Don't forget the subliminal fragrance on the toilet paper," Parker quipped. It took the staid scientist a moment to recognize the joke. He smiled feebly.

"I'm heading over to research and leaving from there. Send a feed of tomorrow's lineup to my office later,"

Parker said and walked out the door. He took the elevator to level eighteen. He had two disks with him. One was a video of Zita's last interview with Rama that had a readout of the scalar wave activity in the room at the time, and the other was a scalar readout by itself. He had Walther Kauss's analysis from their Bonn laboratory, but he wanted to cross-check it with his own people. The lab covered one entire floor of the complex, as a dozen scientists worked on the next generation of sub-liminal technology. Parker stepped into Dr. Kroen's office and handed the grey-haired, impeccably dressed scientist the readout disk.

"And you're looking for the scalar wave signature?" he said, trying to remember their phone conversation.

"It's a wave readout of two people in a confined area. I want to know if they're telepathically communicating."

"It'd be easier to read with full video."

"I don't have one," Parker lied facilely. Kroen shrugged his shoulders.

He took the disk from him. "Follow me. Hornig has the scalar equipment." They walked across the floor, around tables of electronic equipment being tuned, past psychics hooked up to frequency modulators, to a corner office where a young man wearing old-fashioned wire-rimmed glasses was studying a wave chart. He stood up with their entrance.

"Charlie, run this tape through a scalar analyzer and tell us what we have here," Van Horn said without introductions.

Hornig nodded his head and nervously took the tape. He placed it inside an audio/video wave scanner. A moment later a series of waves appeared on the green calibrated screen. "They're scalar, all right," Hornig said, and pointed out a loop in one of the waves. "See the spikes." He spoke into the microphone, "Separate by frequency." The screen showed two distinct set of waves. "Full spectrum sweep," he continued. The screen changed to a broad range of waves including those in the human brain wave frequency. "I'd say you have two people talking while also communicating telepathically."

Both men looked back at Parker, whose blank expression revealed nothing. "Okay, that helps." There was a moment's pause. "I'll take the disk back."

"Sorry, of course," Hornig said self-consciously, and hurriedly removed the tape. "I'll erase my temp memory of it."

"Do that, and gentlemen this inquiry is classified Above Top Secret. In fact, it never happened."

Both men solemnly nodded their heads and secretly wished that indeed it never had. With disks in hand, Parker turned and walked out of the office across the lab heading for the train terminal at level five. The twelve o'clock bullet would return him to Washington in forty-five minutes.

There were only two other passengers waiting on the short, three-car-lengths-long platform. The man, in his mid-thirties, dressed like a college professor, was in fact a high-level courier. The young woman, an administrative in J-2, was leaning against the wall, her face paler than normal. At mid-day she must be going home sick. Parker took two steps across the platform and into his private compartment, the door sliding open on the visual cue. He sat down in his chair, called up the service menu on the wall monitor, and fingered his order. Switching screens, he viewed the coach car and saw Anne Jones in her seat with her eyes closed. He tapped out her name on the touch-keys and her status appeared: absence due to illness. Parker had handpicked every person at this facility and knew that Anne was single. Under different circumstances, he might have asked her to join him in his compartment, but it appeared they were both indisposed today.

For him it was a security matter that demanded immediate attention and one that made him sick to his stomach. To address it, he would have to escape from the next level of distraction. Parker was tempted to blot out his problem behind video viewer glasses or drown it out with the audio headset. (Signals on the dept train were fairly clean, but subliminal contamination was so pervasive and the technology for stripping the signals so unreliable that he rarely viewed any form of public programming.) But he now removed the photographs from the envelope and again viewed Zita's clandestine meeting with Dr. Halzack at the Aquarium in Geneva. Kauss's Euro agents had been unable to record the conversation due to static interference from the dolphins. (Whales and dolphins, when excited, could emit spurts of brain waves that deflected microwave communication.) When notified, Parker had assumed the evasive tactics were merely to elude the Euros, and he had awaited her report. Zita filed one for the hotel meeting but not for the second one—after her "exchange" with Rama—nor for that matter, on the telepathic communication itself. He could only surmise that his agent was in collusion with the two of them.

Parker had used Zita, and only sparingly, for environmental disinformation, but knowing her ecological fanaticism, he had made the mistake of placing her on the front line, where her loyalties, never one hundred percent, had now been compromised. If she had failed him, Parker could blame only himself. He had had too much confidence in his control over this very willful, independent young woman. While drawing her into this operation, he had tried to protect her from the deadly knowledge that the greater struggle, in which Rama's release was merely a ploy, was with the emergence of the BMIs (biologically mutated individuals). Unfortunately, at least for her, Zita had become a pawn in this conflict and would most likely be sacrificed. Just as the psychic wars of the 2020s had been orchestrated, creating a crisis that allowed authorities to stifle the development of these powers in the general population, so yet another world crisis would have to be arranged to permit the suppression and elimination of the BMIs. If he was saddened by Zita's apparent defection, Parker could console himself with the knowledge that being expendable made her even more exploitable. She was already planted in two adversarial camps, and he would stretch her position by placing her in a third.

Cary Jamison sat in the front row of the courtroom on the government's side. He was watching in amazement as Jacques Beauvoir, presenting the case for Rama's release to the European Supreme Court, gave an impassioned summation. The Justices, six women and five men, sat behind the high oak bar and followed the speech on their vid screens. It appeared to both his external and internal senses that the Justices had already been persuaded by Beauvoir's case and that listening to summations from both sides was a mere formality. Although he had strived to gain Rama's release for his own iniquitous purposes, the supreme ease with which it was accomplished—from Zita Hiller's surprisingly biased articles to the bumbling case presented by the government—relegated today's proceedings to orchestrated drama for video court viewers. Even Rama's taped interview from Bernia was uncompromising both in its harsh denial of criminal complicity and its steely-eyed refusal to plead his case. The last bewildering straw was the government's failure to call for its own expert testimony, used so effectively at Rama's first trail.

"In conclusion," Beauvoir continued, his hand cutting the air with expressive gestures, "I would like to state, a claim that I could validate with expert testimony, that my client is a holy man in every sense of the word. His impassioned environmental advocacy was an attempt to minister to the poor and dispossessed of this world, and he was repaid for his efforts by twenty years of unjust incarceration. That is the way the world sometimes treats the high-minded. But there is a justice even higher than this court's, and it saw fit to reward this man with a Buddha's enlightenment. Today we humbly ask you, the honored justices of this court, to align your law with God's and return this holy man to his ashram."

There was a murmur in the courtroom, and the red-faced Chief Justice, Hilda von Kleist, gaveled the court to order. "That is quite enough from you, Mr. Beauvoir. Have a seat, sir." She turned to the Asian official, Takamasa Yukawa, who was sitting next to Beauvoir at his table. "Mr. Yukawa, is the Asian government prepared to assume responsibility for the prisoner and the consequences of his future activities?"

Yukawa, a rather tall Japanese diplomat, stood up and brushed the lint off his lapel. "Madame Justice, and the other Justices of this esteemed court, we have interviewed the prisoner, and do not believe he poses a criminal threat to society. On the contrary, we believe him to be as he claims: a simple holy man who wishes only to return to his ashram to live out his days in peaceful contemplation. We would ask that you release him, and are prepared to escort him back to India and, as you have stated, assume full responsibility for his conduct there."

This was a more generous endorsement than the court had expected from the cautious Asians. It had an impact on the Justices, reflected in a row of nodding heads and raised eyebrows. The audience could hear the clicking sound of keyboard input—private verbal consultation was impossible—as the Justices exchanged messages. Finally, Justice von Kleist spoke, "Having heard the case for both sides, this court will render a judgment on May 1." She gaveled the proceedings to a close.

Jamison again shook his head in amazement; he turned and looked at Edington, who appeared panicky. Nobody had expected a decision this quickly, and it would require them to accelerate their plans. As they stood and exited down the center aisle, Jamison bumped into Zita Hiller. He had tried to probe her earlier in the month but could not get a clear reading, and assumed she had undergone an initiation. This made her less susceptible to their manipulation but not yet invulnerable. Seeing her in court, their physical proximity allowing more delicate scanning, only confirmed that suspicion.

"Ah Ms. Hiller, come to see your handiwork?" Jamison asked coyly.

The woman gave him a penetrating look. "More than my hands were stirring this pot."

Jamison laughed. "Touché, my dear." He mischievously added, "You did seem to bring out the best in the man. You must be his *soror mystica*."

"Which is?"

"In medieval alchemy, the 'mystical sister' of a spiritual adept."

Zita Hiller turned to Jamison's companion, a picture of studied ennui. "And who's he, your 'bored mystica.'" She turned and walked off before the boy's venomous tongue could lash out at her.

Edington turned to fling a retort at the woman's retreating back. Jamison grabbed the boy's arm and pulled him around. "Ah, Billy, you must learn to appreciate life's little ironies." The boy started to defend himself. "Please, we don't have time for temperament. Call us a cab, and have it meet us at the south entrance. I'll confirm our reservations."

It was a short flight from Luxembourg to Paris, and while his young companion played video chess, Jamison sat back in his seat and attended to the uneasy feelings stirring within him. Rama's release required the cooperation of at least the three dominant members of the World Council: Europe, North America and Asia, and it was proceeding much too easily. Although the Euros had appeared open to it, reviewing his petition with great fanfare, it was generally considered a political ploy in their power struggle with the others. From all indications they were just as leery of the man's transformation and its uncertain potential. Had they discovered, as he had most recently, that their scalar field did not contain him and that from his fourth dimensional state he could affect outside the prison? Jamison sighed in relief. Of course, that was the explanation, and the obvious solution was a World Council decision to release him so they could more easily dispose of him. And, if they were that fearful of Rama, and he had him as an added weapon in his arsenal, Jamison would be in a much better bargaining position, if anything should go awry.

They met George Bates at his warehouse on the Seine. The faded company name stenciled on the window of the side door read: Electronics Distributors Internationale. On the main floor workmen loaded a conveyor belt with crates of electronic equipment that were unloaded at the other end onto a barge docked under a huge environ screen. This legitimate business activity was the cover for the more lucrative sale of outlawed subliminal technology. The market for such equipment from business to private use was expanding, and while the world states made a show of containment, they actually supplied smugglers like Bates with outdated equipment. Research showed that exposure to the different frequency controls of subliminal technologies increased susceptibility exponentially. And, ultimately, without powerful psychic modulators, their effectiveness was limited.

Following Bates' driver, the two men were led down three flights of rickety stairs to a cavernous room located under the riverbed, which offered a degree of psychic protection. When they entered, Bates introduced them to Remy Duprey, the pilot, and Emilio Sanchez, the tech expert, who would accompany them on their mission.

As they sat back down, Duprey, a big burly man with sharp eyes, turned to Jamison. "George tells me you can read a man's mind like a book."

Jamison rolled his eyes and looked at Bates to call off his man, but he appeared disinclined. The psychic turned back to the pilot. "And you want to know if we can obtain the prison access codes, so you won't be hovering in clear view of their disrupters with your pants down." Edington laughed.

Embarrassed, Duprey growled at him, "What's so funny, little man?"

"That you had a mind to read in the first place," Edington replied without flinching.

"Boys, please," Bates piped up. "Save your energy; you're going to need it." He pulled the prison plans out of their tube and unrolled them onto the table, pinning the corners down with wine glasses. Everybody stared at the plans and privately assessed the formidable challenge this prison breakout posed. Bates gave them a moment to be suitability intimidated. He handed Jamison a thin dossier, which he opened and quickly scanned. "This is a list of the access codes we'll need at each stage of the break-in. We don't know who'll be manning the towers or the inside security booths, so we've broken it down by position; what they'd be responsible for, the type of information running through their minds on any given shift. Is that what you wanted?"

Jamison nodded his head. "Excellent, George. Now if you could give us a visual cue as well, where they'd most likely be sitting or standing, it'd help."

"I can do that," Sanchez said. He was a short, wiry man with a look of keen intelligence.

"Would alarms be triggered by codes or manually?" Edington asked.

"They wouldn't be pushing little red buttons if that's what you're asking," Sanchez replied.

"Three-digit or five-digit?"

Sanchez looked to his boss, who shrugged his shoulders. "Five-digit. They'd want somebody to think twice before shutting the place down. Why?"

"If I sense detection, wanna know how much time I've got."

"Right," Sanchez said, nodding his head in agreement.

Edington took a folder out of his pocket and handed it to Bates. "We've supplemented your bios on the Red Cross doctors with some personals." George thumbed through the file. "You know the restaurants they frequent, and I can tell you if it's the food or the waitresses. You know their lovers, and I can tell how serious they are."

"Good. It'll help. Picking them up and switching is half the job."

"We've just gotten back from the hearing, and it looks like they're letting him go, and fast," Jamison added.

"That was easy," Bates said, frowning.

"Yes, it was, George."

"Could this be some kind of elaborate set-up?"

"No. They want him dead, just not there."

"Unless they use the break-in as a cover, getting all three of us at once."

"They'd lose too much face with any attempt, even an aborted one. No. They want the public to think they're invulnerable."

"They've got me fooled," Duprey quipped.

Jamison and Bates exchanged looks. This man would be replaced. "The Red Cross has already been asked, if needed, to send a team on two weeks' notice."

"And they're rendering a judgment by May 1."

"Okay. I'm moving my teams into place for the pick-ups," Bates said.

"Everybody but me will be in Geneva by the end of the month," Jamison added.

"Okay. Next time we meet, it's in Switzerland with everybody prepared to go at a moment's notice." They all nodded their heads in agreement.

Chapter Seventeen

The child went deeper, down, down into the material web, layer after layer, sticky like mucous membranes, suffocating, each layer trembling in terror, grasping, holding on to every movement of life, infusing it with its fear, crippling it with its accidents, killing it with its deaths, but this movement was vital, its wavelength long, and it whipped its way through the layers, suffering each agonizing outcry, lashing it with its don'ts and cannots and should've-beens and always-will-be's, matter's universal habits strangling every movement toward freedom, and life and light, and as he passed through each layer and it gave up its hold, it snapped back into place like a rubber band stretched to its limits in one moment and in the next at rest in its old, static immobility, and he knew that nothing could reform this ungiving matter, only complete and total transformation would change it, in the blink of an eye or a millennium's constant erosion, and finally, suddenly, the child broke through the barrier between two worlds, into a silent empty vastness that stretched to infinity, and the child could feel his wavelength shorten, shorter and shorter, and his body, what he could feel of it, had the density of infinite mass but was as light as air, and with the higher vibration, his body spread through the formless vastness, his cells as wide as sunflowers, until he was inside of everything, and a small voice spoke. . .

"I am there," Baba said.

In the control booth of the electronic modulation lab, Halzack and Cosgrove stood back and watched a dozen technicians reading their needle gauges and observing their green scopes. The boy's mother, Roya, showing grave concern—her son was very vulnerable in this state—viewed the testing through a window in the visitors' gallery above them. The technicians began bombarding the boy with a range of EM waves. They moved up the scale in wavelength, hoping to define this state by the refraction of waves passing through it, but there was no discernible bending. He did react, however, to a burst of scalar waves by absorbing them.

Finally, Dr. Cantor, the businessman's scientist, looked up from the control board and turned to his two colleagues. "Nothing in the EM range seems to affect him. And he eats scalar waves like spaghetti. Next, we're going to pipe in a modified subliminal recording. The technology's generations old, but it makes a normal person hum the Star-Spangled Banner. Guess where we got it? It's in the scalar range, which is the only radiation he reacts to." Cantor told one of his assistants, "Go ahead and play it, Jean."

The young man pushed the play button on the audio feed, and he and the others watched their monitors and strained to hear the customary humming. The boy showed no response. In thirty seconds, Cantor turned on his microphone.

"Baba, do you hear. . .anything?"

"Somebody is telling me to sing a song," said the boy, as Dr. Cosgrove translated, "but it is silly and I will not sing for them."

"Okay, we're going to have them suggest other things to you." Jean played a series of ten short subliminal suggestions, but Baba did not respond to any of them.

Jean said, "DI would love this kid."

Cantor frowned and turned on his microphone. "Computer log, erase last remark." The young technician hunkered down over his console. The scientist turned to Dr. Halzack. "I've gotten response on these subliminals from everybody we've tested. You should hear the regional governor hum the Yankee tune. He made us destroy the recording afterwards. But Baba just absorbs scalar, which, if we could figure out how he does it, would be worth something to somebody."

"He's not to be used in that way, I thought we agreed to that," Halzack said.

"Sorry," Cantor said, and turned back to his subject. He hit a switch and the curtain in the next room pulled back to reveal a middle-aged woman reclining in a doctor's chair. "Baba, there's a woman in the next room. Can you tell me what's ailing her?"

"Her head hurts," Baba said, and Cantor nodded his head in agreement. "I can stop the hurt."

This was not on the agenda, but Halzack leaned over and spoke into the microphone, "Go ahead, Baba. Make it better."

Suddenly, the woman's EEG reading showed a burst of activity, and a moment later, she was heard to say, "My headache's gone."

"Okay, Joyce, Ms. Rine will take you back." As she got up, Cantor looked down the row of technicians. "Anybody get anything on him?"

"Nothing," said one man, and the woman next to him, "Ditto."

"How can he affect without a change in brain-wave frequency?" one of the technicians asked. Someone else added, "Must be some comfy place."

They brought in three more patients with increasingly severe ailments, with the same results. "I know you said no, but if I ran a terminal past him, and. . ."

"And the flood wouldn't end," Halzack said.

Showing his temper, Dr. Cantor stood up from his console. "Well, Henry, he beats me. He doesn't react to EMs, and he eats scalar. I can't enhance what I can't detect. Offhand, I'd say he goes dimensional, but I can't prove it, and if I could, I wouldn't know what to do with it anyway."

Dr. Cosgrove took his seat and began to bring Baba out of his "sacred place." While Dr. Halzack tried to reassure Cantor, Dr. Benjamin Burke, the cross-specialist, former child prodigy, nicknamed, "Genius of Milo," for excited arm-waving, walked down the stairs into the tank. Burke was short, rotund with a scraggly brown beard. Women found his teddy-bear looks and cuddly warmth irresistible. He explained it to dumbfounded colleagues as the "butterball effect."

"Can I check my watch, kid?" Burke said.

Baba did not understand the words but knew what the man wanted. He undid the watch band and handed it back to him. Burke glanced up at Dr. Cosgrove in the control booth. "Dana, translate for me." He turned back to Baba. "Let me check the time, and you can have the watch for keeps." Baba's eyes lit up. Although he could not read the foreign numbers, he was greatly impressed with all the little dials that showed time zone differences.

In the control booth, Dr. Halzack turn to see Dr. Burke talking with Baba in the tank. "What's he doing?"

Cantor watched his colleague for a moment. "Probably asking the kid's astrological sign."

Burke hurried back up the stairs into the booth and picked up a telephone. He hit the record button and tapped out an eleven-digit number from memory. He listened while he looked at his watch. The look of amazement appearing on his face had been seen before by his colleagues and created a little anticipation. Burke placed the receiver head onto a printer-feed, played back the message and obtained a quick transcription. He cross-checked it with his watch, making a mental calculation.

"Burke, you late for a date?" Cantor said.

Benjamin Burke stared at his sometimes antagonistic boss, and slowly replied with a raised voice so everybody in the room could hear him, "If I were, I'd be 1.389737525 seconds early." Dr. Halzack did not at first see the implications of the man's retort, but Cantor understood it.

"That was the atomic clock in Boulder?" Cantor asked, his voice cracking, and Burke nodded his head. "Okay, call it and put it on the screen." Burke tapped out the number and routed the call to the overhead display. "On my mark, everybody." The technicians had their watches in hand; fingers poised over stop buttons. "One, two, three!" Cantor shouted. Everybody compared their time to the frozen ten-digit number on the screen. Their watches were all off by the same factor. A chorus of "aaaahhh's" filled the room.

"Somebody call local time," Cantor said. "Okay, one group call time in New York, Montreal, and Detroit. They're all equidistant. The other three moved out in increments of a thousand miles." Cantor finally looked back at Burke in grudging acknowledgement. "Anything I missed?"

"If the effect were cumulative," Burke said, his hands making nervous notations in the air, "the variance would be greater, since he's been in and out of this state for months now. So the field snaps back at some point, and its duration would be helpful to know. And my guess is that it's localized. I'd get another team to start from ground zero and call out in twenty-five-mile increments."

Dr. Cantor nodded his head in agreement and picked up the telephone to round up more calling teams. Halzack and Cosgrove had stood back and stayed out of the way during the outburst of activity, but Henry now pulled Burke aside. "Ben, I assume the time difference means some kind of dimensional shift?"

"That's my guess," Burke said in continued amazement. "And, wherever he goes, the place must have tremendous acceleration to shift the third dimension into its space."

"In this dimension, will things be. . .different," Halzack asked uncertainly.

Burke laughed at his colleague's expression. "No. To us, everything will seem normal, but like astronauts traveling at the speed of light, we will appear to have slowed down to those outside the zone, relative to our position, and when we return to 'proper' time, we'll have aged less, if only in nanoseconds."

"The Twin Paradoz applies here?" Halzack asked.

"Our reality, whatever its boundaries, has been accelerated, and we'll experience the effects of Einstein's relativity the same as the twins in his time distortion explanation."

"But, like the astronaut, will we come home?"

"I assume it's only a temporary shift."

Halzack thought for a moment. "And if you could put a hundred Babas into that 'accelerated' state, could you make it permanent?"

Dr. Burke laughed. "You're not serious?"

"Let's say I'm curious," Halzack replied.

"You are serious," Burke said, and then thought about this remarkable possibility. "There're some more dimensional freaks in the physics department, and we could give you an educated guess. But I'm going to want to know the whys of the situation before I help you warp time and space."

"You want whys," Halzack, running his hand through his hair and feeling overwhelmed. "I've got plenty of whys."

Baba was finally retrieved from the tank by his mother, and he walked into the control booth and up to Dr. Burke, who took one look at the boy and handed him the watch. Baba wrapped it around his lower arm, inches above his wrist, where there was enough girth to affix the band.

They watched him staring at his new toy. He held up the face for all to see. "Soon, all the clocks will spin together." Dr. Burke looked at his two colleagues, and seriously wondered, for the first time in his life, if he had not ventured into a strange intellectual territory from which there was no return.

Dr. Burke had determined that the dimensional shift was indeed localized to a 215-mile radius around Toronto, and that it had lasted for twenty-three minutes. At that point, clocks inside the circle caught up with those outside the affected area. Nobody felt a shift; no instruments registered shock waves, magnetic waves, or any quantifiable effects. Burke had a camera trained on the university's own electron clock (calibrated to nanoseconds), and it showed the moment of the shift, a jump of 1.3 seconds from one vid frame to the next, now registering standard time. No exterior force should have been able to affect the clock's operation, but the video clearly showed it. However, given the remarkable nature of the phenomenon and the number of people aware of it, Cantor spent the next two days fielding questions from colleagues and university officials, which he fended off. The government was more persistent, and the National Science Council began an official inquiry into the dimensional experimentation and its effects. Until further notice, Halzack was instructed to stop testing the child. Burke suggested that the staff unplug their home vid feeds and shop for psychotronic protectors. Nobody took him seriously until DI types showed up two days later asking questions.

Burke was astonished by the dimensional shift precipitated by Baba's inner state. As a student of Heim's six-dimensional geometry and the Everett-Wheeler-Graham "Many Worlds Interpretation" of quantum mechanics, he was nonetheless shocked—if delightfully so—by this confirmation of their theories. He understood how Einstein must have felt when observations in 1919 proved the gravitational warping of light and validated his Special Theory of Relativity. But, with the prospect of "arranging" further shifts, Burke was determined that he would not one day look back over a dimensional wasteland with remorse, as Einstein no doubt did after Hiroshima. Dr. Halzack stopped by Burke's office in the speculative or "weird science" department a few days later to talk about dimensional shifting. Burke cleared a spot for his guest on a cluttered sofa, while he paced up and down the narrow walkway between towering stacks of books.

"Everett was a student of John Wheeler at Princeton back in the 1950s. His 'Many Worlds Interpretation' was his Ph.D thesis, later amplified by Wheeler and Graham. It suggests that when a wave function collapses (when one subatomic particle in a stream is identified—or actualizes) the others don't vanish—the orthodox interpretation—they actualize in coexistent worlds or, for our purpose, other dimensions."

"Or with each action the universe splits into two worlds, or two time lines."

"Yes, repeatedly, as the theory suggests, and into discrete separate branches of reality," Burke said. "Later, Bijorsky showed in his Unified Field Theory that the different branches can cross over or merge, as paranormal phenomena would suggest or, in his example, create 3-D matter from 4-D energy."

"I remember reading about it in a survey course. How the 'Many Worlds Interpretation' was overlooked in its day."

"Yes, even Wheeler used to say he could believe it only on Monday, Wednesday, and Friday, but not any other time."

"It sounded pretty farfetched to me, at the time, but I was a hard-science man."

"As no doubt Relativity or the Quantum Theory would sound to nineteenth-century scientists," Burke said, pausing for a moment. "Now the psychotronic interpretation that encompasses the MWI, pioneered by Thomas Bearden back in the 1970s, says that mind and matter exist in separate dimensions, mind in its own dimensional world spatially removed from our physical world, and that the commonality between them is time. But for mind to affect matter, which happens constantly, like negative thinking affecting your blood pressure, the mental dimension must rotate into or synchronize with, a simple exercise in Heim's geometry, the physical dimension, and pass its momentum onto the object it affects. The classic example is a psychic's mind synchronizing or tuning into the EM frequency of an object and modulating it. And, when you realize that the EM dimension is actually the morphic field dimension that forms everything from stars to embryos, you see that our reality is actually made up of many intersecting dimensions, and that organic life is sustained by subtly meshing them together."

Burke looked over at Dr. Halzack, who nodded his head in acknowledgement. "And the different dimensions," he continued, "are not as discrete as they may seem. Movement, or velocity, in one dimension crosstalks, as Bearden called it, into all others. Speculation has it that movement of sufficient momentum can actually alter other dimensions."

"Permanently?" Halzack asked.

"One would assume that for crosstalk and rotation to occur, there must be a commonality between dimensions besides time. And, although they may operate according to different laws, one would assume that other dimensions like our own third dimension are in flux, evolving, changing, interconnected and affected by everything in the universe, as we are."

"And that's how Baba was able to heal your patients without us detecting an 'exchange' between them?"

"Yes, and how Rama can 'affect' outside the Tesla fields," Burke added. "One of the great challenges of science is Bell's Theorem, the mathematical proof—later verified by experimental data—of a hypothetical experiment proposed by Einstein and two colleagues in 1935, which became known as the EPR Paradox. It suggested that two particles *some distance apart* could affect each other without a casual connection. Bell showed that, when emitted together, they will always have opposite spins, no matter what happens to either of them, or how great the distance between them. Scientists have changed the spin of one particle from up to down, right to left, and the other always changes to its opposite. This undermines the whole casual basis of science, and suggests that the separate parts of our universe are connected in noncasual ways."

"And you're saying," Halzack said, "that dimensional shifting explains that connection."

"Yes, and not an idea original to me."

"And Rama's keepers?"

"Persist, as most of contemporary science, in the view," Burke sneered, "of separate but causally connected parts."

"Which brings us to the experiment at hand."

"It does," Burke added, smiling mysteriously. "From my reading, mystics, especially the ancient Tibetans, describe a light world as the ground being of existence. I believe it's a realm woven from our feelings and intuitions, and it's where Baba and the other Ramas go.

He described it as 'the well at the bottom of the earth'?"

"Yes. At first I took him literally."

"No, it's dimensional. And it must have incredible mass and acceleration for him to cause a time shift. I would say that the longer he stays there, and the more friends he brings with him, the longer and more pervasive the shift."

"Could they move the third dimension into that realm?" Holzack asked.

"Again, it's a matter not of force and momentum, but synchronization. They could merge the two or, to be more precise, create a temporary merge where objects or people, vibrating high enough, would shift over before it snapped back. But whether it would take 100 people 100 years to shift it, or if ten could do it in ten minutes, I couldn't tell you," Burke said. He added pointedly, "And there's the question of why you'd want to do it to begin with."

"We've always thought of evolution as the adaptation to a changing physical world. If the hot African sun kills off fruit-bearing trees and turns the jungle into a grassy savannah, you either eat grass and become efficient at it, developing flat grinding teeth, or die. If a competing species is eating your porridge, you either kill it off or eat cake. The brain's neocortex has been considered the supreme adaptive organ. It helped us not only kill off the competition, but actually remodel the physical world to suit our needs. At first it proved to be a smashing success, taking us from the African plains to the moon in 10,000 years, but eventually it cut us off and isolated us from the natural world, with catastrophic results. If you're telling me now that the neocortex is merely a finer tuning device to pick up the mental world's broadcast, then adaptation has not been between Homo sapiens and the physical environment, but between the mental and physical dimension, which the mental has totally dominated."

"If so, Baba and his friends, by tuning into the light dimension or realm or spiritual world, are evolving not only the physical world but its mental counterpart as well," Burke added. He thought for a moment. "Well, Henry, this satisfies my qualms about further 'experimentation.'"

"Yes, the program seems to be unfolding without our help, but I for one don't mind giving it a little nudge," Halzack said. His colleague nodded his head conspiratorially.

Chapter Eighteen

As they fell from a cloudless sky, the snowflakes were light and fine, each with its own sacred geometric design, a million unique creations, sparkling in the rainbow-colored light, as if filtered through a prism, each flake a different blend of colors, and then the snow stopped and lay along the ridges and down the slopes and on the swells of the finely sculpted mountains; its sinewy hills stretched along the lowlands, and its granite heart drew them upward into the lofty realms where the brown earth kissed the pale blue sky, hanging low and cloudless, with unblinking stars peeking through the sun's spangled light, and the moon rose over the horizon, and it was huge and bright, and its craters and canyons were fully lit, and it moved swiftly across the sky and the earth felt no shadow and it was gone.

Rama stood at the observation window in the arboretum. In a small self-contained circle that he had shifted into the fourth dimension, the holy man viewed the world around him. Slowly, he shifted the dimensional wavelengths within the circle, and its two occupants found themselves viewing the mountainscape with its now bare peaks and slopes. Rama turned and smiled at Ms. Hiller. "It is not quite as spectacular without the snow."

"It's fine," Zita said breathlessly.

"Shall we?" Rama said. They turned and walked back to the wicker chairs and their steeping tea.

"So where did we leave off?" Rama asked, pouring them both a cup of tea.

"You were describing a society of people living in the natural state, and said that there would be no need for police or security forces. Will you elaborate?"

"I used to tell my devotees that if you follow the prescribed teachings of Buddhism, you'll become a good Buddhist, but you'll never become a Buddha. And, I could add, that if you follow the civil laws of any state, you'll become a model citizen but no Thomas Jefferson.

"The problem is we take children coming to us 'trailing clouds of glory' and assume that something is wrong with them. The priest would repress their desires and appetites; the guru would quiet the mind's restless chatter; the policeman would arrest darker impulses toward larceny and mayhem. But we create in them, project onto them, in the development of their ego, all our own sordid appetites and impulses. Instead of nurturing their divine seed and letting it unfold in its own time and way, we pull them away from their natural functioning and turn them into stiff outward-directed social creatures. It is an awful trick we play on them. In a way, we keep the priest and the policeman employed by creating desires in the child, such as lust by repression and sex-based advertising, that lead them, twenty years later, to beat their neighbors over the head and steal their wives."

"But children would become savages without discipline," Zita insisted.

"Am I a savage?"

"No. And I would rather have a world populated by Ramas than some people I know, but that's not to say that left alone, children will naturally develop their divine qualities."

"Well, I arrived here, at the natural state, by dropping the falseness that society bred into me, by reclaiming my divine child, as it were. If you recognize those qualities in the child, nurture and develop them, they will remain in the blessed state."

"But science tells us that some people have a genetic propensity toward criminal behavior."

"And other ancestral genes would have us howl at the moon, eat raw meat, and swim in tidal pools. I would replace both nature and nurture with varying wavelengths. Everything, including our impulses and desires, vibrates at certain wavelengths. By changing the wavelength of a larcenous impulse, you transform it into something altogether different. And I do not mean a desire to steal from the rich and give to the poor. This is not repression or modification. It is the complete transformation of energy.

"When the mind stops in the adult, or never begins in the child, when this explosion happens the first time or every time a thought arises, the cells of the body become realigned, the whole vibration of the body changes. Anger, lust, greed is washed out of your system, or placed on hold; it gets transformed. People in this state could not kill to save their lives, or steal to feed their stomachs; they would die or starve instead, and not because they are obeying the ten commandments or Buddha's thirteen precepts. It is the mind, the ego that separates you from your. . .soul, the source of your natural moral response, and reduces you to followers of rules. Freed of it, recognizing your connection to the whole, you would naturally honor and respect the divine in all that you touch. You would not need to follow Christ's precept to 'love your neighbor as yourself,' because you would experience it every moment of your life. You would not need priests or policemen telling you to behave yourself; you would naturally act in harmony with others and the whole. Does that answer your question?"

Zita felt a twinge of pain in her head, as her perspective shifted.

- *And this is how you would transform an entire civilization,* she thought.

- *Yes. Everything physical, mental, and emotional is made up of energy, vibrating at its own wavelength. If you jumped them up an octave or two at once, those who could withstand the shift would walk into another world, a mirror of the one they just left.*

- *The fourth dimension?*

- *I am not a physicist, but that is as good a name as any.*

"Yes, it does," Zita said. "I think my readers would be interested in how people would personally relate to each other. Would they have relationships? Would they get married?"

"Relationships based on love, not obligation. Marriage is already an outdated institution."

"Excuse me for asking, but would people still have sex?"

"I would imagine procreation would work much the same way. Sex can be a divine experience and was meant to be all along."

- *And those who couldn't withstand it?* Zita thought.

- *I believe a collective shift would send a wave through matter, affecting the vibration of every atom. Those that resisted the shift would start to wobble chaotically. These people would feel the quickening but would not shift over. Left behind in a third-dimensional world of increasing destructiveness, they would experience earthquakes, tidal waves, the poisonous atmosphere, and the social breakdown the others would escape.*

- *Wouldn't they notice those who shift out?*

- *The world is reformed with each breath, and I would imagine you would take with you every trace of your existence in the previous state. You go, and in that moment, the world gets reformed around your never having been there to begin with.*

- *Would you be creating a whole new world or dimension, or stepping into a preexisting one?*

- *Our world has always been the inner levels of a greater dimensional world. Throughout history, people able to raise their vibrations have walked through or ascended into it.*

"And you're saying that love, as a vibration, is the frequency of change, not just between people but for the earth, for ourselves?" Zita asked.

"Just look at its transformative effects on us."

"And yet people also do hideous things to each other in its name."

"They appropriate the word for their use, but when moved by its vibration, you could do no harm."

- *So you would just walk through totally conscious into a mirror world?*

- *No, at first, you would not see the difference, or most people would not.*

- *Even if you woke up and the skies were clear?*

- *The changes might be uneven, but your perspective would*

*shift to accommodate the changes. You might sense that some-
thing was odd, but the feeling would pass.*

- But others would be aware of the changes?

*- Consciousness is the only matrix: the more levels you
have integrated, the more you are aware of.*

"But, if people were mainly 'feeling' oriented, moved
by strong feelings, wouldn't there be conflicts?" Zita
asked.

"Conflicts are based on mutual exclusion. I want something you want, and we both cannot have it. But, in
a unified state, that would be telling the right hand it
cannot have what the left hand has."

"And if two men were in love with the same woman?"
Zita asked.

"Loving themselves, or the God in them, makes loving
others less compulsive or exclusive."

*- Could you fall from such a state, lower your vibration
and find yourself back in the old world?*

- I seem able to live in both worlds, heaven and hell.

- Sounds like quantum religion.

*- Old time religion's heaven, hell, and bardo might be
just that.*

Rama paused for a moment, his face straining, as
he sensed a disturbance. "Something is happening. We
need to leave here immediately."

As the turbocopter flew through the valley in shadow,
rock steeples rising into the sky on either side, the
domed prison appeared above, reflecting the afternoon
light. Stuck atop the towering peak, it looked like the
glass head of a long-necked doll. Then the copter rose
quickly in an updraft of mountain air. The pilot, Pietro
Ghiberti, the newest member of the assault team, tried
to maneuver the craft into the electronic approach path
on his scope but leveled off 100 feet too high, requiring
an awkward and dangerous descent.

"Know this is your first fly-in, Mendes. But lose it
again, and it'll be your last," said Colonel Stutter, the
control tower supervisor. "Now everybody stick their
badges and their faces up to the camera."

One by one, Jamison, Edington, and Bates, dressed as Red Cross doctors, held up their IDs and smiled for the vid camera. Viewing the substituted photographs, Stutter checked the names off his list. He next received a visual on the pilot and co-pilot, and when the correct ten-digit code was entered, he approved the copter for landing. There were still three more levels of security checks, but the prison's confidence in its inside security and the Alps' unpredictable wind currents, making it dangerous for copters to hover outside, led to old-fashioned visual identification for entrance through the outer defenses. Once inside, however, the crew would be subjected to the most sophisticated battery of ID tests imaginable.

But, once they passed through the scalar field and were inside its impenetrable psychic barrier, the local photonic field protecting the security booth, its personnel and its computers was no match for two of the world's most powerful unguarded psychic minds. Before the four-man security team could implement the next level of checks, Jamison and Edington had used telepathic hypnosis to have the men enter first-, second-, and third-level clearances on their crew, freeing them from the copter.

They were walking across the floor to the prison entrance, when Colonel Stutter, taking a break after the day's last fly-in, saw the copter crew and the contingent of doctors. It had only been fifteen minutes since they landed. Normally, security clearance took at least an hour. He stepped into the control booth.

"Lowell, what's going on with them?" he asked the shift chief. The man did not answer. "Lieutenant, I'm talking to you." When the man failed to respond, Stutter hurried over and turned him around in his chair. He was fixed-eyed catatonic. Before he could grab the computer microphone, the five-digit code on his tongue, a wave of mental confusion hit him. He slumped to his knees, holding his head before he passed out.

An electronic short-circuit, blanking out the long-range radar, kept the control-tower crew occupied and unaware of Stutter's long absence. The night shift for the security booth would not come on duty for another two hours, and the doctors' escort was not expected for forty-five minutes. An electronic signal was sent that disrupted the prison's phone system, making unanswered calls to the booth appear part of the general breakdown.

A quick command to the security computer opened the third-floor door into the prison. Sanchez and Ghiberti slipped into the security crew's locker room, stole guard uniforms and quickly changed. Outside they escorted the three Red Cross doctors to their appointment with Dr. Cherenkov in the first-floor infirmary. Edington searched the computer code files and keyed in the second-floor code. The elevator door opened, and they walked down the corridor toward the control booth for the prison's main cell block. Here, along the outer wall, encased in their own private scalar wave fields, were the psychic marauders they had come to free. Jamison could not resist the temptation to run his hand along the wall, in anticipation of seeing his "boys" soon. The cells were blocked to his psychic probing and their firmaglass windows were darkened, but knowing they were only inches from him was comforting to the touch.

From inside the control booth, Joseph Murdock saw the contingent of doctors walking down the corridor toward him. This floor was off bounds to outside personnel, and these guards should not have had access to the daily floor code. And the tall doctor running his hand along the wall struck him as very odd. Although he felt invulnerable behind his steel door and psychically impenetrable scalar field, Murdock placed a finger near the alarm button.

"You guards, identify yourselves!" Murdock barked over the corridor speaker.

Jamison, in extended fourth-dimensional time, was able to review the prison's guard roster and identify guards who matched their men's description and who had never logged second-floor duty. He checked the day's schedule, identified Joseph Murdock as the duty officer, and did not note any contact with the selected guards. He made computer notations of their current duty and starting time. He telepathically relayed their names and ID numbers to Sanchez and Ghiberti. It took less than a second.

"Sir, Edouard Girard, ID number 2564783," Sanchez said.

"Vincent Palladio, ID number 4024639," Ghiberti said.

Murdock called up the day's duty roster and confirmed their present assignment, but that did not explain their presence in restricted areas. "Girard, can you tell me what you're doing here?"

"Sir, Dr. Dunbar expressed a wish to visually check the conditions of the prisoners before reviewing their records in the infirmary," Sanchez replied.

Murdock stared in cool disbelief at the guard's flimsy explanation. "Gentlemen, hold your positions."

Jamison dropped his medical case, and Sanchez pushed it up against the door with his foot. The men backed down the hallway.

"Gentlemen, I'm warning you. One more step, and you're neutralized," Murdock said. As they retreated, he pushed the alarm button that sounded off throughout the prison and activated the psychotronic defense system. It flooded the hallway with nerve-blocking sound waves that should have reduced them to puddles of flesh. He was amazed to see the men stop halfway down the hall and turn back to him, apparently blocking the psychotronic effects. Murdock unsheathed the plasma guns mounted inside the hallway walls. It was now apparent that the men were advanced psychics, who could fight off the sound wave assault but could not breach the scalar field and reach him, and that they must be planning to force their way inside. Joseph Murdock looked down and spotted the case a moment before it exploded, blowing open the door and rupturing the scalar barrier. Murdock soon proved more vulnerable to assault than his assailants, his nerve impulses blocked and his heart stopped, falling to the floor. As he lost consciousness, he heard a familiar voice calling him out of the darkness and he followed.

Standing back, Jamison and Edington psychically neutralized the other guards in the booth, while Sanchez and Ghiberti ran down the hallway and entered the control center. Jamison was able to scan the dying man's mind to obtain the codes needed to shut down the local scalar fields around the second floor cells. He telepathically relayed the codes to Sanchez, who entered them and released the fields. Guards were already moving down the hallway and up the cleared elevator shaft toward their positions. Jamison contacted the half-dozen psychics in their cells; together they sent out a neuron-disrupting wave of energy that knocked out everybody in the prison except his men. Almost everybody. Two people were unaffected by the assault, holed up in the infirmary biding their time.

By the time Rama and Zita had reached the infirmary, Dr. Cherenkov and his staff were lying on the floor in catatonic states. Rama checked and saw that there was no permanent damage, and waited to treat them while he assessed the situation. He felt the awful, deranged minds freed of their restraints probing the prison, inflicting pain and slow agonizing death on those identified as their chief oppressors, including Dr. DeWitt, the warden, whose disembodied soul Rama also helped over the threshold and out of their tormenting control. He now slightly shifted the surrounding space into the fourth dimension. Psychic probes by the prisoners would find the doctors and nurses but would leave him and the woman undetected, although still visible. Who would think to search for him in the place he was scheduled to be examined?

"What's happening?" Zita finally asked.

"Jamison has freed the others, but it is only a matter of time before they find us."

"Will they kill us? Can they kill us, I should say?"

"If you can maintain your inner focus, and remain in the Sacred Space, they cannot harm us, but they can force us to go with them."

"As hostages?"

"I have not been able to probe their minds, but I would assume as much." Rama raised his hand, as he closed his eyes, and Zita felt herself shift again. "I could play this game with them, and they might give up and leave without us, but they would take their anger out on the others."

Zita thought for a moment. "I'd rather take my chances and free the others."

Rama nodded his head; it was the answer he expected. "I will stretch it as far as I can. An alarm has already been set off at the base command, so they do not have much time."

In the arboretum, Jamison and Misho, his samurai psychic, as he called him, were scanning the prison in search of Rama and the woman.

"He's doing dimensional shifts to hide from us, I'm sure of it," Jamison said.

"He is that advanced?"

"Yes, much has happened with him, and if we could learn what he knows. . ."

"Yes, but I sense his heart has not changed, and that makes him vulnerable," Misho said. He psychically tortured one of the captured guards. The man screamed in his unconscious state; the pain was so intense. Jamison nodded his head in agreement; Rama would not allow lives to be sacrificed for his own safety.

"I've got him," Jamison said triumphantly. "They're in the infirmary after all. Wait." He received a message from Edington. "We don't have much time. Apparently, he was able to alert the base command. We need to grab them and go."

"Maybe we should forget them," Bates said.

"And not collect your reward?" Jamison said in mock surprise. "I won't hear of it."

"Yeah, well, I'd rather live to spend what I've got."

"Then let's hurry. You round up the others, get them on the copter, and we'll collect Rama and the girl."

When Jamison and Misho walked into the infirmary, Rama and Ms. Hiller were sitting in chairs apparently waiting for them. The two men stared at each other for a long moment. "We don't have much time. Are you prepared to go with us?"

"I'd rather stay, but you can at least leave Ms. Hiller. She's of no use to you."

"Very touching," Jamison said. "No, her DI boss, Parker, is the mastermind who's been keeping you under wraps and keeping the world in deep sleep for years. No, with what she knows, she'll be quite valuable indeed." Jamison motioned for them to go ahead out the door. Rama and Zita stood up and followed Misho out the door of the infirmary.

"Excuse me," Jamison said at the door as he turned back to the doctors and nurses lying on the floor. "This one knows too much," Jamison said, as he focused on Dr. Cherenkov. The doctor's unconscious body began to shake and tremble; Zita turned her head away, looking to Rama for help. She could feel the slight shift and saw Cherenkov's body go limp. Rama had shifted him, and Jamison could not detect it. Zita sighed in relief. Jamison turned back and hurried them out the door.

Part Four
Emergence

The Rama Journal

15 October 39. It appears my medical crisis is over, at least in their minds. Blood tests no longer show stray cancer cells, or any of the other innumerable ailments they have so carefully charted. Just letting them examine me was a deadly mistake. If I was merely indisposed before walking into their disease-minded clinic, I was definitely disposed of afterwards. The medical mind, or any mind for that matter, projects its history on every new situation. If it is conditioned to see illness, that is what it will see. And if it is not there, and the projecting mind is powerful enough, it will shift the person into it. Fortunately, my transformation shifted me out of my mind—no joke—which is the tool it uses to mold the other person. No mind, no influence.

20 October 39. They are preparing to move me back to my cell. No doubt another Renault is tending to another Rama in another clinical world. One where the doctor-patient relationship meets both their expectations. Maybe not. Watching my transformation has stopped Renault's world, as they say. Maybe his adjustment, which has been considerable, helped push me over. No doubt there is a synergy of sorts in these situations. And if one were to push the world over? You would first have to engage it. But, going deep enough, the many becomes the one, and if you can affect at that level, it is done.

2 November 39. I was sitting on my perch again viewing the mountainscape. It was beautiful. How I missed it. And then I shifted my consciousness. I was viewing these mountains from this perspective in another world or dimension. The change was subtle but glorious.

I now turned—in this world—back to viewing my cell and its contents. I shifted: it changed slightly; I shifted again, then again, and finally to a world or dimension where this prison's inherent vibration did not translate. How interesting. Are these inbetween states mirror worlds of increasingly higher vibration, each filtering out incompatible elements? Is the universe composed of layered worlds, stacked on top of each other, or somehow meshed together?

10 November 39. I have been experimenting. I find that, depending on my vibration, I can shift out into any number of dimensions. Shifting while thinking negative thoughts, I end up in a prison much worse than Bernia. There they treat me like an animal. How horrible. In another I walk with enlightened beings in a place of incomparable beauty. We are all Buddhas in one dimension, gangsters in another. All connected, all one. We must slide between these many worlds, tuning them as we past through. None can be saved, as they say, unless all are saved.

25 November 39. It is now apparent that my transformation, entering the no-mind state, is merely a second class ticket. I still have much to do. Yes. This world, ruled by thought, can no longer contain me. But my entrance into those more sublime dimensions, which I can only glimpse now, requires another ticket of sorts. Here I can develop my intuition, but how am I to develop my feelings. My human contact is so restricted. There is a friendly guard, Joseph Murdock, and my mother who visits, which provide some contact. Of course my feelings extend to my love of God and Earth, but I sense in this regard that I must reenter the human world to refine them. Maybe they will let me out one day. It is ironic that now they could just as easily confine me in a local jail in Geneva. I can evade their scalar fields, but it is human contact that I need, and even adobe walls can restrict that. Making my request, I must release it, wait on the shore for the universe to wash its answer back to me.

Chapter Nineteen

From an underground cellar, Rama stretched his etheric body through the trembling earth. He could feel the awful harshness of the accelerated mental energies from the freed psychics, whipping through its clay flesh, lashing it until the body writhed in pain. Each negative thought carried by a singular scalar wave sought out its complement in the earth's naturally generated waves: from the rotation of its inner core to the movement of tectonic plates, hooking up with them and depositing its load of energy on each formation, building up its stress. Rama could feel the earth's pain in the throbbing beat of its quickened pulse, and he shifted the planet out of phase with its previous vibration to forestall temporarily the disastrous union of waves. He alone could not effect a permanent shift, nor could he contend with the massive assault of wave activity, generated by the coming mental warfare, that would lower the planet's vibration with the attendant results. Rama would need assistance. However, the children, who could accomplish this task, were not responding.

From across the room, Zita watched the holy man meditating. The light level in the damp cellar was low, but she was aided in her scrutiny by the light of the man's aura which, although it did not illuminate his physical presence, reflected what was more discernible to her. It had been three days since their capture, and they were being kept together in this stone cellar. Rama had made a gallant but unnecessary appeal for separate quarters. Sharing the same space with the master, caressed by his sweet energies, was worth the inconvenience of a joint cell, if not the peril of their detention.

Zita could see from his limbering-up movements that Rama had finished his meditation. She waited for the holy man to speak.

"The earth suffers much," Rama said.

"Have the psychics begun?"

"No, but just their stray thoughts make her screech in agony."

"Can we do anything to stop them?"

"I cannot fight them, but with the others I might be able to shift the planet out of harm."

"The children?"

"Yes, but their intent may be different."

"You're not linked up with them?"

"They do not seek it," Rama said.

"And you trust their. . .knowingness?"

"As much as my own, but as parents say, they have a will of their own."

Zita found this uncertainty less than reassuring. "What will become of us?"

Rama smiled at the woman. "Hopefully, you will get us out of here."

Zita stared back at him. "You know."

"It was not so difficult to discern."

"Well, I'm no longer. . .working for them."

"But they did teach you such things?"

Zita nodded her head. "From what I've seen," she said, "this place is not. . .secured very well."

"Good. Then I can plan our vacation. I have some 'friends' in India who would put us up."

Zita laughed. "And I was thinking Paris would be a. . . stretch."

"It is always good, my dear," Rama said with a mischievous smile, "to stretch yourself to your absolute limits."

On the top floor of the old manor house, located on a sprawling estate in the French countryside near Lyon, a nurse was administering sedatives to six sleepless patients. Outside the impenetrable silence of their scalar cells, the freed psychics were having trouble functioning in a world constantly bombarding their delicate brain receptors with stimuli. Bates had taken the precaution of hiring a nurse and stocking their hideaway with an assortment of drugs used on the mentally disturbed. Upon their arrival, he had had blood samples drawn and analyzed by a psychopharmacologist. It appeared, by the residual drugs in their blood, that the prison doctors had been more concerned with their patients' psychic potentials than with their psychotic disorders. Bates' position was the reverse. To liberate the former, he had to subdue the latter. Jamison, who had thought the precautions unnecessary, was impressed with the man's foresight and concluded that Bates was still useful to him.

Downstairs, in the old drawing room, Edington and Gordon sat at two terminals tapped into the world's financial computer systems and telepathically gathered the access codes for normal on-line systems and for off-line systems considered invulnerable to computer hackers. For two years they had supplied these codes to a team of analysts mapping out the world's stock, commodities, and banking markets. Jamison and his psychics would need to know exactly where to attack these systems to bring them down, pilfer their assets, destroy their records, and insert viruses that would make them inoperable without their cooperation. Given the severity of the last assault by the psychics, it was amazing that more of these critical computer systems were not protected by photonic barrier modulators. But the world had grown arrogant with the perpetrators safely confined behind their scalar fields and with the world's security forces weeding out any psychic successors.

Jamison and Bates walked down the wide sweeping marble staircase between floors and went into the operation room. The half-dozen analysts in firmaglass cubicles were busy studying their monitors. Jamison asked Edington and Wernher Ehrlich, their chief analyst, to follow them. The group walked down the hall to the den. They entered, closing the door behind them, and took seats at an old oak table, oval-shaped and engraved with elaborate dragon designs. Ehrlich passed around disks of his final report and nervously tapped the table leg with his boot as they read it.

"Excellent, Wernher," Jamison finally said looking up from his computer notepad. "Are we seeing any added security on these systems?"

"Nothing extraordinary, surprisingly enough," Ehrlich replied. "Most of the codes have been changed since the breakout. An exercise in futility, and they know it. I had at least expected them to take some of the more vulnerable systems off-line to make it more difficult for us, but I am not seeing signs of that."

"If I were expecting an attack," Bates said, stroking his chin, "I'd be fortifying my defenses, unless I was setting a trap."

"We've checked and they don't have backup systems," Edington said.

Bates turned to Jamison. "Then what's their game?"

"Parker knows we're coming, and so he must be baiting the hook. He wants to engage us, and while we're exposed, attack with his subliminal teams."

"He has that much confidence in them?" Bates asked in alarm.

"Apparently."

"And you're prepared for them?"

"Yes, George, we were rather looking forward to it. Weren't we Billy?"

"We've been keeping tabs on them for the past two years, and they don't have anybody at our level," Edington said.

"You mean nobody as strong as your whacked-out friends upstairs," Bates snapped.

"George, please. We can handle them, and our 'friends' will be just fine." Jamison turned to his analyst. "Wernher, are we on schedule?"

"Late Wednesday. To catch both Asian and Euro markets trading. Of course the North American markets won't be open, and they won't open once the others crash."

"I would've thought we'd want to crash them on-line?" Bates asked.

"That's what Parker's waiting for," Jamison said. "He has his own systems wired more closely. He sees us coming, draws us into an exchange, while they take the Euros and Asians off line."

"If I had my choice," Ehrlich interjected, "I'd do the North Americans first, but we need to crash at least two of the big three for our plan to work."

Jamison turned to Bates. "And how long before they find us, George?"

"Apparently the jamming worked. Euro air traffic could only narrow it down to a thousand-kilometer-wide circle. If they can't trace your psychic signals back to the source, as you claim, I'd say we have at least a week."

"And everything's set for the move?"

"The barge is ready, and the villa in Majorca."

"Good. I want to be able to move out on a moment's notice."

In Tokyo the World Council convened an emergency session to address the mounting crisis. Although the freed psychics had not made blackmail demands nor mounted an attack on the financial markets, the general population, expecting the worst, had made a run on banks and stock markets worldwide. The rather weak assurances from the council that the situation was under control did little to slow down the frenzy of cashing-in and selling-off. This World Council session should have been a rallying point for governments trying to calm panicked citizens, but the world states were publicly blaming each other for the catastrophe, and their petty bickering made concerted action appear highly unlikely.

Protesters, wearing bright yellow environ coats and hoods, their faces covered by sunglasses and globs of sunscreen lotion, had been crowding the streets around the World Council building in downtown Tokyo for two days. News teams from around the globe, barred from the council session itself, were roaming among the frantic protesters taping live interviews and adding their own mostly negative commentary. The subdued World Council members, riding the underground bullet train from the airport, were able to avoid the anxious crowds and slipped unnoticed from their cars in the basement of this steel and smoked-glass shrine to world order. The interior elevator quickly lifted them to the top floor. Here they entered the much-photographed council chamber with its equally famous round table of Japanese red cypress. The seven members took their seats. Now, in total privacy, they were able to relax their hostile stance and talk cordially with each other.

Contrary to their public display of rivalry and contention, the world states were unified in defense of their common security interests. When Michael Parker stepped up to the podium, the council members greeted him with light applause.

"Thank you, gentlemen. It has been a trying time for us all, so let me get to the point. The psychics have been freed from Bernia and are set up somewhere in the French Province of Europe. We are expecting the first attack at any time. One of our objectives is to minimize the damage from their attack on the targeted banking and stock markets, but I must emphasize again that unless the population thinks another economic collapse is imminent, they will not respond with sufficient emotional distress to trigger, we believe, the balancing strategies of the Biologicals."

"Well, if the markets do crash, and it's irrecoverable, killing off the BMIs becomes a moot operation as far as I'm concerned," said Ian Sutherland, representing the Australian Islands.

"As you know, we've been setting up this operation for quite some time. In the last two years we've managed to disguise key financial assets and, where deemed necessary, withdraw or liquidate them. But we have had to leave a sufficient amount intact, the liability spread evenly among the seven states, or their analysts would have become suspicious."

"I just hope you left us enough of a base to rebuild from," Sutherland replied.

"Mr. Parker," said Antonio Serra, the Brazilian, who represented South America. "We agreed to cooperate with your scheme, because of the common threat to humanity and its religious and cultural heritage, but as you and the others gathered here know, South America is by far the poorest of the world states, and we stand to suffer the most."

"Mr. Serra, you should take this protest. . ." Parker replied.

"Sir, I am not complaining. Our people know the face of deprivation better than yours. I just want the assurance that you can contain the psychics, who have already wrecked my country's economy once, before they ruin us again."

"The Europeans have agreed to use nuclears if the situation gets out of hand."

Serra was impressed and looked to Paul Lafontaine, the European council member. "If it becomes necessary. . .you can count on us." The man nodded his head in polite reply, while wondering what possible help they could render.

Huan Wei, the Asian member and chairman of the council, turned from this exchange back to Michael Parker. "My scientists have read your report on the dimensional shift by the boy in Toronto. They wonder if you can really spot the shift as fast as you claim. If you cannot, your plan to overwhelm them is doomed to failure."

"We have placed atomic clocks in proximity to all known biologicals. Any shift will be immediately detectable," Parker said adamantly, as the others considered his explanation.

Wei shook his head. "They agree that, once the shift has commenced, flooding the fourth dimension with scalar waves could destroy them, but again can we act quick enough with a sufficient load?"

"Mr. Wei, I have already covered the science in a previous briefing to this council."

"Then please indulge me again," the chairman replied.

Parker gathered himself. "My scientists tell me that the fourth dimension or spacetime is not filled with virtual charge or charged particles, like sunlight in our dimension, but that it is composed of this finer scalar energy. It would be as if the energy locked away in solid matter were readily available."

"Or as if all matter on the planet were radioactive," Wei added.

"Yes. The next concept is that, when we speak of the fourth dimension, we are not talking of infinite space, but of a localized part of the spacetime continuum, a mirror image, as it were, of the third-dimensional space it reflects."

"So it is composed of energy and exists in a confined space."

"And by flooding it with scalar waves from our generators, we can stress it with this additional charge, like pumping air into an inner tube, expanding it to the breaking point or bursting its bubble, as it were." Parker looked around the table, and the council members nodded their heads. He continued, "And the biologicals must operate from this dimension to effect change, and while there they are totally vulnerable."

Mr. Wei smiled wanly. "I believe the question is whether you can pump the air in fast enough to trap them there."

"In the estimation of our scientists," Parker said, taking a deep breath, "who have been working with scalars for twenty-five years, along with the best minds in dimensional physics, it is. And I trust their judgment."

"Well sir," Wei said, his voice straining. "I hope this council has not erred in trusting yours."

Arthur Hays, the North American council member, stood to voice a protest on Parker's behalf, when the doors to the chamber opened and an assistant rushed up to Mr. Wei. This extraordinary breach in protocol by the stiffly proper Asians silenced the diplomat, who patiently awaited the results of their consultation. Having relayed his message, the assistant bowed to the members of the council and hurried out.

"It appears, Mr. Parker, that your theory and those of your colleagues will soon be put to the test," Wei said obliquely, making the other members hang on his words.

Hays finally asked, "They've begun the attack?"

"Begun and ended," Wei said. Glaring at Parker, he added, "They have crashed the Asian and European financial markets in the time it took you to give us your explanation."

"We expected as much," Parker replied coolly.

"Well, I hope we can expect as definite a reply from you. And, until then, this council is adjourned."

The council members hurried from the chamber to their offices in the building for updates on the attack and the damage to their respective countries. Hays asked Parker to accompany him, but Parker respectfully declined, saying he needed to return to his command center on the DI spaceplane. In the basement, he hurried onto the train waiting to take the council members to the airport. He entered a private compartment reserved for him and his staff. Mark Owens, his operational analyst, who acted as his assistant on trips abroad, glanced up from his notepad.

"Guess you heard?"

Parker nodded his head. "What's the damage?"

Owens entered a three-letter code into the computer and brought up the damage assessment report on today's attack. He handed the notepad to his boss. "There's not much yet." Sitting down on the opposite bench, Parker took the notepad and scanned the report. Owens added, "It could be worse than we expected."

"Jamison's done his homework, and the speed and precision of their attack indicates that the Bernia boys have recovered from their drug treatment and are as effective as ever."

The train slid out of the underground station on its ten-minute run to the airport. Owens asked, "I wonder if it's the new recruits?"

Parker looked up from the computer. "Some of Jamison's students are as advanced as our psychics, but not to this degree." He thought for a moment. "Did Zandar call? Are the clocks on-line?"

"Yeah, he said to tell you the clocks were ticking."

"As if atomic clocks ticked," Parker said shaking his

head. "I think Peter is already in the fourth dimension."

Owens laughed but knew not to join in debunking the Chief, who was fair game for Parker but not for him. The train arrived; they were met by a limousine and driven halfway around the outer rim of the airport to the spaceplane terminal. As soon as they boarded, the plane taxied out and waited for clearance. In minutes it wás racing down the long runway and flying off into the night sky. They soared above the twinkling lights of Tokyo, and when the scramjets kicked in, hurled toward the region of the unblinking stars above.

The on-board command center was buzzing with activity. Michael Parker was the man of the moment. He had been waiting for this moment his entire career, but he was caught out of place for the moment flying above a world he had left devastated by his devious plan. When the children were discovered and their progress secretly monitored, he had been the first to see the threat they posed to the world governments' control over their benumbed populations. Parker had campaigned long and hard to convince the politicians that the biologicals (his term) were a far more serious threat to that control than Rama or the lunatics in Bernia. His colleagues in the intelligence community eventually had been won over by the mounting evidence, and they in turn had convinced the world state leaders to draw up contingency plans. It was Baba's dimensional shift that had finally convinced them to activate their plan to allow Jamison to free the psychics and set up the present confrontation. The World Council held Parker and his colleagues accountable for its success, and security chiefs were nervously calling for assurances.

Owens transferred a call from Walther Kauss in Europe to Parker's small office at the back of the plane. "Yes, Walther," Parker answered.

"We discovered a plant at the prison. Grilling him now. Might come up with something soon. If we can locate Jamison, how far should I stay back? I don't want to risk losing him."

"Are you still at Bernia?"

"No, we brought him back with us."

"I hope you're blocking out the 'interview,'" Parker said with alarm.

"No, but we will."

"Whatever you get, don't act on it yet. Don't even think about it, as they say."

"Okay, I can wait. Remember, the man is in my backyard, and I will have to bring him in."

"Maybe not, maybe we can eliminate him from this end."

"That would be helpful. But, as you Americans say, I will believe it when I see it." He broke the connection.

Owens stuck his head in the door. "I've got Wang on the line."

"I can't mollycoddle everybody. You talk to him, Mark." Owens stepped back and closed the door.

Parker turned to his computer monitor and punched up the readings, relayed by satlink, from the atomic clocks positioned around the globe. They were all synchronous. Apparently the shift had not begun. He now sat back and reviewed his plan of attack. Their psychics would not attempt to reclaim financial markets worldwide, to bring downed market systems back on-line, or to seek out the pilfered assets. They would instead attack their opponents directly; the power of a hundred psychic minds would be focused on the six outlaws from Bernia. The object, as with the lost assets, was not to kill them or prevent another attack, but to engage them in a deadly exchange of mental scalar waves that would hopefully draw the children into the battle. When the biologicals sought to counterbalance the effects of their warfare with a dimensional shift, Parker would switch on his underground scalar generators located in bunkers around the world and flood their fourth-dimensional world with a massive influx of scalar waves that hopefully would either trap them there or destroy that world—and them along with it.

Chapter Twenty

His eyes wandered from one rock formation to another, sweeping across the white sand, along flat stretches onto rippled hills and into raked trenches, until he came upon another jagged colossus rising upward from the sand unexpectedly, on no known chart, part of no known pattern, its sheer physicality drawing the eyes like a magnet from the desert world below. He climbed upward from crevice to crevice to the top and down the other side, and again his eyes traveled the white sand, but now intoxicated with its featureless vista, his mind expanding across this endless terrain. Another rock, several small ones in a row, like steppingstones, drew his focus and his eyes jumped them, one after the other, and the joy of it made his eyes dance and stilled his mind.

Dr. Henry Halzack, sitting alone on a bench, looked up from the Japanese rock garden on the roof of the science building. The roof was otherwise deserted, as was most of the building; colleagues and students were staying in the safer confines of their homes, waiting for further news and clinging to their small parcels of security. Halzack spread his feeling web out into the world, as Baba had shown him, and felt the fear and terror around him, in his family and friends, and then he went deeper, touching the battered soul of his race. Its pain was nearly unbearable, and he expected it, like a man in his death throes, to roll over and release its dying breath at any moment. Halzack refused to allow this awful pressure to build any further. If he could release it—he was certain of it—and reclaim that soul, he was bound by conscience to proceed. Some would ask what right had he to make such a momentous decision? He would reply that access sometimes denoted right, and in this case, he would act as if circumstances had chosen him for whatever reason, and he would not shrink from it.

Halzack stood up from his bench and walked over to the elevator. At the twelfth floor, he stepped out and walked around the curving outside corridor to the conference room where he had left the others an hour earlier. Dr. Burke was conferring with Cosgrove when Halzack stepped into the room. He turned to him. "Henry, we were getting ready to call the rescue squad."

Dr. Halzack smiled faintly. "Where's Baba?"

Everybody stopped and looked at their steely-eyed colleague before Dana Cosgrove replied, "He's in his quarters back at the dorm."

"Well, I'm going to get him, and if he's willing, we're going to go through with it, with or without your support."

The others were momentarily flabbergasted. Benjamin Burke was the first to respond. "I'll go down and prepare the lab."

Malcolm Beaton shook his head. "Your resolve is commendable, Henry, but you don't have the authority to. . ."

"Malcolm, shut up," Halzack said. He looked over at Dr. Cosgrove. "Dana, I'll need you to translate."

She nodded her head in reply. "You go along with Ben. I'll get Baba."

Halzack turned back to Beaton, his long-time friend. "Do you go home and forget you were here, or do I lock you up in the bathroom?"

Beaton was stunned by his colleague's threat. "Okay, I'm leaving, but whatever happens, don't talk to the press."

"All right," Halzack said. He looked to the others. "Let's go." He turned, and they followed him out the door.

When Dana Cosgrove arrived at the college dormitory, she knocked on the boy's door, and Roya answered it immediately. "Baba said you were coming for him."

Dana could see the woman's apprehension, and she

reached over and took her hand. "It'll be fine, Roya. Trust me."

Baba came out of the bathroom zipping up his pants. He smiled at Dana. "In case we get stuck."

"Thanks for the warning," Dana replied.

At the university, Burke was in the third floor modulation lab setting the electronic feedback equipment in the tank. He ran one of the electrodes down his sweater to create measurable static electricity. "Henry, can you read that?"

Dr. Halzack, out of his element, tentatively leaned over the electronic board with its array of lights, dials, and switches, and saw a blinking indicator. "The little red light in the right corner," said Halzack. He added, "Why aren't they marked?"

"So people like you can't sneak in here and use the board," Burke said from the tank. He finished checking the rest of the array, and went up the stairs into the control room. He walked over to Dr. Halzack.

"Well, I hope you know what you're getting us into," Burke said.

"I was hoping you could tell me," Halzack said half-seriously.

"Hell, I know more about dimensional shifting than anybody, and it beats me," Burke replied. He could see his colleague's trepidation. "Don't blanch on me now, Henry. Look, I go along with your evolutionary explanation: they're the next step, and this is what they do, this is their process, like ours is dissecting lab rats. So, let them do it and hold on for the ride."

Halzack had to laugh. "This is what I get for throwing in with weird science."

Dr. Cosgrove stepped into the control room. The boy and his mother followed after her. When Baba saw Dr. Burke, he raised his watch in the air, and the two scientists came over.

"So have all the hands begun to spin together?" Burke asked the boy.

"No, Dr. Ben, but they will soon," Baba said, and Cosgrove translated.

Halzack turned to Cosgrove. "Did you say anything to him?"

Cosgrove shook her head. "He knew we were coming, and I assumed he knew why."

Burke squatted and spoke to Baba. "So you're going to call your friends together."

"Yes, we have been waiting for you to ask."

"This place, the well, where you meet, you're going to take us there?"

"'Down the rabbit's hole we shall go.'"

Burke was puzzled by the reference, and Dana Cosgrove said, "*Alice in Wonderland.*"

Roya added, "It is his favorite story."

"It must be a very large hole for all the world to fit," Burke said.

Baba's expression turned serious. "Dr. Ben, you are already there, this is wonderland, if you could see it." Baba stepped over and gave the scientist a hug. He pulled back and said, "I hear them calling."

Dr. Burke stood up and, taking the child by the hand, led him down the steps into the modulation tank. Burke attached the electrodes to his head and asked Baba if he minded the monitoring devices.

"Baba, the lab rat," he said, astounding Dr. Burke. "Do you hear everything?"

Baba put his cupped hands over his ears and mimicked listening to music on a headset. "All the tunes."

He stepped back and stared at this smiling Buddha-boy. The remote monitors with their tiny antennas stuck out from his head, giving him the appearance of a high-tech bushman. "Just tune in, Baba; we're with you." The boy smiled enigmatically. The scientist turned and ran up the steps to the control room. The others had watched the curious exchange, and they waited for their colleague to speak.

"He's ready, if we are," Burke said.

Sitting in the controller's seat, Halzack leaned forward and spoke into the microphone. "Okay, Baba, go to 'The Well,' and answer their call."

The boy closed his eyes and immediately the monitoring equipment registered the lower frequency brain-wave patterns that characterized his journey into fourth-dimensional space. Dr. Burke was monitoring the live feed to the atomic clock in Boulder in the western province, and he saw the two digital clocks clicking off. "Well, there goes the first shift. It's only a one-hundred-millionth of a second, but it's starting."

In the cellar of the manor house, Rama could feel the harsh mental energies directed at the psychics, passing through the earth and engulfing the house. The woman, lying on a cot pushed up against the far wall, again stirred restlessly in her sleep. Rama had extended his aura to surround and protect her, but he could not totally shield her from the vicious wave of attacks. He felt a slight earthquake tremor that shook the house. This was the third that night, and they were hitting closer. The shaking woke Zita. She sat up and shivered in the damp morning air, wrapping the wool blanket around herself.

"What was that?" she asked.

"An earthquake tremor."

"They're striking back?"

"Yes, back and forth for hours now," Rama said. "It is a curious strategy."

"Michael's going after them directly, isn't he?"

Rama nodded his head. "This Michael; he was your boss?"

"Yes, and more."

"You know he is as. . .bad as the others. Maybe worse."

"Yes, as I discovered fairly late."

"Do not worry," Rama said. "When we get to Asia, I will introduce you to a nice Brahman boy."

Zita laughed. "How close was that tremor?"

"Close."

"We'd better get out of here before the house falls on us," Zita said, standing up and straightening her clothes. She went over and looked out the barred glass window. Peitro Ghiberti, an old-fashioned hunting rifle lying on his lap, sat in a chair propped up against the stone wall. She turned back to Rama, "He's not one of them?"

"No. Just a hired thug."

Zita knelt down and examined the lock. "I could pick this, if you could. . ."

"I can not use force myself, nor can you harm anybody on my behalf."

"Well, that makes it a lot harder."

"It just requires more imagination."

Zita thought for a moment, and a plan came to her. "Could you create a. . .disturbance down the hall?"

Rama nodded his head. "To draw him away?"

"Yes, and then I'll pick the lock and swing the door open. Hopefully, when he comes back, he'll think we've fled and won't check the cell."

"And if he sticks his head in here?"

"We're caught, unless you can make us disappear."

Rama smiled. "Let me see what I can do." The holy man sat down on one of the metal folding chairs and closed his eyes. Zita watched him in nervous anticipation. Rama popped open one eye. "Don't forget the lock."

Standing up against the wall, Zita peeked out the window at the guard. Suddenly, there was a loud pop. Ghiberti jumped up from his chair, and it crashed to the floor. He glanced down the hall, then back at the cellar door. There was another pop. He stepped over and tested the door knob. He turned and jogged off down the hall, rifle in hand. Zita knelt down. She stuck the pin from her belt buckle into the old mechanical lock, jiggling it. In a moment she turned the knob and cracked open the door.

Zita looked back at Rama, amazed to discover him standing under the light fixture, a shoe and sock in either hand. "Sorry, but it is the best I can do." He slipped the sock through the wire grate and worked it over the bulb with his fingers. He hit the fixture with the heel of his shoe, breaking the bulb and darkening the room. Zita slowly swung open the door; the light, edging around its end, formed a rectangle on the stone floor. Rama and Zita slipped into the shadows of the opposite corners. In a minute, Ghiberti stuck his head into the cellar and tried switching on the overhead light. He cursed in Italian and stepped back.

After a moment, Zita saw the holy man walking out of the shadow. She almost yelled out to him, but caught herself. Zita closed her eyes and shifted into the other space.

- *Go back. This could be a trick.*
- *Yes, of course.*

A moment later Ghiberti's rifle barrel preceded him into the room. He looked around the cell, shook his head, and hurried out the door. This time they could hear him cursing as he ran down the hall. Zita stepped out from the darkened corner and slowly approached the door, her hands up ready to take or to deliver a blow. She stuck her head out into the hall, looking both ways. It was clear. Turning back to Rama, she said, "Let's get our coats, and get out of here."

They ran down the hall in the opposite direction from the guard's exit. Around the first corner, they spotted a door with a window at the end of another long hall. When she came up on it, Zita broke a window pane with her elbow and opened the door from the outside. They scampered up the steps that led to the grounds. Although it was still night, the glow of first light could be seen at the edge of the enveloping darkness. Several lights on the outbuildings revealed an outline of the compound. Zita quickly surveyed the surroundings.

"Our best hope is to steal a car and try to reach a thoroughfare," Zita said, anticipating resistance.

"Stealing I can live with. Just don't run anybody over," Rama said. Zita hurried off toward the barn with the holy man following after her. Inside, there were an assortment of electric vehicles. At the front was an old Renault two-seater. Zita leaned over the driver's seat and checked the battery charge. It had three-quarters of a full charge. She went over to open the barn doors. Surprisingly enough it was unlocked. She swung the door open and went back to the car. Rama had seated himself in the passenger's side. Zita quickly dismantled the steering cover and hot-wired the electrical engine.

"Yes, the practical arts," Rama said. He paused for a moment. "There are men coming out of the main house."

"Okay, hold on to your restrainer." Zita drove the car out of the barn and down the driveway. Ghiberti jumped in front of the car with his rifle pointed at them. "Bend down," Zita shouted. She swerved the car around the man, jumped a ditch, ran through a wire fence and headed across the open field.

Rama sat up in his seat until he heard bullets zinging past them. "The man?" he asked.

Zita shook her head in amazement. "He's shooting at us." Suddenly the engine of the car died out. She reached over and tapped the amp meter, but it showed a good charge.

Rama reached over and touched an exposed wire in the ignition assembly. The car started up. "We make a good team."

"But will it land us back in prison," Zita retorted. She drove the car across the field and onto an adjoining country road and sped away.

The sun was rising over the fields directly in front of them, shining through the windshield tint. Zita ran her finger behind the brown cover. "It's pretty thin. Wouldn't want to drive very long in this light." They approached a sign for Lyon, France, twenty-five kilometers ahead. "Good. They have a notorious sub-culture. We could find a fleabag hotel, no questions asked, and hole up for awhile." She waited, but the holy man did not reply. "You weren't serious about trying to make India?"

"Your people will be after us too?"

"I would imagine," Zita said. The holy man nodded his head. "Just walking into a train station would be announcing our presence."

"Invitations to a dance," Rama said obliquely.

"More like a hanging."

"Some people have to stretch their necks to see the true territory."

Zita shook off the suggestion. "Are you sure?"

"Ms. Hiller, one is never sure of anything. We can only propose and allow God to dispose." Rama turned his head and stared out the window at the passing countryside. "Besides, how else would we meet up with your Brahman boy?"

When Ghiberti raced up the stairs to the living quarters hunting for Bates, he walked into a scene of wild pandemonium. Half the psychics had been subdued and were strapped to their beds. One was cowering in the corner psychically lashing out at the men trying to restrain him. Another, strapped to a doctor's chair, was receiving an injection. The last lay dead on the floor, shot in the forehead by Bates, who still held the revolver in his hand. Ghiberti hesitantly approached his boss. "They got away."

"Damn it, man. He's worth a million pounds to us," Bates said, glaring back at his pilot, his finger closing around the revolver's trigger before it eased off. He went over to Jamison, who sat in a circle with his two companions, trying to shield the group from their attackers. Bates tapped the man on the shoulder. "They've escaped."

Jamison opened his eyes long enough to acknowledge him, then closed them and continued with his visualization. A moment later, Edington snapped out of his trancelike state. He shook his head and blinked his eyes several times. He stood up. "I saw them in the barn taking a car; we'll have to hurry to catch them."

The three men ran down the stairs and out the front door of the manor house just as the Renault sped up the driveway. Ghiberti stepped out in front of the car and leveled his rifle at the driver. He heard Edington telling him to take the shot; he squeezed the trigger of the rifle. But, at the last moment, the barrel was knocked out of line. The car swerved around him and jumped the ditch, heading out across the field. Ghiberti knelt down and took aim at the car but the barrel kept dipping, causing him to shoot short of the target.

Bates had headed for the barn to start up another car and pursue them, but all the car batteries were dead. When Ghiberti came back and reported to him, he threw a fit. "Pietro, you just cost me a ton of money." In frustration, Bates punched the young man in the face, breaking his nose.

Jamison was furious about Rama's escape. Unlike his greedy partner, he was more concerned about the man's strategic value. Had he evaded Ghiberti in the cellar, like he had hid from them during the break-in, by dimensional shifting? What else was he capable of doing? Jamison assumed that his keepers had discovered just such a capability and found it too lethal to contain. He had no doubt that they had planned to release Rama in order to kill him. If his plans succeeded, would his future domain be threatened as well? He had hoped to learn the secret to dimensional shifting, but realized that if it were teachable, Rama could instruct others, and he and his psychic friends would be back to square one. The World Council was right. The man was too dangerous to be kept alive.

At this point, however, Jamison's chief concern was his battle with the World Council and its psychic force. The night of sustained attacks had taken its toll. He had lost one of his fragile friends, and he did not know how severely the others were affected. Sustaining and reinforcing an auric field was different from focused visualization. Their long incarceration and drug treatment had left the men so emotionally unstable that they could barely defend themselves. Since their powers were undiminished, it appeared that their only defense would be an unrelenting offense.

The men met for a late breakfast in the kitchen of the old manor house with its copper pots and pans hanging from the ceiling. Sanchez, who had had more than one stint as an undercover cook in his checkered career, scrambled eggs and fried substitute bacon for the crew. While they ate, Jamison gave them his analysis of the situation.

"I assumed since they were so advanced they could ward off any attack," Bates said,

"It's their instability; they're much worse than I thought."

"I think their keepers saw this possibility, destabilized them with drugs, in case they were ever pitted against them. Dr. Jurgens said he's found some very exotic compounds in their blood."

"It appears so, George," Jamison said. "Although their powers are unaffected, their ability to focus them is eroding."

"Which makes them useless."

"Yes, if that were our only strategy."

"Oh really," Bates said, his voice edged with sarcasm. "We have another? Whatever could that be?"

"It was edited out of my scalar books, but Parker should've dug a little deeper: scalar waves, hooking up with naturally occurring waves in tectonic plates, can precipitate earthquakes."

"You just spray the vicinity with scalars, letting the quakes knock out their underground facilities."

Jamison nodded his head. "However, it is something of a 'Doomsday Device,' since the unabsorbed waves can bounce back in our direction."

"Well, professor, I don't see where we have a choice. If they keep knocking us out, we lose anyway. And, if I'm going down, I don't mind taking the world with me."

"George, you're a real scourge," Edington said in grudging admiration. Bates smiled, his gold front tooth reflecting the light of the overhead incandescents.

Chapter Twenty-one

At North America's eastern subliminal facility, Michael Parker stood at the window in the command booth and watched the psychics in their glass booths during a break in their ongoing battle. Some were listening to music on headsets or viewing virtual reality tapes. Others had gone down the hall to the cafeteria or were napping in their sleeping quarters. All were on instant callback, and in an emergency they could actually "send" from anywhere in the facility. Dr. Jan Van Dorn stepped over and took a look at his crew.

"I gave them an hour break."

"They can use it," Parker said sarcastically. "What do your follow-ups show?"

"They were hit pretty hard; we definitely nailed one of them."

Parker turned and glared at his assistant. "That's not the objective."

"It wasn't us directly; they either killed them or they did themselves in."

"That makes a difference?" Parker asked incredulously. His assistant looked away. "Tell your people to monitor them more closely; this isn't target practice." The man nodded his head.

"Oh, we're getting a lot of stray scalar activity. Can't tell if it's natural or them missing."

"Just here?"

"It's pretty broad-ranged, but more intense around our facilities, so it must be them."

Parker thought for a moment. "I don't like the sound of that. Hit them with a low-grade sweep and see if that affects the level."

The vidphone buzzed in the background. Van Dorn turned and saw that it was the red security phone. "It's yours. I'll round the others up."

Parker walked back to the desk. "If I'm not here, I'll be down the hall checking the clocks." Van Dorn nodded his head and hurried off.

Parker flipped on the vidphone. Walther Kauss's grey-bearded, dour face stared back at him. "Is it him?"

"It is Rama and the woman. Got on the TransEuro at Lyon."

"Hope they're having a comfortable train ride."

"They are in a private first-class compartment. Easier for us to apprehend them but also easier for him to 'operate.'"

"Yes, that tells us something. She'd know that third-class seating was safer."

"Do we pick them up in Munich, or let the honeymoon continue?"

Parker laughed. "That's funny, Walther." He thought for a moment. "Our last attack knocked out some of Jamison's capability, and that might've slowed down their timetable. If we take Rama out, especially if he's in contact, the BMIs might speed things up before the others chime in."

"Okay," Kauss said. "In Munich, I will catch the train and watch them myself."

"And I'll have my people monitor them from here and keep you posted."

Kauss groaned. "I'd rather see the whites of their eyes."

"Well, if Rama blinks, grab him," Parker joked, but Kauss did not catch the reference. "Call me, when you're in place."

Parker looked up and saw the psychics coming back into the operation's room and taking their places. He hurried out the door and down the hall, heading for the communications room. It had been augmented with a half-dozen digital wall clock monitors, calibrated to one-billionth of a second, linked with atomic clocks from around the world set up to detect any shift into the fourth dimension. The room also served as Parker's satellite link-up with the scalar wave generators located in bunkers at strategic locations worldwide. It was their estimate that portals into the next dimension, which these generators were set up to penetrate, would most likely first appear in unstable fissure zones along earthquake faults. The heightened scalar activity here was evidence, some scientists thought, of tears in the space/time continuum.

When Parker walked into the room, Charles Hornig, the scalar wave expert who headed the 4-D monitoring team, looked up from his control board. Parker immediately turned to view the clocks. There was a small discrepancy, only one-hundred-millionth of a second, in four of the six clocks.

He turned sharply to Hornig. "Why wasn't I notified?"

"We agreed it wasn't a shift until all the clocks registered it."

Parker groaned. This was such a typical attitude; these scientists could be so dense. He started to reprimand him, when Hornig's expression changed. Parker turned and stared in amazement at the wall of clocks. They were all spinning through their numbers finally ending with one-ten-millionth of a second shift from standard time.

Parker said, "Hey Charlie, anything to report?" Dr. Hornig thought of a snappy reply, but the digital clocks caught him open-mouthed, as they spun through another series of numbers.

"Tell me this isn't happening in one massive shift," Parker said in alarm.

"Remember," Hornig added, "they have to spin through a lot of numbers to reach even one-millionth of a second."

Four of the clocks stopped, registering five-hundred-thousandth of a second. In a moment, the last two stopped spinning at one-hundred-thousandth of a second. Parker turned around to Hornig. "Since distance isn't a real factor, the uneven shifting amazes me."

"These are buffer zone shifts, remember. You'd expect

a lot of fluctuation back and forth until everything gets shifted over," said Hornig excitedly.

The man's enthusiasm annoyed Parker. "Which, if you'll remember, is what we're here to prevent."

"Yes, of course," Hornig replied, his eyes dimming. Suddenly, the room started to shake violently, knocking one of the digital clock monitors off the wall and cracking its firmaglass cover. Parker grabbed hold of the doorjamb for support, and Hornig held the side of the metal communication's board. The shaking lasted ten seconds.

"Was that another shift?" Parker asked, brushing the plaster dust off his suit coat.

"No, it felt more like an earthquake tremor." Hornig checked his board, tapping a dial and recalibrating the gauge. He was startled when the teleprinter hummed into action, quickly printing out a half-dozen messages. Parker leaned over and read the monitor as Hornig pulled the hard copies from the printer. They finished reading together and looked up.

"How can it be earthquakes if everybody is getting hit at the same time?" Parker asked.

Hornig thought for a moment. "There is a way." He scooted his chair over to his desk and talked to his monitor screen, "Master File: Jamison: Theories: Scalar Waves: Earthquakes: Call up and Print." The file appeared on his screen and began to fill his printer bin. Hornig quickly scanned the report.

"Dammit man, just give it to me," Parker finally snapped.

The scientist looked up at him. "Jamison claimed that stray scalar waves passing through the earth could hook up with their natural complement in tectonic plate zones, causing further stress."

"Yeah, I remember, and we dismissed it because. . ."

"Because, based on equal values for all scalar waves, whatever their source, the amount needed, for even one earthquake, would be astronomical."

Parker nodded his head. "But Jamison claimed they differed by source. What the MIT boys called his 'Psycho Theory.' Even in their current unstable state, when they can't focus on individual targets, they could still spray the earth with, let's call them 'heavy' scalars, and depending on their value, precipitate earthquakes worldwide."

The facility was hit by a massive earthquake that lifted the room vertically as well as moving it horizontally. This splintered the firmaglass windows in the office and in those across the hall, splattering them with tiny plastic slivers. The teleprinter and its stand, attached to the floor, was ripped up and flung across the room. The other computer equipment, though still attached to tables and stands, was destroyed. The shaking stopped, and Parker, his face cut and bleeding, stepped over to the emergency satlink phone. He tapped out the combination on the metal box, opened the compartment and picked up the phone. He was immediately connected to the Director in Washington.

"Michael, is that you?" Peter Zandar asked from the other side.

"Yeah, what's left of me," Parker said. "How're things at your end?"

"Not bad. Only a 2.5 tremor, but there're 8.0s all over the place, and both Utah and Mexico's been knocked out."

"That leaves only us and Ontario?" Parker said in astonishment. "What about the generators, we lost contact?"

"Two down so far."

"Look, the shift's only starting, but we can't wait. . .," Parker said, his voice broken up by static.

"I agree," Zandar said. "Take out as many as we can before. . ."

The emergency lights blinked out. Parker heard what sounded like a torrent of water breaking through a damn and rushing onward. In the next moment, the ceiling and walls of the office caved in; Parker and Hornig were buried under an avalanche of dirt and stone. Five hundred feet of earth, tons of loose rock and crystal, the deflection barriers for the facility's sensitive psychic work, had poured through the huge cracks in the outer walls of the underground fortress, killing everybody inside.

At the other end, the satlink went dead. "Michael, you still there?" Zandar asked. There was no reply. He hung up the phone in the emergency command center and walked over to the communication's board. His assistant, who entered all the initial enabler codes, stepped aside. Zandar took the microphone, "Peter Zandar: Operation Flood: activation code WC 3965679321: Commence." The board lit up and showed that the six operational scalar wave generators, located around the world, had received the command and were charging up.

In France at their country estate, Jamison and his cohorts had little time to celebrate their apparent victory over the World Council. As with most of the world, they were picking up after a string of earthquakes—aftershocks were still shaking southern Europe—and volcanic eruptions along the Pacific Ring, precipitated by the psychic exchange between the two sides, had killed hundreds of millions worldwide and caused massive damage. But, with the destruction of North America's four underground subliminal facilities, including most of their psychics, Michael Parker and his top aides, Jamison appeared to be in a superior position in his negotiations with the World Council and its chairman, Huan Wei. However, the man was amazingly resistant to their demands. This was as unnerving as it was threatening. Was the war in fact over, or did the WC have recourse to more lethal weapons?

Jamison sat at his makeshift desk in the den of the manor house replaying Huan Wei's taped reply to their monetary and ecological demands on his portable video monitor. The man was sitting at the oval table of red Japanese cedar at the World Council Building in Tokyo flanked by the other six council members, their dour faces lined up like cemetery stones along either side.

"Mr. Jamison, you have placed us in a very untenable position in regard to your demands. It is true that you have brought the world states to their knees with your wanton attacks on our financial institutions. But the resulting ecological damage to the planet, not to mention the millions killed by earthquakes and those who will die from exposure to the lethal natural elements, has compromised your position. We find it ironic that you would begin your journey to ecological paradise by aggravating—almost beyond repair, our scientists tell us—the very conditions you seek to ameliorate. You, sir, are a terrorist, despite your high-minded agenda and your pseudo-religious stance, and while you have the upper hand today, history has shown us that your superior power will find its answer, and with it your demise, in yet a greater force to come.

"We could await that day, step from the scene, and allow you the thankless task of implementing your own agenda. But gangsters like you are usually poor administrators, and more will suffer due to your incompetent handling of these duties, including further ecological degradation, than by the present attacks. We are therefore willing to accede to some of these demands, including complete amnesty for you and your hooligans. It will take time to determine how we can redirect our resources for a quicker reclamation of the environment, but you must be patient and bear with us during this difficult changeover. And, we must have assurances that you will not forcibly interfere with our efforts.

"We will allow a watchdog committee appointed by you to oversee this implementation, but it will have no legal force nor will you or any of your representatives be seated on this or any other governing body. Now, if you wish, you can destroy what is left of our civilization with your superior force, along with the earth you claim to love, but we will not be your puppet World Council, and the people of world, we believe, would rather die at your hands than be ruled by the likes of you. That, sir, is our reply in full."

Wei looked up from the prepared statement and stared at the camera. Jamison wished he could read the man's mind, but the World Council chamber was surrounded by a psychically impenetrable scalar wave field. He would have to rely on his own equally inaccessible intuition to answer these nagging doubts. Jamison reached over and turned off the monitor screen, and the tombstoned faces bleeped out. He was certain Wei had drawn up contingency plans for a conventional attack against them, using nuclear or satellite lasers, if he should knock out their psychic force. At this moment, Bates was ferrying equipment and personnel to a barge on the Rhone river that would take them south to the Mediterranean and their island hideaway. Unless the World Council was willing to destroy the southeast sector of the French Province, they would escape. Jamison sensed that Wei was in possession of secret knowledge, which threatened the man himself. Was it their own doomsday device, or a possible third party? No doubt this explained the man's insistence on a disk exchange rather than a live satlink hookup—which would leave him more vulnerable, despite precautions, to psychic probing. The World Council's position was untenable indeed, and yet they were obviously stalling for time.

Edington opened the door to the den and stepped inside. "We're almost ready to leave."

Jamison removed the video disk and placed it in its case. He tossed the case to Edington. "Go ahead and pack it. Damn if I can figure it out."

"We've been scanning. . .everybody, or the few people they've exposed. Nothing. The fact that they've gone to this length to shield so many scientists and government officials says something in itself."

"Yes, William. All is not what it seems."

"There is one thing," Edington said, stepping over and sitting down in one of the old-fashioned feather-cushioned chairs. "We found Rama and the Hiller woman on a train crossing the Middle East. There must be a dozen Euro agents on the train stalking them, but nobody's making a move, even with the game over."

Jamison narrowed his eyes. "You'd think they'd grab them just to get our location." He thought for a moment, then spoke aloud, "Why wouldn't our location be of importance?" Edington shrugged his shoulders. "Either they know it," Jamison added, "and haven't moved on us, or he's more important to them free."

"He does have. . .capabilities. We should've killed him when we had the chance."

"But, if he's their secret weapon, which I doubt—he'd never cooperate—why not grab him and at least try."

Edington thought about it. "There's something else. We're picking up a lot of scalar wave activity around earthquake faults. We thought it was from tectonic plate movement, but it's keeping up long after the rupture. And in some places where there aren't any."

"Will it block us out?" Jamison asked in alarm.

"It is interfering with our scans."

"I've always thought, and made it a point not to publish my theory, that flooding the fourth dimension with scalar waves might be one way to block a wholesale psychic offensive."

"You mean scalar generators?" Edington asked.

"Yes. But, if that's their weapon, why use it now, after the fact?" His colleague thought for a moment, but could only shake his head in consternation. "Well, it appears that Rama holds the key to this puzzle. And if they don't want to grab him, maybe George can."

Rama shifted back from a fourth-dimensional world of clear skies and grain-filled fields to the overcast gloom of this world with its encroaching sand-blown desert and the threat of physical violence lurking in the dark corridors of the train. He realized that the "children" had precipitated this shift and that the barriers between these two worlds were rapidly breaking down. Rama could see that they planned to shift the world and the ready ones—those capable of holding the higher vibration—out of its present crisis. It was a bold undertaking fraught with risk, both for them and those they wished to save. He hoped that they had compensated for matter's incredible inertia to its own elevation, be it the matter of human flesh or solid granite mountains.

Zita opened the door and peeked inside their compartment. She saw that Rama had returned. He was staring out the window, sipping a cup of water. Closing and locking the door behind her, she came over and sat on the bench across from him.

"See more of your friends?" Rama asked.

"Yeah, and they're still keeping their distance."

"And I was hoping to invite them for. . .warm water."

"Not in this. . .world," Zita said tentatively. Rama laughed in reply. She added, "Stuck my head in earlier, but you were. . . elsewhere."

"It's amazing how rapidly the shift's progressing. I'm finding it harder to come back."

"Given the situation, I can understand that."

Rama smiled. "If I should. . .shift out spontaneously, don't be alarmed."

"And if it becomes permanent?"

"The situation here will reform without my having ever been part of it."

"Well, it's been nice knowing you," Zita said half-seriously. She was alarmed by that prospect.

"Hopefully, you'll shift over as well."

Zita stared back at the holy man. "So, at any moment, I could find myself riding another train in another world without these goons to contend with?"

"Or at least with ones more inclined to drink with us."

There was a knock on the door, and Zita looked wild-eyed at Rama. He shrugged his shoulders. "We're still here." She stepped over to the door.

"Miss Hiller, I would advise both of you to remain in your compartment."

"Who is this speaking?"

"You would know me by name," he said obliquely.

Zita placed her ear against the door. Putting her hand on the knob, she turned it slightly, as if to open it, listening for a response but there was none. She stepped back. "He's gone, I think."

"One of your 'friends'?" Rama asked.

"He had a slight German accent; I'd say it was Walther Kauss, head of European security."

"Curious warning, if he is indeed out to apprehend us."

Zita sat back down on the cushioned bench. "He's

had plenty of opportunity for that, and hasn't made a move."

Rama closed his eyes, spread himself out probing the train. "It's Jamison's people, who've boarded the train, that he's warning you about."

"That tells us something," Zita said, as the holy man opened his eyes. She added, "From what you've sensed, Jamison's won the battle, and yet he's still fighting. My guess is that he knows about the children and wants to grab you for security."

Rama sighed, "These people grow very tiresome. Both sides would destroy the world to keep anyone else from ruling it. The cost in human suffering, the loss of the natural world and its beauty, all mean nothing to them."

Suddenly Rama felt the others calling to him in distress. "Something has happened, and I must go over. Sit tight and wait." He took her hand. "Don't let them move me—as long as you can." He let go, closed his eyes and appeared to withdraw into a deep meditation.

Rama shifted out of this world into its mirror opposite in the fourth dimension. He was temporarily immobilized by the conditions he encountered. Much had changed in the intervening time. Massive amounts of scalar waves were bombarding this dimensional world, hooking up with its natural scalar component and creating a barrier that allowed energy into its net but created an impenetrable barrier to its release. The result was that Rama and everybody here were trapped in this world. At the same time, by hooking up with its scalar matrix, the waves were draining the energy from this world and building up a charge that could explode and destroy it. It appeared that most of the children, attempting to shift the third-dimensional world here, were trapped and would eventually be drained dry and die. To save them and avert the destruction of this sacred fourth-dimensional world, Rama would need to discover some way of stopping the bombardment.

After an hour had passed and Rama had not moved from his position on the bench across from her, Zita assumed that he was lost to her and that she would not be claimed by this shift to the fourth-dimensional world. When there was a knock on the door, and this world now claimed her attention, Zita stood up and walked over to the door. She resisted the temptation to take the revolver out of her purse and confront these people on their own terms.

"Miss Hiller," the same voice called out to her.

"I'm here," she said.

"If Rama has joined his friends, which I suspect he has, he won't be coming back."

"Actually, I just sent him out for ice cream," Zita said with mock unconcern.

The man laughed. "Yes, Michael said you had a cool head."

"Well, I'm not buying it."

"You can wait for him, but when we stop at the Asian border, you will be escorted off the train."

"Rama will be hard to explain."

"Not in a body bag," the voice said.

Zita heard the man turn and walk back down the corridor. She suspected that he had accurately described Rama's predicament. The holy man would have come back or contacted her by now. His warning about their removal prior to the border crossing also made sense. The Asian border guards would grant asylum to Rama, or to her vouching for him, and would protect them from their pursuers. Zita used her phonewatch to get a satellite fix on their location and the speed of the train. By her calculation they had three hours before arriving at the border. It would be a difficult escape, given the number of agents from both sides tracking them, for her alone. Toting her catatonic friend would complicate matters immeasurably, but if she were stranded in this world, she would not give up without a fight.

Chapter Twenty-two

When Baba walked out of the science building and glanced up at the sky, it was clear blue without clouds and the sun shone brightly, and he strolled down the hedge-lined stone walkway; the people passing by, mostly college students and their teachers, seemed happy and content, and they waved and smiled back at him, and a few bowed their heads in prayerful greeting; and when he reached the crowded sidewalks of the city and walked along, everybody was friendly, though few knew of him, and several people stopped and asked if he were lost or took his hand and led him across the busy intersections, and he felt at home here with these people and would be happy to share this world, as they no doubt would, if asked, with those who sought sanctuary in this higher dimensional world; but then he felt the slight shift and the tremor and knew that something was wrong, and he looked up to see the first clouds scurrying across the skies, and the people began to hurry along their way—he could feel the pace of life quickening—and he saw the dull glow of milky light at the edge of the world and its static sparks, and he sensed that it would soon engulf this world and drain it of its light and life; he hurried along to the park where the other children had gathered under the oppressive milky-white cloud cover that had now descended like a misty fog hanging over the world, its static charge building, its sparks now constant streaks of lightning lashing out at them, and they huddled together and sought a way to reverse the impending collapse. . .

Halzack had become alarmed when he saw the boy's vital signs eroding. A few minutes later, Benjamin Burke reported that the dimensional shift, as noted by the time variance, had stopped and had begun to reverse itself. He informed the others. They had a group meeting and discussed their options and decided that it would be premature, given the danger, to intercede. Burke disagreed with them and paced the floor, while Halzack sat at the control board and monitored the boy's condition. Finally, he swiveled around and watched his colleague for a moment.

"Ben, sit down, would you, you're giving me a headache."

"Yeah, well a little pain'll keep you alert," Burke snapped back.

Halzack sighed. "Look, if you can think of anything else, I'm open to it."

Burke stopped and thought for a moment. "I need to know more about his condition, what's happening over there."

"Okay, how do we get it, or who would know more?" Halzack asked.

"Somebody who can shift back and forth," Burke said, and then had a sudden recognition. "Rama!"

"Yeah, right. Let's just call his captors, ask to speak with him."

"They've got the reporter too. Zita Hiller. She might be with him," Burke said.

Halzack nodded his head. He remembered his meeting with her at the aquarium. "She did give me her satlink number, but. . ."

Burke laughed. "What the hell, let's call her. I'm sure she's got a phonewatch."

Halzack was stunned by the suggestion. "What if some goon answers?"

"Then I'll order dinner," Burke said in wild-eyed delight.

The two men looked at each other and nodded their heads. Halzack swiveled around to the computer. The man hesitated, and then spoke into the microphone, "Call 247-8526: Access code: 6398453: Search Mode: Hiller, Zita."

The woman's name appeared on the screen along with her nine-digit satlink number. Halzack froze. Finally, Burke turned the monitor screen, stepped over to the phone and tapped out his four-digit access code and her satlink number. A moment later, Zita Hiller spoke over the speaker.

"Is this a joke?"

Dr. Halzack was speechless, and Burke replied, "No, I'm calling on behalf of Henry Halzack, whom I believe you know. The sit. . ."

Halzack interrupted, "Zita, it's Henry here. Are you all right?"

"Well, I'm riding the Euro Express with a catatonic holy man, and some very nasty fellows just gave me an ultimatum. How's the weather there, Henry?" she asked mockingly.

He heard her tone. "Sorry, but it's important." Halzack glanced at Burke, who nodded his head. "Okay, here's what's happening. The boy we talked about, Baba, and some friends of his, were trying to shift the world out of this crisis. But, they've gotten stuck in the fourth dimension."

"Well, that's what happened to Rama," Zita said. "He went back and forth, but this last time, he didn't return."

"Did he say anything about what he saw?"

"He said he was responding to a call for help, probably from them." There was a pause. "And the Euro agents claim they've done something to fix him there."

Halzack glanced back at Burke, who now asked, "What's happened with the war?"

"The other side appears to have won the day."

"Do you know how?"

"Something to do with the earthquakes. They precipitated them and killed off the council's psychics."

"And the World Council just conceded?"

"Apparently," Zita said impatiently. "Who is this, and what're you getting at?"

Burke turned to Dr. Halzack, "Think I know what they've done." He turned and hurried back to his computer console and started working.

"He's the colleague I mentioned. . .Benjamin Burke."

He paused for a moment. "Look, let us toss it around on this end and get back to you."

"Okay, but I've got two hours before things turn ugly," Zita said.

"Within the hour," Halzack said and broke the connection.

Halzack turned and walked over to Burke's console. He stood back and observed the scientist. He was calling up journal papers, reviewing them, dictating notes, and finally testing his theory with a graphic model. The speed at which the man worked was truly breathtaking. Burke finally stopped; it appeared he had drawn his conclusion. He turned to Halzack. "My guess is that the World Council arranged this crisis to draw the children into a fourth-dimensional world, which they've flooded with scalar waves, consuming its energy source and creating a charge that could literally blow it apart.

"How's that?" Halzack asked.

"The singular waves from the generators—I assume that's what they're using—combined with those that make up the fourth dimension. The resulting paired scalars or photons will build an immense static charge."

"Similar to what they do with the natural scalars in tectonic fault zones."

"Exactly."

"And you have a way of drawing off the charge?"

"Not exactly," Burke said. "According to Santilli, electric and gravitational fields are not mutually exclusive—they can be converted. It may be possible to use this building with its iron girders buried in the earth, and its circular shape, as a gravity well, to suck the excess energy from their fourth-dimensional world back into this dimension and ground it in the earth."

"What will the effect be here?"

"The only way it'd work would be to wire it counter to the earth's gravitational field. This is created by the rotation of the earth's inner and outer cores and the planet's rotation around them. The result would slow down that rotation, and could even stop it. Since time is also a function of the earth's rotation, it would stop time as well."

"That sounds pretty radical," Halzack said in alarm.

"It's what happens every time the earth switches its magnetic poles, which has occurred fourteen times in the geologic record."

"What will the effect be on us?"

"It's the earth's gravity that contains the body's electrical impulses. As they become lower, those electrical impulses will speed up. Your vibration will increase."

"So time will slow down, but our perception of it will speed up," Halzack said.

"Bringing us into closer synchronization with the fourth dimension for crossing over."

"I bet that's the effect the children had intended to create."

"No doubt," Burke said. "It's interesting to note that the initiation chambers in the Giza Pyramid and other megalithic sites do just that, lower magnetics to increase vibratory rate."

"So these children, or anybody for that matter, can reverse the process: lower magnetics—with the attendant effects—by raising their vibration."

"Yes, and what I propose will merely facilitate a naturally occurring process."

"And what do we do?" Halzack asked.

"We use Baba, who's straddling both dimensions, as the conduit, and us as the link. We form a human electrical chain between Baba and the iron girder in the corner. I'd wire the girder, so the electricity running through it creates a magnetic field running opposite the earth's."

"Burke, that's crazy. The charge would fry us," Halzack said in alarm.

"While we stay linked with Baba, we'd be interdimensional—ethereal, if you will—and our bodies would offer no resistance to the flow of electrons." Burke smiled mischievously. "We'd be the world's first true superconductors."

"Okay, but they have to set it up at their end as well. How do we contact them?" Halzack asked.

"Well, Henry, somebody has to go over there and tell them."

When Rama arrived at the park, the milky-white fog had settled, enveloping everything. The children had detected his presence in this dimension and had guided him to them. They gathered around their master, whom many were seeing for the first time. Although the children had been frustrated in their attempt to shift the world into a fourth-dimensional space and could feel the life force being drained from this world by the scalar wave bombardment, they had not given up hope.

- *Master,* Baba thought, *it is good to see you.*

- *Yes, it is good to see all of you. Would that it be under clearer skies.*

- *Do you know what drains the life from this world?*

Rama looked up at the flashes of static electricity.

- *The Negatives in the lower realm are mechanically sending energy that combines with this world's.*

- *If we do not stop them, all may be lost here,* Baba thought.

- *Baba, a voice calls you,* Christina thought.

The boy closed his eyes and heard a faint but familiar voice calling to him.

- *Your friend, the scientist, has come. Help me direct him.*

Rama and the children located Dr. Halzack and led him through the deserted byways of this world to the park. Baba met him at the edge of the trees and took the man's hand. It was shaking.

- *So you've come to meet my friends.*

"And to help you save this world," Halzack said.

- *Just think the thought, Dr. Zack, and we will hear you.*

- *Okay, I can do that.*

They walked back to Rama and the children, who had seated themselves in a circle on the grass. Two places were left open for Baba and his friend. They seated themselves, and Halzack looked around at the children, some of whom he had been in psychic contact with these past few months. Names were easily matched with faces by feeling their harmonic connection.

- *I assume this is more than a social call,* Rama thought.

The children giggled.

- *You must be Rama. It is an honor, sir.*
- *Here, we are all Ramas. Pleased to meet you.*
- *Yes, of course,* Halzack thought. *I think we have a way to remedy your situation here. We need to channel this electrostatic charge back into the third dimension.*
- *It won't destroy it?* Baba asked.
- *My colleague calls it a gravity well. By seeding the earth with this charge, we can create a magnetic field opposite the earth's, slow its rotation, slowing time, and create the ideal conditions for your shift.*

Rama and the children conferred. Halzack could hear the exchange between them with his inner ear; it sounded like the buzz of a thousand bees. Their deliberation was concluded instantaneously. Rama turned back to Dr. Halzack.

- *There is another factor. Lowering magnetics will speed up the earth's frequency.*
- *Its base resonant frequency?* Halzack asked.
- *That is the geologic term?*
- *Yes. Burke mentioned that, but what will the effect be?*
- *Our bodies vibrate to this frequency, and if it quickens too rapidly, which could occur with your scheme, most people will not adjust.*
- *Creating chaos?*
- *Or more chaos. This has been naturally occurring, and those unable to adjust have been self-destructing.*
- *How do you propose to offset that?* Halzack asked.
- *You are going to channel the charge through Baba's third-dimensional body?*
- *Yes, connecting it to the girders of the building it occupies.*
- *We will use the photons being absorbed to send a pulse through the lower dimension.*
- *Super subliminals.*
- *The difference being: it is being made available and not imposed.*
- *Master, it is time,* Baba thought.

He moved to the center of the circle, as the others closed file and linked up around him. Henry had a nervous moment, wondering if he could resonate with the elevated beings around him. He was reassured by an inner voice, that sounded like all the children speaking together, that in his present state he was able to raise his frequency and attune himself with the greater whole. The milky white energy began to swirl around this matrix grid, drawn in through the top of their heads, running through their bodies into those around them, collectively modulating its particles, then directing it like spokes in a wheel into Baba at the hub, poised between both worlds, circulating through him and into his third-dimensional counterpart in the laboratory chamber of the circular building. . .

Roya sat next to Baba in the tank, her hand clasped around her son's. Benjamin Burke stood next to her, linked to Dana Cosgrove, who held the exposed iron girder at the outer rim of the chamber, it having been decided, for the purpose of reversing the electrical flow, to have a woman as the final link in the chain. Burke had contacted Zita Hiller to tell her their plans and suggest she remain in physical contact with Rama during the experiment to facilitate her shift into the fourth dimension. But, standing between these two women, who were growing impatient with the long wait, holding hands and feeling foolish, he wondered if he had really lost his mind. Burke was about to voice this suspicion when he felt a surge of energy pass through Roya and hit him with huge static charge.

"Okay, everybody, whatever you do," Burke shouted over the humming pulse, "don't break the link until I say so, or we'll fry."

The three of them saw their hardened solid bodies grow increasingly lighter and lighter, interpenetrated by a crystalline grid of light, that conducted the energy passing through them without resistance. The fear-ridden chatter in their minds stopped immediately. There was a slight pressure between the eyes, and their heads felt tight, as if nothing else could fit inside, and they were quiet and still as a pond on a summer's day. But it was the feeling center that was activated and became the ruling principle of their being. With the mind stilled, they extended their feelings out into the world and felt their feeling connection not only to each other, but to that great chain of being grounded in this living earth, with its own sentient identity, through the lower forms of life, from the mineral through the plant to the animal and up to the human world and through it to the spiritual world that they had contacted. They felt this shift and saw a vision of a new earth and sensed that here there was unity and harmony, and that the great chain of being was respected and all living creatures honored.

The energy channeling through them into the iron girder had spread through the superstructure of the building and created the desired gravity well. Building in intensity, it created a rift or portal through which ever greater amounts of fourth-dimensional energy could be drawn. It was now self-sustaining. The result lessened the need for the human conduit, which appeared to be a catalytic operation.

Benjamin Burke felt the energy flow along the chain subsiding, and he turned to Dr. Cosgrove. "Dana, I feel we can break it off."

"Okay, but what happens to us?" Cosgrove asked, looking down at her less than solid body.

"I think we've already shifted, and wouldn't expect much of a change."

Dana glanced around the room, seeing a subtle difference: the physical objects had a soft glow. "Things look more alive, that's for sure."

"Okay, Dana, Roya, let's break. . .now." They broke the circuit and watched as their bodies began solidifying in a slightly less ethereal form. Trying to walk, they felt like babies taking their first awkward, tentative steps. Roya stumbled and Burke caught her, holding up her lighter body with little effort. He sat her down on the steps to the control room and made his way up to the booth. He checked the atomic clock monitors and called down to the others, "From what I can tell, we're about ten hours out of sync." The others looked puzzled. He added, "Trust me, we're there."

"What about Baba, when does he come back?" Roya asked.

"He's here, just preoccupied. He'll come out when he's ready."

Roya nodded her head. This felt right. The two women walked up the steps and went out into the hall. Burke sensed something, turned and took one step before hearing Dana Cosgrove think—Ben should see this. He walked into the hallway as she turned to call him. They realized that speech was no longer necessary. The others immediately understood as well. He went over to her at the window overlooking the atrium. The circular well of the building was still funneling a torrent of light from a tear in space just above the building through this shaft and into the earth below.

They turned and walked down the hallway to an outside window where Roya was viewing downtown Toronto. They responded to her excited state before she thought to call them. From the twentieth floor, they observed two cities overlapping each other. The perspective was drastically different. The old world, with its overcast skies and its hanging layer of brown smog, was interpenetrated by the same world in another dimension. Here the skies were clear, the air clear, and the buildings bright and shiny. On the streets of one world, people were trudging along hunched over with the burden of their broken world and their shattered lives, while in the other the people appeared genuinely happy, practically skipping along the tree-lined boulevard.

- I don't know about you, Burke thought, but I'll take the one with the sunny skies.

At that moment, there was a shift, and the other world was completely phased out of their existence. A moment later, they felt somebody coming down the hall toward them. It was Baba. He smiled but did not say a word, stepping up to the window. He turned and looked up at Dana Cosgrove.

- Dr. Cos, can we go to lunch? I'm hungry.

As the earth's rotation slowed and its magnetic field

decreased, each a function of the other, time itself began to stretch out. However, instead of life moving in slow motion (relative to an observer outside the zone) the pulse of life quickened as people responded to the higher frequency of the earth's resonant pulse. Those aspects of matter—physical, mental, or spiritual—that could not match this rate of increase, began to separate out from the whole. People who could not raise lower vibrational aspects of self became trapped by them and remained behind in a third-dimensional world that matched this frequency and wavelength. They would continue to experience: the earth's equivalent in earthquakes and volcanoes, air and water pollution; society's equivalent in poverty and violence, and the politics of control and suppression. But those who were willing to confront the totality of themselves—not only their negative dark shadow but the possibilities of their positive white shadow—and to raise their vibratory level, passed into a fourth-dimensional world of greater peace and harmony. This was not in any sense an ultimate state devoid of negativity, but one whose mid-range vibration was higher than the third dimension's highest states.

This transition period lasted for three days; the ready ones quickly shifted over. However, it was a tumultuous period for those who were forced to confront their own negativity, or who had regressed from previous levels of self-development. Those who had hidden their dark selves behind rigid religious or political ideologies, suppressing disowned aspects of self they projected onto the world—human, planetary, or divine; those who had failed to integrate countersexual selves, or who embraced a world of light devoid of shadow, were made to live out and claim in a few days, at this greatly accelerated pace, their totality. They then either shifted into the greater world—more here than beyond—or perpetuated the split in consciousness and the pull toward lower vibrational energies and re-inhabited an even darker third-dimensional world.

In Europe, riding a barge down the Rhone River heading for their island hideaway in the Mediterranean,

Cary Jamison and his team of psychics were among the first to detect the dimensional shift. Psychics, who were more attuned to vibration and thus other dimensional worlds, whose development was often accelerated by negative childhood experiences, felt more keenly the separation in themselves of elements vibrating at the different wavelengths. Their split-off child selves, often precipitated by abuse, cried out to be recognized, healed, and integrated. These crippled selves formed the deep dark pockets, vibrational wells, that like magnets pulled these shattered souls, with their transcendent aspects, into its archaic domain, and bound them to their own dimensional hell.

Jamison, whose childhood abuse and subsequent denial, which closed down some aspects of self and led to the development of others, was a classic example of this pattern. As the shift rapidly progressed and the separation widened, he could not suppress these denied selves after a lifetime of accumulated repression, and they surfaced and demanded attention. Jamison stared into the faces of a thousand disowned selves, ugly and hideous, begging for acceptance, for integration into the greater totality. But the man could not claim them. Their energies could have transformed his being, but they would now slither back into their wells, dragging the man down, cutting him off from his higher psychic faculties, and fixing him in a third-dimensional world reformed to match his conflicts, receptive to his projections.

When the shift began, the Euro Express had been traveling across the Middle East heading toward the Asian border in the province of Iran. After hearing back from Dr. Burke, Zita had moved across to Rama's seat and taken the holy man's hand. In itself, this did not mitigate the effects of the shift, the separation of elements by their wavelengths and her confrontation with those still unresolved, denied aspects of self. Zita had already taken the first step after her Watcher crisis, and with the help of Julia, her analyst, had begun to integrate these selves. This had started a cascade effect in the past month where she was given further opportunity—in conflicts with Michael, her capture and imprisonment, her initiations with Rama—to accelerate the process. Now, with the shift in effect, Zita was one of the ready ones and soon found herself along with the holy man in a fourth-dimensional world devoid of these previous conflicts.

When the train had stopped at the Asian border, there were no knocks on the door, no forced entry and abduction by burly underworld types. Zita had released the holy man's hand and walked through the train but found no sign of Walther Kauss and his Euro agents. She made inquiries but the porters did not remember anybody by his description having boarded the train. Zita returned to her compartment to find Rama ordering lunch over the dinerphone.

- *Would you like something to eat?*

Zita shook her head in amazement, and he completed the order and hung up. She sat down across from the holy man but waited for him to speak.

- *You look like you have seen a ghost,* Rama said.

- *Well, aren't you?*

- *Feels real to me.*

Rama pinched his skin, and then reached over and clasped Zita's hand. The touch of warm skin on skin was reassuring.

- *It appears that the shift is completed.*

- *I went looking for Kauss and his boys, but nobody remembers them.*

- *Yes, you will find. . .divergence between the two worlds.*

- *And where exactly are they?*

- *On another train in another world, chasing somebody else no doubt.*

- *With no memory of us?*

- *Their world has been reformed without us, or any trace of us having been there.*

- *But we remember them.*

- *Our dimension encompasses theirs.*

- *And if I call DI in Washington?*

- *I doubt that it translated. Probably get the Library of Congress.*

Zita nodded her head. She looked out the window at the sunny blue skies and the beautiful mountain landscape. They passed through a small village in what was previously, as she recalled, one of the world's most impoverished areas, but was now, or in this world, clean and well-kept with warmly attired peasants of a cheerful disposition. This scene was repeated in village after village, and when they had traveled down from mountains to the Indian plains below, Zita saw none of the abject poverty she had associated with India. There were no lines of armless untouchables or starving children waiting on the train platforms, or flies swarming around diseased discards lying in ditches or along the side of country roads.

- *You see an improvement?* Rama asked his awe-struck companion.

- *Miraculous.*

- *There never was any lack, even in our world. Just our inability to tap the bountiful universe around us.*

Zita spent the rest of the afternoon viewing this world and its wondrous sights. By late morning, she saw a mileage sign for Bombay.

- *Are we traveling to your ashram in Bombay?* Zita asked.

- *I would assume so.*

- *And what are the circumstances of our journey?*

- *I would guess that you are a reporter writing an article about me.*

- *After your release from prison?*

Rama glanced down at his clothes, and Zita now noticed his European suit and shoes. In fact, he was dressed more like a college professor than a guru.

- *After my European tour, I would guess.*

Zita sat back in her seat and sighed deeply; it was indeed a new world, and she would have to chart its old and new territory day by day. In an hour the train pulled into the station in Bombay. Rama pointed out his mother and a small group of friends waiting for them.

- I would've expected a larger reception, Zita said.

- You might find my status less elevated in this world.

The train stopped and the two of them stood up. Rama went to open the door, and escorted her out the door and down the corridor. Zita stepped off the train onto the platform and looked up into the clear blue sky, the sun in golden display high in its natural domain, the air she breathed clean and crisp. Walking beside her friend on this clear day, Zita took his arm, remembering her dream in that other world, only months ago by some reckoning, a lifetime by others, and she knew that she had finally arrived in her world.

Reference Material

Bearden, Thomas E. *Excalibur Briefing*. San Francisco: Strawberry Hill Press, 1980.

Bobroff, Rabbi Alvin, ed. *The Mystique of Enlightenment: The Unrational Ideas of a Man Called U.G.* Farmingdale, NY: Coleman Publishing, 1984.

Braden, Gregg. *Awakening to Zero Point*. Questa, NM: Sacred Spaces/Ancient Wisdom, 1993.

Lovelock, James. *The Ages of Gaia*. New York: W.W. Norton & Company, 1988.

Marciniak, Barbara. *Bringers of the Dawn: Teachings from the Pleiadians*. Santa Fe, NM: Bear & Company, 1992.

McKibben, Bill. *The End of Nature*. New York: Random House, 1989.

McRae, Ronald M. *Mind Wars: The True Story of Government Research into the Military Potential of Psychic Weapons*. New York: St. Martin Press, 1984.

Rajneesh, Bhagwan Shree. *Dimensions Beyond the Known*. London: Sheldon Press, 1975.

Rajneesh, Bhagwan Shree. *When the Shoe Fits. Talks on Stories of Chuang Tzu*. Poona, India: Rajneesh Foundation, 1976.

Ralphs, John. *Exploring the Fourth Dimension: Secrets of the Paranormal*. St. Paul, MN: Llewellyn Publications, 1992.

Satprem. *The Mind of the Cells*. New York: Institute for Evolutionary Research, 1981.

Satprem. *Sri Aurobindo or The Adventure of Consciousness*. Mt. Vernon, WA: Institute for Evolutionary Research, 1981.

Targ, Russell, and Harold Puthoff. *Mind-Reach: Scientists Look at Psychic Ability*. New York: Delacorte Press, 1977.

White, John. *Poleshift: Predictions and Prophecies of the Ultimate Disaster*. New York: Doubleday, 1980.

White, John, ed. *Psychic Warfare: An Investigation Into the Use of the Mind as a Military Weapon*. London: Aquarian Press, 1988.

Yatri. *Unknown Man: The Mysterious Birth of a New Species*. New York: Simon & Schuster, 1988.

Yogananda, Paramhansa. *Autobiography of a Yogi*. New York: Philosophical Library, 1946.

Zukav, Gary. *The Dancing Wu Li Masters*. New York: William Morrow, 1979.